# Exam Ref 70-483:
# Programming in C#

Wouter de Kort

Published with the authorization of Microsoft Corporation by:
O'Reilly Media, Inc.
1005 Gravenstein Highway North
Sebastopol, California 95472

ISBN: 978-0-7356-7682-4

2 3 4 5 6 7 8 9 10  QG  8 7 6 5 4 3

Printed and bound in the United States of America.

Microsoft Press books are available through booksellers and distributors worldwide. If you need support related to this book, email Microsoft Press Book Support at mspinput@microsoft.com. Please tell us what you think of this book at *http://www.microsoft.com/learning/booksurvey*.

Microsoft and the trademarks listed at *http://www.microsoft.com/about/legal/en/us/IntellectualProperty/ Trademarks/EN-US.aspx* are trademarks of the Microsoft group of companies.  All other marks are property of their respective owners.

The example companies, organizations, products, domain names, email addresses, logos, people, places, and events depicted herein are fictitious. No association with any real company, organization, product, domain name, email address, logo, person, place, or event is intended or should be inferred.

This book expresses the author's views and opinions. The information contained in this book is provided without any express, statutory, or implied warranties. Neither the authors, O'Reilly Media, Inc., Microsoft Corporation, nor its resellers, or distributors will be held liable for any damages caused or alleged to be caused either directly or indirectly by this book.

**Acquisitions and Developmental Editor:** Russell Jones

**Production Editor:** Melanie Yarbrough

**Editorial Production:** Box Twelve Communications

**Technical Reviewer:** Auri Rahimzadeh

**Copyeditor:** Ginny Munroe

**Cover Design:** Twist Creative • Seattle

**Cover Composition:** Ellie Volckhausen

**Illustrator:** Rebecca Demarest

[2013-08-09]

*Dedicated to my parents who encouraged me to start programming when I was 7.*

—WOUTER DE KORT

# Contents at a glance

# Contents

---

**What do you think of this book? We want to hear from you!**

Microsoft is interested in hearing your feedback so we can continually improve our
books and learning resources for you. To participate in a brief online survey, please visit:

**www.microsoft.com/learning/booksurvey/**

**What do you think of this book? We want to hear from you!**

Microsoft is interested in hearing your feedback so we can continually improve our
books and learning resources for you. To participate in a brief online survey, please visit:

**www.microsoft.com/learning/booksurvey/**

# Introduction

The Microsoft 70-483 exam focuses on a broad range of topics that you can use in your work as a C# developer. This book helps you understand both the basic and the more advanced areas of the C# language. It shows you how to use the C# language to create powerful software applications. This book also shows you how to use the new features that were added to the C# language, such as support for asynchronous code. This book is aimed at developers who have some experience with C# but want to deepen their knowledge and make sure they are ready for the exam. To use the examples in this book, you should be familiar with using Visual Studio to create a basic Console Application.

This book covers every exam objective, but it does not cover every exam question. Only the Microsoft exam team has access to the exam questions themselves and Microsoft regularly adds new questions to the exam, making it impossible to cover specific questions. You should consider this book a supplement to your relevant real-world experience and other study materials. If you encounter a topic in this book that you do not feel completely comfortable with, use the links to find more information and take the time to research and study the topic. Great information is available on MSDN, TechNet, in blogs, and in forums.

## Microsoft certifications

Microsoft certifications distinguish you by proving your command of a broad set of skills and experience with current Microsoft products and technologies. The exams and corresponding certifications are developed to validate your mastery of critical competencies as you design and develop, or implement and support, solutions with Microsoft products and technologies both on-premise and in the cloud. Certification brings a variety of benefits to the individual and to employers and organizations.

> **MORE INFO**  **ALL MICROSOFT CERTIFICATIONS**
>
> For information about Microsoft certifications, including a full list of available certifications, go to *http://www.microsoft.com/learning/en/us/certification/cert-default.aspx*.

# Who should read this book

This book is intended for developers who want to achieve certification for the C# programming language. This book prepares you to take and pass the exam 70-483: Programming in C#. Successfully passing the 70-483 exam also counts as credit toward the Microsoft Certified Solution Developer (MCSD): Windows Store Apps Using C#.

# Assumptions

You should have at least one or more years of experience programming the essential business/application logic for a variety of application types and hardware/software platforms using C#. To run the examples from this book you should be able to create a console application in Visual Studio. As you progress with your learning through this book and other study resources, you will become proficient at developing complex applications. You will be able to use all features that C# offers. This book is focused on helping those of you whose goal is to become certified as a C# developer.

You can find information about the audience for Exam 70-483 in the exam preparation guide, available at *http://www.microsoft.com/learning/en/us/exam-70-483. aspx#fbid=x2KPCL1L6z8*.

# Organization of this book

This book is divided into four chapters. Each chapter focuses on a different exam domain related to Exam 70-483: Programming in C#. Each chapter is further broken down into specific exam objectives that have been published by Microsoft; they can found in the "Skills Being Measured" section of the Exam 70-483: Programming in C# website at *http://www.microsoft. com/learning/en/us/exam-70-483.aspx#fbid=x2KPCL1L6z8*.

The material covered by the exam domain and the objectives has been incorporated into the book so that you have concise, objective-by-objective content together with strategic real-world scenarios, thought experiments, and end-of-chapter review questions to provide readers with professional-level preparation for the exam.

# System requirements

Where you are unfamiliar with a topic covered in this book, you should practice the concept on your study PC. You will need the following hardware and software to complete the practice exercises in this book:

- One study PC that can be installed with Visual Studio 2012 (see hardware specifications below) or a PC that allows the installation of Visual Studio 2012 within a virtualized environment. You can use Visual Studio 2012 Professional, Premium, or Ultimate if you own a license for one of these. If you don't have access to a licensed version, you can also use Visual Studio 2012 Express for Windows Desktop, which can be downloaded from *http://www.microsoft.com/visualstudio/eng/downloads*.
- Visual Studio 2012 supports the following operating systems: Windows 7 SP1 (x86 and x64), Windows 8 (x86 and x64), Windows Server 2008 R2 SP1 (x64), Windows Server 2012 (x64).
- Visual Studio 2012 requires the following minimum hardware requirements: 1.6 GHz or faster processor, 1 GB of RAM (1.5 GB if running on a virtual machine), 5 GB of available hard disk space, 100 MB of available hard disk space (language pack), 5400 RPM hard disk drive, DirectX 9-capable video card running at 1024 x 768 or higher display resolution.
- If you plan to install Visual Studio 2012 in a virtualized environment, you should consider using Hyper-V and ensure that the minimum hardware requirements are as follows: x64-based processor, which includes both hardware-assisted virtualization (AMD-V or Inter VT) and hardware data execution protection; 4 GB RAM (more is recommended); network card; video card; DVD-ROM drive; and at least 100 GB of available disk space available to allow for the storage of multiple virtual machines.

# Conventions and features in this book

This book presents information using conventions designed to make the information readable and easy to follow:

- Each exercise consists of a series of tasks, presented as numbered steps listing each action you must take to complete the exercise.
- Boxed elements with labels such as "Note" provide additional information or alternative methods for completing a step successfully.
- Boxed elements with "Exam Tip" labels provide additional information that might offer helpful hints or additional information on what to expect on the exam.
- Text that you type (apart from code blocks) appear in bold.

- A plus sign (+) between two key names means that you must press those keys at the same time. For example, "Press Alt+Tab" means that you hold down the Alt key while you press the Tab key.

- A vertical bar between two or more menu items (for example, File | Close) means that you should select the first menu or menu item, then the next, and so on.

## Acknowledgments

I'd like to thank the following people:

- To Jeff Riley for providing me the opportunity to write this book.

- To Ginny Munroe for helping me through the whole editing process. I learned a lot from your feedback and advice.

- To Auri Rahimzadeh for your technical reviewing skills.

- To my wife, Elise, for your support.

And to all the other people who played a role in getting this book ready. Thanks for your hard work!

## Errata & book support

We've made every effort to ensure the accuracy of this book and its companion content. Any errors that have been reported since this book was published are listed on our Microsoft Press site at oreilly.com:

*http://aka.ms/ER70-483/errata*

If you find an error that is not already listed, you can report it to us through the same page.

If you need additional support, email Microsoft Press Book Support at *mspinput@micro-soft.com*.

Please note that product support for Microsoft software is not offered through the addresses above.

# We want to hear from you

At Microsoft Press, your satisfaction is our top priority, and your feedback our most valuable asset. Please tell us what you think of this book at:

*http://www.microsoft.com/learning/booksurvey*

The survey is short, and we read every one of your comments and ideas. Thanks in advance for your input!

# Stay in touch

Let's keep the conversation going! We're on Twitter: *http://twitter.com/MicrosoftPress*.

# Preparing for the exam

Microsoft certification exams are a great way to build your resume and let the world know about your level of expertise. Certification exams validate your on-the-job experience and product knowledge. While there is no substitution for on-the-job experience, preparation through study and hands-on practice can help you prepare for the exam. We recommend that you round out your exam preparation plan by using a combination of available study materials and courses. For example, you might use this *Exam Ref* and another study guide for your "at home" preparation, and take a Microsoft Official Curriculum course for the classroom experience. Choose the combination that you think works best for you.

Note that this *Exam Ref* is based on publically available information about the exam and the author's experience. To safeguard the integrity of the exam, authors do not have access to the live exam.

# CHAPTER 1

# Manage program flow

If you could build only programs that execute all their logic from top to bottom, it would not be feasible to build complex applications. Fortunately, C# and the .NET Framework offer you a lot of options for creating complex programs that don't have a fixed program flow.

This chapter starts with looking at how to create *multithreaded* applications. Those applications can scale well and remain responsive to the user while doing their work. You will also look at the new language feature *async/await* that was added to C# 5.

**IMPORTANT**

**Have you read page xxi?**

It contains valuable information regarding the skills you need to pass the exam.

You will learn about the basic C# language constructs to make decisions and execute a piece of code multiple times, depending on the circumstances. These constructs form the basic language blocks of each application, and you will use them often.

After that, you will learn how to create applications that are loosely coupled by using *delegates* and *events*. With events, you can build objects that can notify each other when something happens and that can respond to those notifications. Frameworks such as ASP.NET, Windows Presentation Foundation (WPF), and WinForms make heavy use of events; understanding events thoroughly will help you build great applications.

Unfortunately, your program flow can also be interrupted by errors. Such errors can happen in areas that are out of your control but that you need to respond to. Sometimes you want to raise such an error yourself. You will learn how exceptions can help you implement a robust error-handling strategy in your applications.

## Objectives in this chapter:

- Objective 1.1: Implement multithreading and asynchronous processing
- Objective 1.2: Manage multithreading
- Objective 1.3: Implement program flow
- Objective 1.4: Create and implement events and callbacks
- Objective 1.5. Implement exception handling

# Objective 1.1: Implement multithreading and asynchronous processing

Applications are becoming more and more complex as user expectations rise. To fully take advantage of multicore systems and stay responsive, you need to create applications that use multiple threads, often called *parallelism*.

The .NET Framework and the C# language offer a lot of options that you can use to create multithreaded applications.

> **This objective covers how to:**
> - Understand threads.
> - Use the Task Parallel Library.
> - Use the *Parallel* class.
> - Use the new *async* and *await* keywords.
> - Use Parallel Language Integrated Query.
> - Use concurrent collections.

## Understanding threads

Imagine that your computer has only one *central processing unit* (CPU) that is capable of executing only one operation at a time. Now, imagine what would happen if the CPU has to work hard to execute a task that takes a long time.

While this operation runs, all other operations would be paused. This means that the whole machine would freeze and appear unresponsive to the user. Things get even worse when that long-running operation contains a bug so it never ends. Because the rest of the machine is unusable, the only thing you can do is restart the machine.

To remedy this problem, the concept of a *thread* is used. In current versions of Windows, each application runs in its own *process*. A process isolates an application from other applications by giving it its own *virtual memory* and by ensuring that different processes can't influence each other. Each process runs in its own *thread*. A *thread* is something like a virtualized CPU. If an application crashes or hits an infinite loop, only the application's process is affected.

Windows must manage all of the threads to ensure they can do their work. These management tasks do come with an overhead. Each thread is allowed by Windows to execute for a certain time period. After this period ends, the thread is paused and Windows switches to another thread. This is called *context switching*.

In practice, this means that Windows has to do some work to make it happen. The current thread is using a certain area of memory; it uses CPU registers and other state data, and Windows has to make sure that the whole context of the thread is saved and restored on each switch.

But although there are certain performance hits, using threads does ensure that each process gets its time to execute without having to wait until all other operations finish. This improves the responsiveness of the system and gives the illusion that one CPU can execute multiple tasks at a time. This way you can create an application that uses *parallelism*, meaning that it can execute multiple threads on different CPUs in parallel.

Almost any device that you buy today has a CPU with multiple cores, which is similar to having multiple CPUs. Some servers not only have multicore CPUs but they also have more than one CPU. To make use of all these cores, you need multiple threads. Windows ensures that those threads are distributed over your available cores. This way you can perform multiple tasks at once and improve scalability.

Because of the associated overhead, you should carefully determine whether you need multithreading. But if you want to use threads for scalability or responsiveness, C# and .NET Framework offer you a lot of possibilities.

## Using the *Thread* class

The *Thread* class can be found in the *System.Threading* namespace. This class enables you to create new treads, manage their priority, and get their status.

The *Thread* class isn't something that you should use in your applications, except when you have special needs. However, when using the *Thread* class you have control over all configuration options. You can, for example, specify the priority of your thread, tell Windows that your thread is long running, or configure other advanced options.

Listing 1-1 shows an example of using the *Thread* class to run a method on another thread. The *Console* class synchronizes the use of the output stream for you so you can write to it from multiple threads. *Synchronization* is the mechanism of ensuring that two threads don't execute a specific portion of your program at the same time. In the case of a console application, this means that no two threads can write data to the screen at the exact same time. If one thread is working with the output stream, other threads will have to wait before it's finished.

**LISTING 1-1** Creating a thread with the *Thread* class

```csharp
using System;
using System.Threading;

namespace Chapter1
{
    public static class Program
    {
        public static void ThreadMethod()
        {
            for (int i = 0; i < 10; i++)
            {
                Console.WriteLine("ThreadProc: {0}", i);
                Thread.Sleep(0);
            }
        }

        public static void Main()
        {
            Thread t = new Thread(new ThreadStart(ThreadMethod));
            t.Start();

            for (int i = 0; i < 4; i++)
            {
                Console.WriteLine("Main thread: Do some work.");
                Thread.Sleep(0);
            }

            t.Join();

        }

    }

}

// Displays
//Main thread: Do some work.
//ThreadProc: 0
//Main thread: Do some work.
//ThreadProc: 1
//Main thread: Do some work.
//ThreadProc: 2
//Main thread: Do some work.
//ThreadProc: 3
//ThreadProc: 4
//ThreadProc: 5
//ThreadProc: 6
//ThreadProc: 7
//ThreadProc: 8
//ThreadProc: 9
```

As you can see, both threads run and print their message to the console. The *Thread.Join* method is called on the main thread to let it wait until the other thread finishes.

Why the *Thread.Sleep(0)*? It is used to signal to Windows that this thread is finished. Instead of waiting for the whole time-slice of the thread to finish, it will immediately switch to another thread.

Both your process and your thread have a *priority*. Assigning a low priority is useful for applications such as a screen saver. Such an application shouldn't compete with other applications for CPU time. A higher-priority thread should be used only when it's absolutely necessary. A new thread is assigned a priority of Normal, which is okay for almost all scenarios.

Another thing that's important to know about threads is the difference between *foreground* and *background* threads. Foreground threads can be used to keep an application alive. Only when all foreground threads end does the common language runtime (CLR) shut down your application. Background threads are then terminated.

Listing 1-2 shows this difference in action.

**LISTING 1-2** Using a background thread

```
using System;
using System.Threading;

namespace Chapter1
{
    public static class Program

    {
        public static void ThreadMethod()
        {
            for (int i = 0; i < 10; i++)
            {
                Console.WriteLine("ThreadProc: {0}", i);
                Thread.Sleep(1000);
            }
        }

        public static void Main()
        {
            Thread t = new Thread(new ThreadStart(ThreadMethod));
            t.IsBackground = true;
            t.Start();
        }
    }
}
```

If you run this application with the *IsBackground* property set to *true*, the application exits immediately. If you set it to *false* (creating a foreground thread), the application prints the *ThreadProc* message ten times.

The *Thread* constructor has another overload that takes an instance of a *Parameter-izedThreadStart* delegate. This overload can be used if you want to pass some data through the start method of your thread to your worker method, as Listing 1-3 shows.

**LISTING 1-3** Using the *ParameterizedThreadStart*

```
public static void ThreadMethod(object o)
{
    for (int i = 0; i < (int)o; i++)
    {
        Console.WriteLine("ThreadProc: {0}", i);

        Thread.Sleep(0);
    }
}

public static void Main()
{
    Thread t = new Thread(new ParameterizedThreadStart(ThreadMethod));
    t.Start(5);
    t.Join();
}
```

In this case, the value *5* is passed to the *ThreadMethod* as an object. You can cast it to the expected type to use it in your method.

To stop a thread, you can use the *Thread.Abort* method. However, because this method is executed by another thread, it can happen at any time. When it happens, a *ThreadAbort-Exception* is thrown on the target thread. This can potentially leave a corrupt state and make your application unusable.

A better way to stop a thread is by using a shared variable that both your target and your calling thread can access. Listing 1-4 shows an example.

**LISTING 1-4** Stopping a thread

```
using System;
using System.Threading;

namespace Chapter1
{
    public static class Program
    {
        public static void ThreadMethod(object o)
        {
            for (int i = 0; i < (int)o; i++)
            {
                Console.WriteLine("ThreadProc: {0}", i);
                Thread.Sleep(0);
            }
        }

        public static void Main()
        {

            bool stopped = false;
```

```
        Thread t = new Thread(new ThreadStart(() =>
        {
            while (!stopped)
            {
                Console.WriteLine("Running...");
                Thread.Sleep(1000);
            }
        }));

        t.Start();
        Console.WriteLine("Press any key to exit");
        Console.ReadKey();

        stopped  = true;
        t.Join();
    }
  }
}
```

In this case, the thread is initialized with a lambda expression (which in turn is just a short-hand version of a delegate). The thread keeps running until *stopped* becomes *true*. After that, the *t.Join* method causes the console application to wait till the thread finishes execution.

A thread has its own call stack that stores all the methods that are executed. Local variables are stored on the call stack and are private to the thread.

A thread can also have its own data that's not a local variable. By marking a field with the *ThreadStatic* attribute, each thread gets its own copy of a field (see Listing 1-5).

**LISTING 1-5** Using the *ThreadStaticAttribute*

```
using System;
using System.Threading;

namespace Chapter1
{
    public static class Program
    {
        [ThreadStatic]
        public static int _field;
        public static void Main()
        {

            new Thread(() =>
              {
                  for(int x = 0; x < 10; x++)
                  {
                      _field++;
                      Console.WriteLine("Thread A: {0}", _field);
                  }
              }).Start();


            new Thread(() =>
              {
```

```
            for(int x = 0; x < 10; x++)
            {
                _field++;
                Console.WriteLine("Thread B: {0}", _field);
            }
        }).Start();

        Console.ReadKey();
    }
  }
}
```

With the *ThreadStaticAttribute* applied, the maximum value of *_field* becomes *10*. If you remove it, you can see that both threads access the same value and it becomes *20*.

If you want to use local data in a thread and initialize it for each thread, you can use the *ThreadLocal<T>* class. This class takes a delegate to a method that initializes the value. Listing 1-6 shows an example.

**LISTING 1-6** Using *ThreadLocal<T>*

```
using System;
using System.Threading;

namespace Chapter1
{
    public static class Program
    {
        public static ThreadLocal<int> _field =
            new ThreadLocal<int>(() =>
            {
                return Thread.CurrentThread.ManagedThreadId;

            });

        public static void Main()
        {
            new Thread(() =>

            {

                for(int x = 0; x < _field.Value; x++)
                {
                    Console.WriteLine("Thread A: {0}", x);
                }

            }).Start();
            new Thread(() =>
            {
                for (int x = 0; x < _field.Value; x++)
                {
                    Console.WriteLine("Thread B: {0}", x);
                }
```

```
            }).Start();

            Console.ReadKey();
        }
    }
}

// Displays
// Thread B: 0
// Thread B: 1
// Thread B: 2
// Thread B: 3
// Thread A: 0
// Thread A: 1
// Thread A: 2
```

Here you see another feature of the .NET Framework. You can use the *Thread.Current-Thread* class to ask for information about the thread that's executing. This is called the thread's *execution context*. This property gives you access to properties like the thread's *current culture* (a *CultureInfo* associated with the current thread that is used to format dates, times, numbers, currency values, the sorting order of text, casing conventions, and string comparisons), *principal* (representing the current security context), *priority* (a value to indicate how the thread should be scheduled by the operating system), and other info.

When a thread is created, the runtime ensures that the initiating thread's execution context is flowed to the new thread. This way the new thread has the same privileges as the parent thread.

This copying of data does cost some resources, however. If you don't need this data, you can disable this behavior by using the *ExecutionContext.SuppressFlow* method.

## Thread pools

When working directly with the *Thread* class, you create a new thread each time, and the thread dies when you're finished with it. The creation of a thread, however, is something that costs some time and resources.

A *thread pool* is created to reuse those threads, similar to the way a database connection pooling works. Instead of letting a thread die, you send it back to the pool where it can be reused whenever a request comes in.

When you work with a thread pool from .NET, you queue a work item that is then picked up by an available thread from the pool. Listing 1-7 shows how this is done.

**LISTING 1-7** Queuing some work to the thread pool

```
using System;
using System.Threading;

namespace Chapter1
{
    public static class Program
    {
```

```
public static void Main()
{
    ThreadPool.QueueUserWorkItem((s) =>
    {
        Console.WriteLine("Working on a thread from threadpool");
    });

    Console.ReadLine();
}
}
```

Because the thread pool limits the available number of threads, you do get a lesser degree of parallelism than using the regular *Thread* class. But the thread pool also has many advantages.

Take, for example, a web server that serves incoming requests. All those requests come in at an unknown time and frequency. The thread pool ensures that each request gets added to the queue and that when a thread becomes available, it is processed. This ensures that your server doesn't crash under the amount of requests. If you span threads manually, you can easily bring down your server if you get a lot of requests. Each request has unique characteristics in the work they need to do. What the thread pool does is map this work onto the threads available in the system. Of course, you can still get so many requests that you run out of threads. Requests then start to queue up and this leads to your web server becoming unresponsive.

The thread pool automatically manages the amount of threads it needs to keep around. When it is first created, it starts out empty. As a request comes in, it creates additional threads to handle those requests. As long as it can finish an operation before a new one comes in, no new threads have to be created. If new threads are no longer in use after some time, the thread pool can kill those threads so they no longer use any resources.

> ***MORE INFO*** **THREAD POOL**
>
> For more information on how the thread pool works and how you can configure it, see
> *http://msdn.microsoft.com/en-us/library/system.threading.threadpool.aspx.*

One thing to be aware of is that because threads are being reused, they also reuse their local state. You may not rely on state that can potentially be shared between multiple operations.

## Using *Task*s

Queuing a work item to a thread pool can be useful, but it has its shortcomings. There is no built-in way to know when the operation has finished and what the return value is.

This is why the .NET Framework introduces the concept of a *Task*, which is an object that represents some work that should be done. The *Task* can tell you if the work is completed and if the operation returns a result, the *Task* gives you the result.

A *task scheduler* is responsible for starting the *Task* and managing it. By default, the *Task* scheduler uses threads from the thread pool to execute the *Task*.

*Tasks* can be used to make your application more responsive. If the thread that manages the user interface offloads work to another thread from the thread pool, it can keep processing user events and ensure that the application can still be used. But it doesn't help with scalability. If a thread receives a web request and it would start a new *Task*, it would just consume another thread from the thread pool while the original thread waits for results.

Executing a *Task* on another thread makes sense only if you want to keep the user interface thread free for other work or if you want to parallelize your work on to multiple processors.

Listing 1-8 shows how to start a new *Task* and wait until it's finished.

**LISTING 1-8** Starting a new *Task*

```
using System;
using System.Threading.Tasks;

namespace Chapter1
{

    public static class Program
    {
        public static void Main()

        {

            Task t = Task.Run(() =>
            {
                for (int x = 0; x < 100; x++)
                {

                    Console.Write('*');
                }
            });


            t.Wait();

        }
    }
}
```

This example creates a new *Task* and immediately starts it. Calling *Wait* is equivalent to calling *Join* on a thread. It waits till the *Task* is finished before exiting the application.

Next to *Task*, the .NET Framework also has the *Task<T>* class that you can use if a *Task* should return a value. Listing 1-9 shows how this works.

**LISTING 1-9** Using a *Task* that returns a value.

```
using System;
using System.Threading.Tasks;

namespace Chapter1
{
    public static class Program
    {
        public static void Main()
        {
            Task<int> t = Task.Run(() =>
            {
                return 42;
            });
            Console.WriteLine(t.Result); // Displays 42
        }
    }
}
```

Attempting to read the *Result* property on a *Task* will force the thread that's trying to read the result to wait until the *Task* is finished before continuing. As long as the *Task* has not finished, it is impossible to give the result. If the *Task* is not finished, this call will block the current thread.

Because of the object-oriented nature of the *Task* object, one thing you can do is add a *continuation task*. This means that you want another operation to execute as soon as the *Task* finishes.

Listing 1-10 shows an example of creating such a continuation.

**LISTING 1-10** Adding a continuation

```
Task<int> t = Task.Run(() =>
{
    return 42;
}).ContinueWith((i) =>
{
    return i.Result * 2;
});

Console.WriteLine(t.Result); // Displays 84
```

The *ContinueWith* method has a couple of overloads that you can use to configure when the continuation will run. This way you can add different continuation methods that will run when an exception happens, the *Task* is canceled, or the *Task* completes successfully. Listing 1-11 shows how to do this.

**LISTING 1-11** Scheduling different continuation tasks

```
Task<int> t = Task.Run(() =>
{
    return 42;
});

t.ContinueWith((i) =>
{
    Console.WriteLine("Canceled");
}, TaskContinuationOptions.OnlyOnCanceled);

t.ContinueWith((i) =>
{
    Console.WriteLine("Faulted");
}, TaskContinuationOptions.OnlyOnFaulted);

var completedTask =  t.ContinueWith((i) =>
 {
     Console.WriteLine("Completed");
 }, TaskContinuationOptions.OnlyOnRanToCompletion);

completedTask.Wait();
```

Next to continuation *Tasks*, a *Task* can also have several *child Tasks*. The *parent Task* finishes when all the child tasks are ready. Listing 1-12 shows how this works.

**LISTING 1-12** Attaching child tasks to a parent task

```
using System;
using System.Threading.Tasks;

namespace Chapter1
{
    public static class Program
    {
        public static void Main()
        {
            Task<Int32[]> parent = Task.Run(() =>
            {
                var results = new Int32[3];
                new Task(() => results[0] = 0,
                    TaskCreationOptions.AttachedToParent).Start();
                new Task(() => results[1] = 1,
                    TaskCreationOptions.AttachedToParent).Start();
                new Task(() => results[2] = 2,
                    TaskCreationOptions.AttachedToParent).Start();

                return results;
            });

            var finalTask = parent.ContinueWith(
                parentTask => {
                    foreach(int i in parentTask.Result)
                        Console.WriteLine(i);
                });
```

```
            finalTask.Wait();
        }
    }
}
```

The *finalTask* runs only after the parent *Task* is finished, and the parent *Task* finishes when all three children are finished. You can use this to create quite complex *Task* hierarchies that will go through all the steps you specified.

In the previous example, you had to create three *Tasks* all with the same options. To make the process easier, you can use a *TaskFactory*. A *TaskFactory* is created with a certain configuration and can then be used to create *Tasks* with that configuration. Listing 1-13 shows how you can simplify the previous example with a factory.

**LISTING 1-13** Using a *TaskFactory*

```
using System;
using System.Threading.Tasks;

namespace Chapter1
{
    public static class Program
    {
        public static void Main()
        {
            Task<Int32[]> parent = Task.Run(() =>
            {
                var results = new Int32[3];

                TaskFactory tf = new TaskFactory(TaskCreationOptions.AttachedToParent,
                    TaskContinuationOptions.ExecuteSynchronously);

                tf.StartNew(() => results[0] = 0);
                tf.StartNew(() => results[1] = 1);
                tf.StartNew(() => results[2] = 2);
                return results;
            });

            var finalTask = parent.ContinueWith(
                parentTask => {
                    foreach(int i in parentTask.Result)
                    Console.WriteLine(i);
                });

            finalTask.Wait();
        }
    }
}
```

Next to calling *Wait* on a single *Task*, you can also use the method *WaitAll* to wait for multiple *Tasks* to finish before continuing execution. Listing 1-14 shows how to use this.

LISTING 1-14 Using *Task.WaitAll*

```
using System.Threading;
using System.Threading.Tasks;

namespace Chapter1
{
    public static class Program
    {
        public static void Main()
        {
            Task[] tasks = new Task[3];

            tasks[0] = Task.Run(() => {
                                        Thread.Sleep(1000);
                                        Console.WriteLine("1");
                                        return 1;
                                      });
            tasks[1] = Task.Run(() => {
                                        Thread.Sleep(1000);
                                        Console.WriteLine("2");
                                        return 2;
                                      });
            tasks[2] = Task.Run(() => {
                                        Thread.Sleep(1000);
                                        Console.WriteLine("3");
                                        return 3; }
                                );

            Task.WaitAll(tasks);
        }
    }
}
```

In this case, all three *Tasks* are executed simultaneously, and the whole run takes approximately 1000ms instead of 3000. Next to *WaitAll*, you also have a *WhenAll* method that you can use to schedule a continuation method after all *Tasks* have finished.

Instead of waiting until all tasks are finished, you can also wait until one of the tasks is finished. You use the *WaitAny* method for this. Listing 1-15 shows how this works.

LISTING 1-15 Using *Task.WaitAny*

```
using System;
using System.Linq;
using System.Threading;
using System.Threading.Tasks;

namespace Chapter1
{
    public static class Program
    {
        public static void Main()
        {
            Task<int>[] tasks = new Task<int>[3];
```

```
            tasks[0] = Task.Run(() => { Thread.Sleep(2000); return 1; });
            tasks[1] = Task.Run(() => { Thread.Sleep(1000); return 2; });
            tasks[2] = Task.Run(() => { Thread.Sleep(3000); return 3; });

            while (tasks.Length > 0)
            {
                int i = Task.WaitAny(tasks);
                Task<int> completedTask = tasks[i];

                Console.WriteLine(completedTask.Result);

                var temp = tasks.ToList();
                temp.RemoveAt(i);
                tasks = temp.ToArray();

            }
        }
    }
}
```

In this example, you process a completed *Task* as soon as it finishes. By keeping track of which *Tasks* are finished, you don't have to wait until all *Tasks* have completed.

## Using the *Parallel* class

The *System.Threading.Tasks* namespace also contains another class that can be used for parallel processing. The *Parallel* class has a couple of static methods—*For*, *ForEach*, and *Invoke*—that you can use to parallelize work.

*Parallelism* involves taking a certain task and splitting it into a set of related tasks that can be executed concurrently. This also means that you shouldn't go through your code to replace all your loops with parallel loops. You should use the *Parallel* class only when your code doesn't have to be executed sequentially.

Increasing performance with parallel processing happens only when you have a lot of work to be done that can be executed in parallel. For smaller work sets or for work that has to synchronize access to resources, using the *Parallel* class can hurt performance.

The best way to know whether it will work in your situation is to measure the results.

Listing 1-16 shows an example of using *Parallel.For* and *Parallel.ForEach*.

**LISTING 1-16** Using *Parallel.For* and *Parallel.Foreach*

```
Parallel.For(0, 10, i =>
{
    Thread.Sleep(1000);
});

var numbers = Enumerable.Range(0, 10);
Parallel.ForEach(numbers, i =>
{
    Thread.Sleep(1000);
});
```

You can cancel the loop by using the *ParallelLoopState* object. You have two options to do this: *Break* or *Stop*. *Break* ensures that all iterations that are currently running will be finished. *Stop* just terminates everything. Listing 1-17 shows an example.

**LISTING 1-17** Using *Parallel.Break*

```
ParallelLoopResult result = Parallel.
    For(0, 1000, (int i, ParallelLoopState loopState) =>
{
    if (i == 500)
    {
        Console.WriteLine("Breaking loop");
        loopState.Break();

    }
    return;
});
```

When breaking the parallel loop, the result variable has an *IsCompleted* value of *false* and a *LowestBreakIteration* of *500*. When you use the *Stop* method, the *LowestBreakIteration* is *null*.

## Using *async* and *await*

As you have seen, long-running CPU-bound tasks can be handed to another thread by using the *Task* object. But when doing work that's input/output (I/O)–bound, things go a little differently.

When your application is executing an I/O operation on the primary application thread, Windows notices that your thread is waiting for the I/O operation to complete. Maybe you are accessing some file on disk or over the network, and this could take some time.

Because of this, Windows pauses your thread so that it doesn't use any CPU resources. But while doing this, it still uses memory, and the thread can't be used to serve other requests, which in turn will lead to new threads being created if requests come in.

Asynchronous code solves this problem. Instead of blocking your thread until the I/O operation finishes, you get back a *Task* object that represents the result of the asynchronous operation. By setting a continuation on this *Task*, you can continue when the I/O is done. In the meantime, your thread is available for other work. When the I/O operation finishes, Windows notifies the runtime and the continuation *Task* is scheduled on the thread pool.

But writing asynchronous code is not easy. You have to make sure that all edge cases are handled and that nothing can go wrong. Because of this predicament, C# 5 has added two new keywords to simplify writing asynchronous code. Those keywords are *async* and *await*.

You use the *async* keyword to mark a method for asynchronous operations. This way, you signal to the compiler that something asynchronous is going to happen. The compiler responds to this by transforming your code into a *state machine*.

A method marked with *async* just starts running synchronously on the current thread. What it does is enable the method to be split into multiple pieces. The boundaries of these pieces are marked with the *await* keyword.

When you use the *await* keyword, the compiler generates code that will see whether your asynchronous operation is already finished. If it is, your method just continues running synchronously. If it's not yet completed, the state machine will hook up a continuation method that should run when the *Task* completes. Your method yields control to the calling thread, and this thread can be used to do other work.

Listing 1-18 shows a simple example of an asynchronous method.

**LISTING 1-18** *async* and *await*

```
using System;
using System.Net.Http;
using System.Threading.Tasks;

namespace Chapter1.Threads
{
    public static class Program
    {
        public static void Main()
        {
            string result = DownloadContent().Result;
            Console.WriteLine(result);
        }

        public static async Task<string> DownloadContent()
        {
            using(HttpClient client = new HttpClient())
            {

                string result = await client.GetStringAsync("http://www.microsoft.com");
                return result;
            }
        }
    }

}
```

Because the entry method of an application can't be marked as *async*, the example uses the *Wait* method in *Main*. This class uses both the *async* and *await* keywords in the *DownloadContent* method.

The *GetStringAsync* uses asynchronous code internally and returns a *Task<string>* to the caller that will finish when the data is retrieved. In the meantime, your thread can do other work.

The nice thing about *async* and *await* is that they let the compiler do the thing it's best at: generate code in precise steps. Writing correct asynchronous code by hand is difficult, especially when trying to implement exception handling. Doing this correctly can become difficult quickly. Adding continuation tasks also breaks the logical flow of the code. Your code doesn't read top to bottom anymore. Instead, program flow jumps around, and it's harder to follow when debugging your code. The *await* keyword enables you to write code that looks synchronous but behaves in an asynchronous way. The Visual Studio debugger is even clever enough to help you in debugging asynchronous code as if it were synchronous.

So doing a CPU-bound task is different from an I/O-bound task. CPU-bound tasks always use some thread to execute their work. An asynchronous I/O-bound task doesn't use a thread until the I/O is finished.

If you are building a client application that needs to stay responsive while background operations are running, you can use the *await* keyword to offload a long-running operation to another thread. Although this does not improve performance, it does improve responsiveness. The *await* keyword also makes sure that the remainder of your method runs on the correct user interface thread so you can update the user interface.

Making a scalable application that uses fewer threads is another story. Making code scale better is about changing the actual implementation of the code. Listing 1-19 shows an example of this.

**LISTING 1-19** Scalability versus responsiveness

```
public Task SleepAsyncA(int millisecondsTimeout)
{
    return Task.Run(() => Thread.Sleep(millisecondsTimeout));
}

public Task SleepAsyncB(int millisecondsTimeout)
{
    TaskCompletionSource<bool> tcs = null;
    var t = new Timer(delegate { tcs.TrySetResult(true); }, null, -1, -1);
    tcs = new TaskCompletionSource<bool>(t);
    t.Change(millisecondsTimeout, -1);
    return tcs.Task;
}
```

The *SleepAsyncA* method uses a thread from the thread pool while sleeping. The second method, however, which has a completely different implementation, does not occupy a thread while waiting for the timer to run. The second method gives you scalability.

When using the *async* and *await* keywords, you should keep this in mind. Just wrapping each and every operation in a task and awaiting them won't make your application perform any better. It could, however, improve responsiveness, which is very important in client applications.

The *FileStream* class, for example, exposes asynchronous methods such as *WriteAsync* and *ReadAsync*. They use an implementation that makes use of actual asynchronous I/O. This way, they don't use a thread while they are waiting on the hard drive of your system to read or write some data.

When an exception happens in an asynchronous method, you normally expect an *AggregateException*. However, the generated code helps you unwrap the *AggregateException* and throws the first of its inner exceptions. This makes the code more intuitive to use and easier to debug.

One other thing that's important when working with asynchronous code is the concept of a *SynchronizationContext*, which connects its application model to its threading model. For example, a WPF application uses a single user interface thread and potentially multiple background threads to improve responsiveness and distribute work across multiple CPUs. An ASP.NET application, however, uses threads from the thread pool that are initialized with the correct data, such as current user and culture to serve incoming requests.

The *SynchronizationContext* abstracts the way these different applications work and makes sure that you end up on the right thread when you need to update something on the UI or process a web request.

The *await* keyword makes sure that the current *SynchronizationContext* is saved and restored when the task finishes. When using *await* inside a WPF application, this means that after your *Task* finishes, your program continues running on the user interface thread. In an ASP.NET application, the remaining code runs on a thread that has the client's cultural, principal, and other information set.

If you want, you can disable the flow of the *SynchronizationContext*. Maybe your continuation code can run on any thread because it doesn't need to update the UI after it's finished. By disabling the *SynchronizationContext*, your code performs better. Listing 1-20 shows an example of a button event handler in a WPF application that downloads a website and then puts the result in a label.

**LISTING 1-20** Using *ConfigureAwait*

```
private async void Button_Click(object sender, RoutedEventArgs e)
{
    HttpClient httpClient = new HttpClient();

    string content = await httpClient
        .GetStringAsync("http://www.microsoft.com")
        .ConfigureAwait(false);

    Output.Content = content;
}
```

This example throws an exception; the *Output.Content* line is not executed on the UI thread because of the *ConfigureAwait(false)*. If you do something else, such as writing the content to file, you don't need to set the *SynchronizationContext* to be set (see Listing 1-21).

**LISTING 1-21** Continuing on a thread pool instead of the UI thread

```
private async void Button_Click(object sender, RoutedEventArgs e)
{
    HttpClient httpClient = new HttpClient();

    string content = await httpClient
        .GetStringAsync("http://www.microsoft.com")
        .ConfigureAwait(false);
```

```
using (FileStream sourceStream = new FileStream("temp.html",
        FileMode.Create, FileAccess.Write, FileShare.None,
        4096, useAsync: true))
{
    byte[] encodedText = Encoding.Unicode.GetBytes(content);
    await sourceStream.WriteAsync(encodedText, 0, encodedText.Length)
        .ConfigureAwait(false);
};
}
```

Both *await*s use the *ConfigureAwait(false)* method because if the first method is already finished before the *awaiter* checks, the code still runs on the UI thread.

When creating *async* methods, it's important to choose a return type of *Task* or *Task<T>*. Avoid the *void* type. A *void* returning *async* method is effectively a fire-and-forget method. You can never inspect the *return* type, and you can't see whether any exceptions were thrown. You should use *async void* methods only when dealing with asynchronous events.

The use of the new *async/await* keywords makes it much easier to write asynchronous code. In today's world with multiple cores and requirements for responsiveness and scalability, it's important to look for opportunities to use these new keywords to improve your applications.

**EXAM TIP**

When using *async* and *await* keep in mind that you should never have a method marked *async* without any *await* statements. You should also avoid returning void from an *async* method except when it's an event handler.

## Using Parallel Language Integrated Query (PLINQ)

*Language-Integrated Query* (LINQ) is a popular addition to the C# language. You can use it to perform queries over all kinds of data.

*Parallel Language-Integrated Query* (PLINQ) can be used on objects to potentially turn a sequential query into a parallel one.

Extension methods for using PLINQ are defined in the *System.Linq.ParallelEnumerable* class. Parallel versions of LINQ operators, such as *Where, Select, SelectMany, GroupBy, Join, OrderBy, Skip,* and *Take,* can be used.

Listing 1-22 shows how you can convert a query to a parallel query.

**LISTING 1-22** Using *AsParallel*

```
var numbers = Enumerable.Range(0, 100000000);
var parallelResult = numbers.AsParallel()
    .Where(i => i % 2 == 0)
    .ToArray();
```

The runtime determines whether it makes sense to turn your query into a parallel one. When doing this, it generates *Task* objects and starts executing them. If you want to force PLINQ into a parallel query, you can use the *WithExecutionMode* method and specify that it should always execute the query in parallel.

You can also limit the amount of parallelism that is used with the *WithDegreeOfParallelism* method. You pass that method an integer that represents the number of processors that you want to use. Normally, PLINQ uses all processors (up to 64), but you can limit it with this method if you want.

One thing to keep in mind is that parallel processing does not guarantee any particular order. Listing 1-23 shows what can happen.

**LISTING 1-23** Unordered parallel query

```
using System;
using System.Linq;

namespace Chapter1
{
    public static class Program
    {
        public static void Main()
        {
            var numbers = Enumerable.Range(0, 10);
            var parallelResult = numbers.AsParallel()
                .Where(i => i % 2 == 0)
                .ToArray();

            foreach (int i in parallelResult)
                Console.WriteLine(i);
        }
    }
}

// Displays
// 2
// 0
// 4
// 6
// 8
```

As you can see, the returned results from this query are in no particular order. The results of this code vary depending on the amount of CPUs that are available. If you want to ensure that the results are ordered, you can add the *AsOrdered* operator. Your query is still processed in parallel, but the results are buffered and sorted. Listing 1-24 shows how this works.

LISTING 1-24 Ordered parallel query

```
using System;
using System.Linq;

namespace Chapter1
{
    public static class Program
    {
        public static void Main()
        {
            var numbers = Enumerable.Range(0, 10);
            var parallelResult = numbers.AsParallel().AsOrdered()
                .Where(i => i % 2 == 0)
                .ToArray();

            foreach (int i in parallelResult)
                Console.WriteLine(i);
        }
    }
}

// Displays
// 0
// 2
// 4
// 6
// 8
```

If you have a complex query that can benefit from parallel processing but also has some parts that should be done sequentially, you can use the *AsSequential* to stop your query from being processed in parallel.

One scenario where this is required is to preserve the ordering of your query. Listing 1-25 shows how you can use the *AsSequential* operator to make sure that the *Take* method doesn't mess up your order.

**LISTING 1-25** Making a parallel query sequential

```
var numbers = Enumerable.Range(0, 20);

var parallelResult = numbers.AsParallel().AsOrdered()
    .Where(i => i % 2 == 0).AsSequential();

foreach (int i in parallelResult.Take(5))
    Console.WriteLine(i);

// Displays
// 0
// 2
// 4
// 6
// 8
```

When using PLINQ, you can use the *ForAll* operator to iterate over a collection when the iteration can also be done in a parallel way. Listing 1-26 shows how to do this.

**LISTING 1-26** Using *ForAll*

```
var numbers = Enumerable.Range(0, 20);

var parallelResult = numbers.AsParallel()
    .Where(i => i % 2 == 0);

parallelResult.ForAll(e => Console.WriteLine(e));
```

In contrast to *foreach*, *ForAll* does not need all results before it starts executing. In this example, *ForAll* does, however, remove any sort order that is specified.

Of course, it can happen that some of the operations in your parallel query throw an exception. The .NET Framework handles this by aggregating all exceptions into one *AggregateException*. This exception exposes a list of all exceptions that have happened during parallel execution. Listing 1-27 shows how you can handle this.

**LISTING 1-27** Catching *AggregateException*

```
using System;
using System.Linq;

namespace Chapter1
{
    public static class Program
    {
        public static void Main()

        {
            var numbers = Enumerable.Range(0, 20);

            try
            {

                var parallelResult = numbers.AsParallel()
                    .Where(i => IsEven(i));

                parallelResult.ForAll(e => Console.WriteLine(e));
            }
            catch (AggregateException e)
            {
                Console.WriteLine("There where {0} exceptions",
                                    e.InnerExceptions.Count);
            }
        }

        public static bool IsEven(int i)
        {
            if (i % 10 == 0) throw new ArgumentException("i");

            return i % 2 == 0;
```

```
            }
        }
}

// Displays
// 4
// 6
// 8
// 2
// 12
// 14
// 16
// 18
// There where 2 exceptions
```

As you can see, two exceptions were thrown while processing the data. You can inspect those exceptions by looping through the *InnerExceptions* property.

# Using concurrent collections

When working in a multithreaded environment, you need to make sure that you are not manipulating shared data at the same time without synchronizing access.

The .NET Framework offers some collection classes that are created specifically for use in concurrent environments, which is what you have when you're using multithreading. These collections are thread-safe, which means that they internally use synchronization to make sure that they can be accessed by multiple threads at the same time.

Those collections are the following:

- *BlockingCollection<T>*
- *ConcurrentBag<T>*
- *ConcurrentDictionary<TKey,T>*
- *ConcurrentQueue<T>*
- *ConcurrentStack<T>*

## *BlockingCollection<T>*

This collection is thread-safe for adding and removing data. Removing an item from the collection can be blocked until data becomes available. Adding data is fast, but you can set a maximum upper limit. If that limit is reached, adding an item blocks the calling thread until there is room.

*BlockingCollection* is in reality a wrapper around other collection types. If you don't give it any specific instructions, it uses the *ConcurrentQueue* by default.

A regular collection blows up when being used in a multithreaded scenario because an item might be removed by one thread while the other thread is trying to read it.

Listing 1-28 shows an example of using a *BlockingCollection*. One *Task* listens for new items being added to the collection. It blocks if there are no items available. The other *Task* adds items to the collection.

LISTING 1-28 Using *BlockingCollection<T>*

```
using System;
using System.Collections.Concurrent;
using System.Threading.Tasks;

namespace Chapter1
{
    public static class Program
    {
        public static void Main()
        {
            BlockingCollection<string> col = new BlockingCollection<string>();
            Task read = Task.Run(() =>
                {
                    while (true)
                    {
                        Console.WriteLine(col.Take());
                    }
                });

            Task write = Task.Run(() =>
                {
                    while (true)
                    {
                        string s = Console.ReadLine();
                        if (string.IsNullOrWhiteSpace(s)) break;
                        col.Add(s);
                    }
                });

            write.Wait();
        }
    }
}
```

The program terminates when the user doesn't enter any data. Until that, every string entered is added by the write *Task* and removed by the read *Task*.

You can use the *CompleteAdding* method to signal to the *BlockingCollection* that no more items will be added. If other threads are waiting for new items, they won't be blocked anymore.

You can even remove the *while(true)* statements from Listing 1-28. By using the *GetConsumingEnumerable* method, you get an *IEnumerable* that blocks until it finds a new item. That way, you can use a *foreach* with your *BlockingCollection* to enumerate it (see Listing 1-29).

LISTING 1-29 Using *GetConsumingEnumerable* on a *BlockingCollection*

```
Task read = Task.Run(() =>
    {

        foreach (string v in col.GetConsumingEnumerable())
            Console.WriteLine(v);
    });
```

**MORE INFO**   IENUMERABLE

For more information about using *IEnumerable*, see Chapter 2.

## ConcurrentBag

A *ConcurrentBag* is just a bag of items. It enables duplicates and it has no particular order. Important methods are *Add*, *TryTake*, and *TryPeek*.

Listing 1-30 shows how to work with the *ConcurrentBag*.

**LISTING 1-30** Using a *ConcurrentBag*

```
ConcurrentBag<int> bag = new ConcurrentBag<int>();

bag.Add(42);
bag.Add(21);

int result;
if (bag.TryTake(out result))
    Console.WriteLine(result);

if (bag.TryPeek(out result))
    Console.WriteLine("There is a next item: {0}", result);
```

One thing to keep in mind is that the *TryPeek* method is not very useful in a multithreaded environment. It could be that another thread removes the item before you can access it.

*ConcurrentBag* also implements *IEnumerable<T>*, so you can iterate over it. This operation is made thread-safe by making a snapshot of the collection when you start iterating it, so items added to the collection after you started iterating it won't be visible. Listing 1-31 shows this in practice.

**LISTING 1-31** Enumerating a *ConcurrentBag*

```
ConcurrentBag<int> bag = new ConcurrentBag<int>();
Task.Run(() =>
{
    bag.Add(42);
    Thread.Sleep(1000);
    bag.Add(21);
});
Task.Run(() =>
{
    foreach (int i in bag)
        Console.WriteLine(i);
}).Wait();

// Displays
// 42
```

This code only displays *42* because the other value is added after iterating over the bag has started.

## ConcurrentStack and ConcurrentQueue

A stack is a *last in, first out* (LIFO) collection. A queue is a *first in, first out* (FIFO) collection.

*ConcurrentStack* has two important methods: *Push* and *TryPop*. *Push* is used to add an item to the stack; *TryPop* tries to get an item off the stack. You can never be sure whether there are items on the stack because multiple threads might be accessing your collection at the same time.

You can also add and remove multiple items at once by using *PushRange* and *TryPopRange*. When you enumerate the collection, a snapshot is taken.

Listing 1-32 shows how these methods work.

**LISTING 1-32** Using a *ConcurrentStack*

```
ConcurrentStack<int> stack = new ConcurrentStack<int>();

stack.Push(42);

int result;
if (stack.TryPop(out result))
    Console.WriteLine("Popped: {0}", result);

stack.PushRange(new int[] { 1, 2, 3 });

int[] values = new int[2];
stack.TryPopRange(values);


foreach (int i in values)
    Console.WriteLine(i);


// Popped: 42
// 3
// 2
```

*ConcurrentQueue* offers the methods *Enqueue* and *TryDequeue* to add and remove items from the collection. It also has a *TryPeek* method and it implements *IEnumerable* by making a snapshot of the data. Listing 1-33 shows how to use a *ConcurrentQueue*.

**LISTING 1-33** Using a *ConcurrentQueue*.

```
ConcurrentQueue<int> queue = new ConcurrentQueue<int>();
queue.Enqueue(42);

int result;
if (queue.TryDequeue(out result))
    Console.WriteLine("Dequeued: {0}", result);

// Dequeued: 42
```

## ConcurrentDictionary

A *ConcurrentDictionary* stores key and value pairs in a thread-safe manner. You can use methods to add and remove items, and to update items in place if they exist.

Listing 1-34 shows the methods that you can use on a *ConcurrentDictionary*.

**LISTING 1-34** Using a *ConcurrentDictionary*

```
var dict = new ConcurrentDictionary<string, int>();
if (dict.TryAdd("k1", 42))
{
    Console.WriteLine("Added");
}

if (dict.TryUpdate("k1", 21, 42))
{
    Console.WriteLine("42 updated to 21");
}

dict["k1"] = 42; // Overwrite unconditionally

int r1 = dict.AddOrUpdate("k1", 3, (s, i) => i * 2);
int r2 = dict.GetOrAdd("k2", 3);
```

When working with a *ConcurrentDictionary* you have methods that can atomically add, get, and update items. An *atomic operation* means that it will be started and finished as a single step without other threads interfering. *TryUpdate* checks to see whether the current value is equal to the existing value before updating it. *AddOrUpdate* makes sure an item is added if it's not there, and updated to a new value if it is. *GetOrAdd* gets the current value of an item if it's available; if not, it adds the new value by using a factory method.

> ## *Thought experiment*
> ### Implementing multithreading
>
> In this thought experiment, apply what you've learned about this objective. You can find answers to these questions in the "Answers" section at the end of this chapter.
>
> You need to build a new application, and you look into multithreading capabilities. Your application consists of a client application that communicates with a web server.
>
> 1. Explain how multithreading can help with your client application.
>
> 2. What is the difference between CPU and I/O bound operations?
>
> 3. Does using multithreading with the TPL offer the same advantages for your server application?

## Objective summary

- A thread can be seen as a virtualized CPU.
- Using multiple threads can improve responsiveness and enables you to make use of multiple processors.
- The *Thread* class can be used if you want to create your own threads explicitly. Otherwise, you can use the *ThreadPool* to queue work and let the runtime handle things.
- A *Task* object encapsulates a job that needs to be executed. Tasks are the recommended way to create multithreaded code.
- The *Parallel* class can be used to run code in parallel.
- PLINQ is an extension to LINQ to run queries in parallel.
- The new *async* and *await* operators can be used to write asynchronous code more easily.
- Concurrent collections can be used to safely work with data in a multithreaded (concurrent access) environment.

## Objective review

Answer the following questions to test your knowledge of the information in this objective. You can find the answers to these questions and explanations of why each answer choice is correct or incorrect in the "Answers" section at the end of this chapter.

1. You have a lot of items that need to be processed. For each item, you need to perform a complex calculation. Which technique should you use?

   A. You create a *Task* for each item and then wait until all tasks are finished.

   B. You use *Parallel.For* to process all items concurrently.

   C. You use *async/await* to process all items concurrently.

   D. You add all items to a *BlockingCollection* and process them on a thread created by the *Thread* class.

2. You are creating a complex query that doesn't require any particular order and you want to run it in parallel. Which method should you use?

   A. *AsParallel*

   B. *AsSequential*

   C. *AsOrdered*

   D. *WithDegreeOfParallelism*

3. You are working on an ASP.NET application that retrieves some data from another web server and then writes the response to the database. Should you use *async/await*?

    **A.** No, both operations depend on external factors. You need to wait before they are finished.

    **B.** No, in a server application you don't have to use *async/await*. It's only for responsiveness on the client.

    **C.** Yes, this will free your thread to serve other requests while waiting for the I/O to complete.

    **D.** Yes, this put your thread to sleep while waiting for I/O so that it doesn't use any CPU.

# Objective 1.2: Manage multithreading

Although multithreading can give you a lot of advantages, it's not easy to write a multithreaded application. Problems can happen when different threads access some shared data. What should happen when both try to change something at the same time? To make this work successfully, *synchronizing* resources is important.

> **This objective covers how to:**
> - Synchronize resources.
> - Cancel long-running tasks.

## Synchronizing resources

As you have seen, with the TPL support in .NET, it's quite easy to create a multithreaded application. But when you build real-world applications with multithreading, you run into problems when you want to access the same data from multiple threads simultaneously. Listing 1-35 shows an example of what can go wrong.

**LISTING 1-35** Accessing shared data in a multithreaded application

```
using System;
using System.Threading.Tasks;

namespace Chapter1
{
    public class Program
    {
        static void Main()
        {
            int n = 0;

            var up = Task.Run(() =>
            {
```

```
                for (int i = 0; i < 1000000; i++)
                    n++;
            });

            for (int i = 0; i < 1000000; i++)
                n--;

            up.Wait();
            Console.WriteLine(n);
        }
    }
}
```

What would the output of Listing 1-35 be? The answer is, it depends. When you run this application, you get a different output each time. The seemingly simple operation of incrementing and decrementing the variable *n* results in both a lookup (check the value of *n*) and add or subtract 1 from *n*. But what if the first task reads the value and adds 1, and at the exact same time task 2 reads the value and subtracts 1? This is what happens in this example and that's why you never get the expected output of *0*.

This is because the operation is not *atomic*. It consists of both a read and a write that happen at different moments. This is why access to the data you're working with needs to be *synchronized*, so you can reliably predict how your data is affected.

It's important to synchronize access to shared data. One feature the C# language offers is the *lock* operator, which is some syntactic sugar that the compiler translates in a call to *System.Thread.Monitor*. Listing 1-36 shows the use of the *lock* operator to fix the previous example.

**LISTING 1-36** Using the *lock* keyword

```
using System;
using System.Threading.Tasks;

namespace Chapter1
{
    public class Program
    {
        static void Main()
        {
            int n = 0;

            object _lock = new object();

            var up = Task.Run(() =>
            {

                for (int i = 0; i < 1000000; i++)
                    lock (_lock)
                        n++;
            });

            for (int i = 0; i < 1000000; i++)
```

```
        lock (_lock)
            n--;

        up.Wait();
        Console.WriteLine(n);
    }
  }
}
```

After this change, the program always outputs *0* because access to the variable *n* is now synchronized. There is no way that one thread could change the value while the other thread is working with it.

However, it also causes the threads to *block* while they are waiting for each other. This can give performance problems and it could even lead to a *deadlock*, where both threads wait on each other, causing neither to ever complete. Listing 1-37 shows an example of a deadlock.

**LISTING 1-37** Creating a deadlock

```
using System;
using System.Threading;
using System.Threading.Tasks;

namespace Chapter1
{
    public class Program
    {
        static void Main()
        {
            object lockA = new object();
            object lockB = new object();

            var up = Task.Run(() =>
            {
                lock (lockA)
                {
                    Thread.Sleep(1000);
                    lock (lockB)
                    {
                        Console.WriteLine("Locked A and B");
                    }
                }
            });

            lock (lockB)
            {
                lock (lockA)
                {
                    Console.WriteLine("Locked B and A");
                }
            }
            up.Wait();
        }
    }
}
```

Because both locks are taken in reverse order, a deadlock occurs. The first *Task* locks *A* and waits for *B* to become free. The main thread, however, has *B* locked and is waiting for *A* to be released.

You need to be careful to avoid deadlocks in your code. You can avoid a deadlock by making sure that locks are requested in the same order. That way, the first thread can finish its work, after which the second thread can continue.

The lock code is translated by the compiler into something that looks like Listing 1-38.

**LISTING 1-38** Generated code from a *lock* statement

```
object gate = new object();
bool __lockTaken = false;
try
{
    Monitor.Enter(gate, ref __lockTaken);
}
finally
{
    if (__lockTaken)
        Monitor.Exit(gate);
}
```

You shouldn't write this code by hand; let the compiler generate it for you. The compiler takes care of tricky edge cases that can happen.

It's important to use the *lock* statement with a reference object that is private to the class. A public object could be used by other threads to acquire a lock without your code knowing.

It should also be a reference type because a value type would get boxed each time you acquired a lock. In practice, this generates a completely new lock each time, losing the locking mechanism. Fortunately, the compiler helps by raising an error when you accidentally use a value type for the *lock* statement.

You should also avoid locking on the *this* variable because that variable could be used by other code to create a lock, causing deadlocks.

For the same reason, you should not lock on a string. Because of *string-interning* (the process in which the compiler creates one object for several strings that have the same content) you could suddenly be asking for a lock on an object that is used in multiple places.

## *Volatile* class

The C# compiler is pretty good at optimizing code. The compiler can even remove complete statements if it discovers that certain code would never be executed.

The compiler sometimes changes the order of statements in your code. Normally, this wouldn't be a problem in a single-threaded environment. But take a look at Listing 1-39, in which a problem could happen in a multithreaded environment.

LISTING 1-39 A potential problem with multithreaded code

```
private static int _flag = 0;
private static int _value = 0;

public static void Thread1()
{
    _value = 5;
    _flag = 1;
}

public static void Thread2()
{
    if (_flag == 1)
        Console.WriteLine(_value);
}
```

Normally, if you would run *Thread1* and *Thread2*, you would expect no output or an output of 5. It could be, however, that the compiler switches the two lines in *Thread1*. If *Thread2* then executes, it could be that *_flag* has a value of *1* and *_value* has a value of *0*.

You can use locking to fix this, but there is also another class in the .NET Framework that you can use: *System.Threading.Volatile*. This class has a special *Write* and *Read* method, and those methods disable the compiler optimizations so you can force the correct order in your code. Using these methods in the correct order can be quite complex, so .NET offers the *volatile* keyword that you can apply to a field. You would then change the declaration of your field to this:

```
private static volatile int _flag = 0;
```

It's good to be aware of the existence of the *volatile* keyword, but it's something you should use only if you really need it. Because it disables certain compiler optimizations, it will hurt performance. It's also not something that is supported by all .NET languages (Visual Basic doesn't support it), so it hinders language interoperability.

## The *Interlocked* class

Referring to Listing 1-35, the essential problem was that the operations of adding and subtracting were not atomic. This because *n++* is translated into *n = n + 1*, both a read and a write.

Making operations atomic is the job of the *Interlocked* class that can be found in the *System.Threading* namespace. When using the *Interlocked.Increment* and *Interlocked.Decrement*, you create an atomic operation, as Listing 1-40 shows.

LISTING 1-40 Using the *Interlocked* class

```
using System;
using System.Threading;
using System.Threading.Tasks;

namespace Chapter1
{
```

```
public class Program
{
    static void Main()
    {
        int n = 0;

        var up = Task.Run(() =>
        {
            for (int i = 0; i < 1000000; i++)
                Interlocked.Increment(ref n);
        });

        for (int i = 0; i < 1000000; i++)
            Interlocked.Decrement(ref n);


        up.Wait();
        Console.WriteLine(n);

    }

}
}
```

*Interlocked* guarantees that the increment and decrement operations are executed atomically. No other thread will see any intermediate results. Of course, adding and subtracting is a simple operation. If you have more complex operations, you would still have to use a lock.

*Interlocked* also supports switching values by using the *Exchange* method. You use this method as follows:

```
if ( Interlocked.Exchange(ref isInUse, 1) == 0) { }
```

This code retrieves the current value and immediately sets it to the new value in the same operation. It returns the previous value before changing it.

You can also use the *CompareExchange* method. This method first checks to see whether the expected value is there; if it is, it replaces it with another value.

Listing 1-41 shows what can go wrong when comparing and exchanging a value in a nonatomic operation.

**LISTING 1-41** Compare and exchange as a nonatomic operation

```
using System;
using System.Threading;
using System.Threading.Tasks;

public static class Program
{
    static int value = 1;

    public static void Main()
    {
        Task t1 = Task.Run(() =>
        {
```

```
            if (value == 1)
            {
                // Removing the following line will change the output
                Thread.Sleep(1000);
                value = 2;
            }
        });

        Task t2 = Task.Run(() =>
        {
            value = 3;
        });

        Task.WaitAll(t1, t2);
        Console.WriteLine(value); // Displays 2
    }
}
```

*Task t1* starts running and sees that *value* is equal to *1*. At the same time, *t2* changes the value to *3* and then *t1* changes it back to *2*. To avoid this, you can use the following *Interlocked* statement:

```
Interlocked.CompareExchange(ref value, newValue, compareTo);
```

This makes sure that comparing the value and exchanging it for a new one is an atomic operation. This way, no other thread can change the value between comparing and exchanging it.

## Canceling tasks

When working with multithreaded code such as the TPL, the *Parallel* class, or PLINQ, you often have long-running tasks. The .NET Framework offers a special class that can help you in canceling these tasks: *CancellationToken*.

You pass a *CancellationToken* to a *Task*, which then periodically monitors the token to see whether cancellation is requested.

Listing 1-42 shows how you can use a *CancellationToken* to end a task.

LISTING 1-42 Using a *CancellationToken*

```
CancellationTokenSource cancellationTokenSource =
    new CancellationTokenSource();
CancellationToken token = cancellationTokenSource.Token;

Task task = Task.Run(() =>
{
    while(!token.IsCancellationRequested)
    {

        Console.Write("*");
        Thread.Sleep(1000);
    }

}, token);
```

```
Console.WriteLine("Press enter to stop the task");
Console.ReadLine();
cancellationTokenSource.Cancel();

Console.WriteLine("Press enter to end the application");
Console.ReadLine();
```

The *CancellationToken* is used in the asynchronous *Task*. The *CancellationTokenSource* is used to signal that the *Task* should cancel itself.

In this case, the operation will just end when cancellation is requested. Outside users of the *Task* won't see anything different because the *Task* will just have a *RanToCompletion* state. If you want to signal to outside users that your task has been canceled, you can do this by throwing an *OperationCanceledException*. Listing 1-43 shows how to do this.

**LISTING 1-43** Throwing *OperationCanceledException*

```
using System;
using System.Threading;
using System.Threading.Tasks;

namespace Chapter1.Threads
{
    public class Program
    {
        static void Main()
        {
            CancellationTokenSource cancellationTokenSource =
                new CancellationTokenSource();
            CancellationToken token = cancellationTokenSource.Token;

            Task task = Task.Run(() =>
            {
                while (!token.IsCancellationRequested)
                {

                    Console.Write("*");
                    Thread.Sleep(1000);
                }


                token.ThrowIfCancellationRequested();

            }, token);

            try
            {

                Console.WriteLine("Press enter to stop the task");
                Console.ReadLine();

                cancellationTokenSource.Cancel();
                task.Wait();
            }
```

```
                catch (AggregateException e)
                {
                    Console.WriteLine(e.InnerExceptions[0].Message);
                }
                Console.WriteLine("Press enter to end the application");
                Console.ReadLine();


        }

    }
}
// Displays
// Press enter to stop the task
// **
// A task was canceled.
// Press enter to end the application
```

Instead of catching the exception, you can also add a continuation *Task* that executes only when the *Task* is canceled. In this *Task*, you have access to the exception that was thrown, and you can choose to handle it if that's appropriate. Listing 1-44 shows what such a continuation task would look like.

**LISTING 1-44** Adding a continuation for canceled tasks

```
Task task = Task.Run(() =>
{
    while (!token.IsCancellationRequested)
    {
        Console.Write("*");
        Thread.Sleep(1000);
    }
    throw new OperationCanceledException();

}, token).ContinueWith((t) =>
{
    t.Exception.Handle((e) => true);
    Console.WriteLine("You have canceled the task");
}, TaskContinuationOptions.OnlyOnCanceled);
```

If you want to cancel a *Task* after a certain amount of time, you can use an overload of *Task.WaitAny* that takes a timeout. Listing 1-45 shows an example.

**LISTING 1-45** Setting a timeout on a task

```
Task longRunning = Task.Run(() =>
{
    Thread.Sleep(10000);
});

int index = Task.WaitAny(new[] { longRunning }, 1000);

if (index == -1)
    Console.WriteLine("Task timed out");
```

If the returned *index* is *-1*, the task timed out. It's important to check for any possible errors on the other tasks. If you don't catch them, they will go unhandled.

## Objective summary

- When accessing shared data in a multithreaded environment, you need to synchronize access to avoid errors or corrupted data.
- Use the *lock* statement on a private object to synchronize access to a piece of code.
- You can use the *Interlocked* class to execute simple atomic operations.
- You can cancel tasks by using the *CancellationTokenSource* class with a *CancellationToken*.

## Objective review

Answer the following questions to test your knowledge of the information in this objective. You can find the answers to these questions and explanations of why each answer choice is correct or incorrect in the "Answers" section at the end of this chapter.

**1.** You want to synchronize access by using a *lock* statement. On which member do you lock?

   **A.** *this*

   **B.** *string _lock = "mylock"*

   **C.** *int _lock = 42;*

   **D.** *object _lock = new object();*

2. You need to implement cancellation for a long running task. Which object do you pass to the task?

   A. *CancellationTokenSource*

   B. *CancellationToken*

   C. Boolean *isCancelled* variable

   D. *Volatile*

3. You are implementing a state machine in a multithreaded class. You need to check what the current state is and change it to the new one on each step. Which method do you use?

   A. *Volatile.Write(ref currentState)*

   B. *Interlocked.CompareExchange(ref currentState, ref newState, expectedState)*

   C. *Interlocked.Exchange(ref currentState, newState)*

   D. *Interlocked.Decrement(ref newState)*

# Objective 1.3: Implement program flow

One important aspect of managing the flow of your program is making decisions in your application, including checking to see whether the user has entered the correct password, making sure that a certain value is within range, or one of the myriad other possibilities. C# offers a couple of statements that can be used when you need to make a decision.

Next to making decisions, another common task is working with collections. C# has language features that help you work with collections by allowing you to iterate over collections and access individual items.

This objective covers how to:

- Work with Boolean expressions.
- Make decisions in your application.
- Iterate across collections.
- Use explicit *jump* statements.

## Working with Boolean expressions

When working with flow control statements, you will automatically work with *Boolean expressions*. A Boolean expression should always produce *true* or *false* as the end result, but in doing so they can be quite complex by using different *operators*.

One such an operator is the *equality operator* (==). You use this one to test that two values are equal to each other. Listing 1-46 shows some examples.

**LISTING 1-46** Using the equality operator

```
int x = 42;
int y = 1;
int z = 42;

Console.WriteLine(x == y); // Displays false
Console.WriteLine(x == z); // Displays true
```

Table 1-1 shows the operators that you can use in C#.

**TABLE 1-1** C# relational and equality operators

| Operator | Description | Example |
|----------|-------------|---------|
| < | Less than | x < 42; |
| > | Greater than | x > 42; |
| <= | Less than or equal to | x <= 42; |
| >= | Greater than or equal to | x >= 42; |
| == | Equal to | x == 42; |
| != | Not equal to | x != 42; |

You can combine these operators by using the *OR* (||), *AND* (&&), and *Exclusive OR* (^) operators. These operators use both a left and a right operand, meaning the left and right part of the expression.

The *OR* operator returns *true* when one of both operands is *true*. If both are *false*, it returns *false*. If both are true, it will return *true*. Listing 1-47 shows an example.

**LISTING 1-47** Boolean *OR* operator

```
bool x = true;
bool y = false;

bool result = x || y;
Console.WriteLine(result); // Displays True
```

If the runtime notices that the left part of your *OR* operation is *true*, it doesn't have to evaluate the right part of your expression. This is called short-circuiting. Listing 1-48 shows an example.

LISTING 1-48 Short-circuiting the *OR* operator

```
public void OrShortCircuit()
{
    bool x = true;
    bool result = x || GetY();
}

private bool GetY()
{
    Console.WriteLine("This method doesn't get called");
    return true;
}
```

In this case, the method *GetY* is never called and the line is not written to the console.

The *AND* operator can be used when both parts of an expression need to be *true*. If either one of the operands is *false*, the whole expression evaluates to *false*. Listing 1-49 uses the *AND* operator to check to see whether a value is within a certain range.

**LISTING 1-49** Using the *AND* operator

```
int value = 42;
bool result = (0 < value) && (value < 100)
```

In this case, it's not required to add the extra parentheses around the left and right operand but it does add to the readability of your code. Just as with the *OR* operator, the runtime applies short-circuiting. Next to being a performance optimization, you can also use it to your advantage when working with *null* values. Listing 1-50 for example uses the *AND* operator to check if the *input* argument is not *null* and to execute a method on it. If short-circuiting wouldn't be used in this situation, the code would throw an exception each time the *input* parameter would be *null*.

**LISTING 1-50** Short-circuiting the *AND* operator

```
public void Process(string input)
{
    bool result = (input != null) && (input.StartsWith("v"));
    // Do something with the result
}
```

The *Exclusive OR* operator (*XOR*) returns *true* only when exactly one of the operands is *true*. Table 1-2 gives the possibilities for the *XOR* operator.

**TABLE 1-2** Possible values for the *XOR* operator

| Left operand | Right operand | Result |
|---|---|---|
| True | True | False |
| True | False | True |
| False | True | True |
| False | False | False |

Because the *XOR* operator has to check that exactly one of the operands is *true*, it doesn't apply short-circuiting. Listing 1-51 shows how to use the *XOR* operator.

**LISTING 1-51** Using the *XOR* operator

```
bool a = true;
bool b = false;

Console.WriteLine(a ^ a); // False
Console.WriteLine(a ^ b); // True
Console.WriteLine(b ^ b); // False
```

# Making decisions

C# offers several *flow control statements* that help you determine the path that your application follows. You can use the following statements:

- *if*
- *while*
- *do while*
- *for*
- *foreach*
- *switch*
- *break*
- *continue*
- *goto*
- Null-coalescing operator *(??)*
- Conditional operator *(?:)*

Using these constructs, you can create flexible applications that enable you to execute different behavior depending on the circumstances. It's important to know these statements and be able to choose between them.

## The *if* statement

The most widely used flow control statement is the *if* statement. The *if* statement enables you to execute a piece of code depending on a specific condition. The general syntax for the *if statement* is this:

```
if (boolean-expression)
    statement to execute
```

The statement to execute is executed only if the *boolean* expression evaluates to *true*. Listing 1-52 shows an example of using *if*.

LISTING 1-52 Basic *if* statement

```
bool b = true;
if (b)
    Console.WriteLine("True");
```

In this case, the application outputs *"True"* because the condition for the *if statement* is *true*. If *b* would be *false*, the *Console.WriteLine* statement would not be executed.

Of course, passing a hard-coded value to the *if statement* is not very useful. Normally, you would use the *if statement* with a more dynamic value that can change during the execution of the application.

When working with program flow statements, it's important to know the concept of a *code block*, which enables you to write multiple statements in a context in which only a single statement is allowed.

A block uses curly-braces to denote its start and end:

```
{
    statements
}
```

Listing 1-52 showed an *if statement* that executes a single line of code only if it's *true*. You can, however, also use a *code block* after the *if statement*. All code in the block is executed based on the result of the *if statement*. You can see an example of this in Listing 1-53.

LISTING 1-53 An *if* statement with code block

```
bool b = true;
if (b)
{
    Console.WriteLine("Both these lines");
    Console.WriteLine("Will be executed");
}
```

Variables defined within a code block are accessible only within the code block and go out of scope at the end of the block. This means that you can declare variables inside a block, and use them within the block but not outside the block. Listing 1-54 shows the scoping differences. Variable *b* is declared outside the block and can be accessed both in the outer block and in the *if* statement. Variable *r*, however, can be accessed only in the *if* statement.

LISTING 1-54 Code blocks and scoping

```
bool b = true;
if (b)
{
    int r = 42;
    b = false;
}

// r is not accessible
// b is now false
```

You can also execute some code when the *if* statement evaluates to *false*. You can do this by using an *else* block. The general syntax looks like this:

```
if (boolean-expression)
    statement
else
    statement
```

Listing 1-55 shows an example of using an *else* statement. This outputs *"False"*.

**LISTING 1-55** Using an *else* statement

```
bool b = false;

if (b)
{
    Console.WriteLine("True");
}
else
{
    Console.WriteLine("False");
}
```

You can use multiple *if/else* statements as shown in Listing 1-56.

**LISTING 1-56** Using multiple *if/else* statements

```
bool b = false;
bool c = true;

if (b)
{
    Console.WriteLine("b is true");
}
else if (c)
{
    Console.WriteLine("c is true");
}
else
{
    Console.WriteLine("b and c are false");
}
```

You can also nest *if* and *else* statements. For readability, it's nice to outline your code correctly. The following code is perfectly legal, but on first sight it's hard to see what the code really does:

```
if (x) if (y) F(); else G();
```

When outlined correctly, the code is equal to the one in Listing 1-57, which is much easier to understand.

**LISTING 1-57** A more readable nested *if* statement

```
if (x)
{
    if (y)
    {
        F();
    }
    else
    {
        G();
    }
}
```

The compiler optimizes your code and removes any unnecessary braces and statements. Under normal circumstances, you should worry more about readability than about the number of lines you produce. Team members especially appreciate it when you write code that's not only correct but also easier to maintain.

## The null-coalescing operator

The *?? operator* is called the *null-coalescing operator*. You can use it to provide a default value for nullable value types or for reference types.

The operator returns the left value if it's not *null*; otherwise, the right operand.

Listing 1-58 shows an example of using the operator.

**LISTING 1-58** The null-coalescing operator

```
int? x = null;
int y = x ?? -1;
```

In this case, the value of *y* is *-1* because *x* is *null*.

You can also nest the null-coalescing operator, as Listing 1-59 shows.

**LISTING 1-59** Nesting the null-coalescing operator

```
int? x = null;
int? z = null;
int y = x ??
        z ??
        -1;
```

Of course, you can achieve the same with an if statement but the null-coalescing operator can shorten your code and improve its readability.

## The conditional operator

The *conditional operator* (?:) returns one of two values depending on a Boolean expression. If the expression is *true*, the first value is returned; otherwise, the second.

Listing 1-60 shows an example of how the operator can be used to simplify some code. In this case, the *if* statement can be replaced with the conditional operator.

LISTING 1-60 The conditional operator

```
private static int GetValue(bool p)
{
    if (p)
        return 1;
    else
        return 0;

    return p ? 1 : 0;
}
```

## The *switch* statement

You can use the *switch* statement to simplify complex *if* statements. Take the example of Listing 1-61.

**LISTING 1-61** A complex *if* statement

```
void Check(char input)
{
    if (input == 'a'
        || input == 'e'
        || input == 'i'
        || input == 'o'
        || input == 'u')
    {
        Console.WriteLine("Input is a vowel");
    }
    else
    {
        Console.WriteLine("Input is a consonant");
    }
}
```

The *switch* statement can be used to make this code more comprehensive. A *switch* statement checks the value of its argument and then looks for a matching label. Listing 1-62 shows the code from Listing 1-59 as a *switch* statement.

**LISTING 1-62** A *switch* statement

```
void CheckWithSwitch(char input)
{
    switch (input)
    {
        case 'a':
        case 'e':
        case 'i':
        case 'o':
        case 'u':
            {
                Console.WriteLine("Input is a vowel");
```

```
            break;
        }
    case 'y':
        {
            Console.WriteLine("Input is sometimes a vowel.");
            break;
        }
    default:
        {
            Console.WriteLine("Input is a consonant");
            break;
        }
    }
}
```

A *switch* can use one or multiple *switch-sections* that can contain one or more *switch-labels*. In Listing 1-62, all the vowels belong to the same *switch-section*. If you want, you can also add a *default label* that is used when none of the other labels matches.

The end point of a *switch* statement should not be reachable. You need to have a statement such as *break* or *return* that explicitly exits the *switch* statement, or you need to throw an exception. This avoids the fall-through behavior that C++ has. This makes it possible for *switch* sections to appear in any order without affecting behavior.

Instead of implicitly falling through to another label, you can use the *goto statement* (see Listing 1-63).

**LISTING 1-63** *goto* in a *switch* statement

```
int i = 1;
switch (i)
{
    case 1:
        {
            Console.WriteLine("Case 1");
            goto case 2;
        }
    case 2:
        {
            Console.WriteLine("Case 2");
            break;
        }
}

// Displays
// Case 1
// Case 2
```

# Iterating across collections

Another subject that has to do with the flow of your program is iterating across collections. Collections are widely used in C#, and the language offers constructs that you can use with them:

- *for*
- *foreach*
- *while*
- *do while*

## The *for* loop

You can use a *for loop* when you need to iterate over a collection until a specific condition is reached (for example, you have reached the end of a collection). Listing 1-64 shows an example in which you loop through all items in an array.

**LISTING 1-64** A basic *for* loop

```
int[] values = { 1, 2, 3, 4, 5, 6 };
for (int index = 0; index < values.Length; index++)
{
    Console.Write(values[index]);
}

// Displays
// 123456
```

As you can see, the *for* loop consists of three different parts:

```
for(initial; condition; loop)
```

- The initial part is executed before the first iteration and declares and initializes the variables that are used in the loop.
- The condition is evaluated on each iteration. When the condition equals *false*, the loop is exited.
- The loop section is run during every iteration and is normally used to change the counter that's used to loop over the collection.

None of these parts is required. You can use for(;;) {} as a perfectly legal *for* loop that would never end. You can also use multiple statements in each part of your *for* loop (see Listing 1-65).

LISTING 1-65 A *for* loop with multiple loop variables

```
int[] values = { 1, 2, 3, 4, 5, 6 };
for (int x = 0, y = values.Length - 1;
    ((x < values.Length) && (y >= 0));
    x++, y--)
{
    Console.Write(values[x]);
    Console.Write(values[y]);
}

// Displays
// 162534435261
```

It's also not required to let the loop value increment or decrement with 1. For example, you can change Listing 1-64 to increment *index* with 2 to only display the odd numbers, as Listing 1-66 shows.

LISTING 1-66 A *for* loop with a custom increment

```
int[] values = { 1, 2, 3, 4, 5, 6 };
for (int index = 0; index < values.Length; index += 2)
{
    Console.Write(values[index]);
}

// Displays
// 135
```

Normally, the *for* loop ends when the condition becomes *false*, but you can also decide to manually break out of the loop. You can do this by using the *break* or *return* statement when you want to completely exit the method. Listing 1-67 shows an example of the *break* statement.

LISTING 1-67 A *for* loop with a *break* statement

```
int[] values = { 1, 2, 3, 4, 5, 6 };
for (int index = 0; index < values.Length; index++)
{
    if (values[index] == 4) break;

    Console.Write(values[index]);
}

// Displays
// 123
```

Next to breaking the loop completely, you can also instruct the *for* loop to continue to the next item by using the *continue* statement. Listing 1-68 shows an example in which the number *4* is skipped in the loop.

**LISTING 1-68** A *for* loop with a *continue* statement

```
int[] values = { 1, 2, 3, 4, 5, 6 };

for (int index = 0; index < values.Length; index++)
{
    if (values[index] == 4) continue;

    Console.Write(values[index]);
}

// Displays
// 12356
```

## The *while* and *do-while* loop

Another looping construction is the *while loop*. A *for* loop is nothing more than a convenient way to write a *while* loop that does the checking and incrementing of the counter. Listing 1-69 shows an example. Notice the extra parenthesis to restrict the scope of the *loop* variable.

**LISTING 1-69** Implementing a *for* loop with a *while* statement

```
int[] values = { 1, 2, 3, 4, 5, 6 };

{
    int index = 0;
    while (index < values.Length)
    {
        Console.Write(values[index]);
        index++;
    }
}
```

As you can see, a *while* loop checks an expression and executes as long as this expression is *true*. You should use a *for* loop when you know the number of iterations in advance. A *while* loop can be used when you don't know the number of iterations.

If the condition of the *while* loop is *false*, it won't execute the code inside the loop. This is different when using a *do-while* loop. A *do-while* loop executes at least once, even if the expression is *false*. Listing 1-70 shows an example of using a *do-while* loop.

**LISTING 1-70** *do-while* loop

```
do
{
    Console.WriteLine("Executed once!");
}
while (false);
```

Within a *while* or *do-while* loop, you can use the *continue* and *break* statements just as with a *for* loop.

## The *foreach* loop

The *foreach loop* is used to iterate over a collection and automatically stores the current item in a *loop* variable. The *foreach* loop keeps track of where it is in the collection and protects you against iterating past the end of the collection.

Listing 1-71 shows an example of how to use the *foreach* loop.

**LISTING 1-71** *foreach* loop

```
int[] values = { 1, 2, 3, 4, 5, 6 };

foreach (int i in values)
{
    Console.Write(i);
}

// Displays 123456
```

As you can see, the *foreach* loop automatically stores the current item in a strongly typed variable. You can use the *continue* and *break* statements to influence the way the *foreach* loop works.

The *loop* variable cannot be modified. You can make modifications to the object that the variable points to, but you can't assign a new value to it. Listing 1-72 shows these differences.

**LISTING 1-72** Changing items in a *foreach*

```
class Person
{
    public string FirstName { get; set; }
    public string LastName { get; set; }
}

void CannotChangeForeachIterationVariable()
{
    var people = new List<Person>
    {
        new Person() { FirstName = "John", LastName = "Doe"},
        new Person() { FirstName = "Jane", LastName = "Doe"},
    };

    foreach (Person p in people)
    {
        p.LastName = "Changed"; // This is allowed
        // p = new Person(); // This gives a compile error
    }
}
```

You can understand this behavior when you know how *foreach* actually works. When the compiler encounters a *foreach* statement, it generates some code on your behalf; *foreach* is syntactic sugar that lets you write some code in a nice way. Listing 1-73 shows what's happening.

**LISTING 1-73** The compiler-generated code for a *foreach* loop

```
List<Person>.Enumerator e = people.GetEnumerator();

try
{
    Person v;
    while (e.MoveNext())
    {
        v = e.Current;
    }
}
finally
{
    System.IDisposable d = e as System.IDisposable;
    if (d != null) d.Dispose();
}
```

If you change the value of *e.Current* to something else, the iterator pattern can't determine what to do when *e.MoveNext* is called. This is why it's not allowed to change the value of the iteration variable in a *foreach* statement.

> **MORE INFO** **ENUMERATORS**
>
> For more information on how the *GetEnumerator* method works and how you can implement your own enumerators see Chapter 2.

## *Jump* statements

Another type of statement that can be used to influence program flow is a *jump statement*. You have already looked at two of those statements: *break* and *continue*. A *jump* statement unconditionally transfers control to another location in your code.

Another *jump* statement that can be used to change the flow of a program is *goto*. The *goto* statement moves control to a statement that is marked by a label. If the label can't be found or is not within the scope of the *goto* statement, a compiler error occurs.

Listing 1-74 shows an example of using *goto* and a *label*.

**LISTING 1-74** *goto* statement with a label

```
int x = 3;
if ( x == 3) goto customLabel;
x++;

customLabel:
Console.WriteLine(x);
// Displays 3
```

You cannot make a jump to a label that's not in scope. This means you cannot transfer control to another block of code that's outside of your current block. The compiler also makes sure that any *finally* blocks that intervene are executed.

The *jump* statements such as *break* and *continue* can have their uses in some situations. If possible, however, you should try to avoid them. By refactoring your code, you can remove them most of the time and this will improve the readability of your code.

The *goto* statement is even worse. It is considered a bad practice. Although C# restricts the way the *goto* operator behaves, as a guideline, you should try to avoid using *goto*. One area where *goto* is used is in generated code like the code the compiler generates when you use the new *async/await* feature in C# 5.

---

**MORE INFO**   **JUMP STATEMENTS**

For more information about *jump* statements, see *http://msdn.microsoft.com/en-us/library/d96yfwee.aspx*.

---

**Thought experiment**

**Choosing your program flow statements**

In this thought experiment, apply what you've learned about this objective. You can find answers to these questions in the "Answers" section at the end of this chapter.

You are updating an old C#2 console application to a WPF C#5 application. The application is used by hotels to keep track of reservations and guests coming and leaving. You are going through the old code base to determine whether there is code that can be easily reused. You notice a couple of things:

- The code uses the *goto* statement to manage flow.
- There are a lot of long *if* statements that map user input.
- The code uses the *for* loop extensively.

1. What is the disadvantage of using *goto*? How can you avoid using the *goto* statement?

2. Which statement can you use to improve the long *if* statements?

3. What are the differences between the *for* and *foreach* statement? When should you use which?

## Objective summary

- Boolean expressions can use several operators: ==, !=, <, >, <=, >=, !. Those operators can be combined together by using *AND (&&), OR (||) and XOR (^)*.
- You can use the *if-else* statement to execute code depending on a specific condition.
- The *switch* statement can be used when matching a value against a couple of options.

- The *for* loop can be used when iterating over a collection where you know the number of iterations in advance.

- A *while* loop can be used to execute some code while a condition is true; *do-while* should be used when the code should be executed at least once.

- *foreach* can be used to iterate over collections.

- *Jump* statements such as *break*, *goto*, and *continue* can be used to transfer control to another line of the program.

## Objective review

Answer the following questions to test your knowledge of the information in this objective. You can find the answers to these questions and explanations of why each answer choice is correct or incorrect in the "Answers" section at the end of this chapter.

1. You need to iterate over a collection in which you know the number of items. You need to remove certain items from the collection. Which statement do you use?

   **A.** *switch*

   **B.** *foreach*

   **C.** *for*

   **D.** *goto*

2. You have a lot of checks in your application for *null* values. If a value is not *null*, you want to call a method on it. You want to simplify your code. Which technique do you use?

   **A.** *for*

   **B.** Conditional operator

   **C.** Null-coalescing operator

   **D.** The short-circuiting behavior of the and operator

3. You are processing some data from over the network. You use a *HasNext* and *Read* method to retrieve the data. You need to run some code on each item. What do you use?

   **A.** *for*

   **B.** *foreach*

   **C.** *while*

   **D.** *do-while*

# Objective 1.4: Create and implement events and callbacks

An *event* can be used to provide notifications. You can subscribe to an event if you are interested in those notifications. You can also create your own events and raise them to provide notifications when something interesting happens. The .NET Framework offers built-in types that you can use to create events. By using delegates, lambda expressions, and anonymous methods, you can create and use events in a comfortable way.

> **This objective covers how to:**
> - Understand delegates.
> - Use lambda expressions.
> - Create and raise events.

## Understanding delegates

In C#, *delegates* form the basic building blocks for events. A *delegate* is a type that defines a method signature. In C++, for example, you would do this with a function pointer. In C# you can instantiate a *delegate* and let it point to another method. You can invoke the method through the *delegate*.

Listing 1-75 shows an example of declaring a *delegate* and calling a method through it.

**LISTING 1-75** Using a delegate

```
public delegate int Calculate(int x, int y);

public int Add(int x, int y) { return x + y; }
public int Multiply(int x, int y) { return x * y; }

public void UseDelegate()
{
    Calculate calc = Add;
    Console.WriteLine(calc(3, 4)); // Displays 7

    calc = Multiply;
    Console.WriteLine(calc(3, 4)); // Displays 12
}
```

As you can see, you use the special *delegate* keyword to tell the compiler that you are creating a *delegate* type. *Delegates* can be nested in other types and they can then be used as a nested type.

Instantiating *delegates* is easy since C# 2.0 added the automatic creation of a new *delegate* when a method group is assigned to a delegate type. An instantiated *delegate* is an object; you can pass it around and give it as an argument to other methods.

Another feature of *delegates* is that you can combine them together. This is called *multi-casting*. You can use the + or += operator to add another method to the *invocation list* of an existing delegate instance. Listing 1-76 shows an example.

LISTING 1-76 A multicast delegate

```
public void MethodOne()
{
    Console.WriteLine("MethodOne");
}

public void MethodTwo()
{
    Console.WriteLine("MethodTwo");
}

public delegate void Del();

public void Multicast()
{
    Del d = MethodOne;
    d += MethodTwo;

    d();
}
// Displays
// MethodOne
// MethodTwo
```

You can also remove a method from an invocation list by using the decrement assignment operator (- or -=).

All this is possible because delegates inherit from the *System.MulticastDelegate* class that in turn inherits from *System.Delegate*. Because of this, you can use the members that are defined in those base classes on your delegates.

For example, to find out how many methods a multicast delegate is going to call, you can use the following code:

```
int invocationCount = del.GetInvocationList().GetLength(0);
```

When you assign a method to a *delegate*, the method signature does not have to match the *delegate* exactly. This is called *covariance* and *contravariance*. Covariance makes it possible that a method has a return type that is more derived than that defined in the delegate. Contravariance permits a method that has parameter types that are less derived than those in the delegate type.

Listing 1-77 shows an example of *covariance*.

LISTING 1-77 Covariance with delegates

```
public delegate TextWriter CovarianceDel();

public StreamWriter MethodStream() { return null; }
public StringWriter MethodString() { return null; }

CovarianceDel del;
del = MethodStream;
del = MethodString;
```

Because both *StreamWriter* and *StringWriter* inherit from *TextWriter*, you can use the *CovarianceDel* with both methods. An example of contravariance can be seen in Listing 1-78.

LISTING 1-78 Contravariance with delegates

```
void DoSomething(TextWriter tw) { }
public delegate void ContravarianceDel(StreamWriter tw);

ContravarianceDel del = DoSomething;
```

Because the method *DoSomething* can work with a *TextWriter*, it surely can also work with a *StreamWriter*. Because of contravariance, you can call the delegate and pass an instance of *StreamWriter* to the *DoSomething* method.

---

> **MORE INFO  COVARIANCE AND CONTRAVARIANCE**
>
> For more information on covariance and contravariance and how they are implemented in C#, see the excellent series of blog posts that Eric Lippert wrote at *http://blogs.msdn. com/b/ericlippert/archive/tags/covariance+and+contravariance/*.

---

# Using lambda expressions

Sometimes the whole signature of a method can be more code than the body of a method. There are also situations in which you need to create an entire method only to use it in a delegate.

For these cases, Microsoft added some new features to C#. In C#, 2.0 *anonymous methods* were added. In C# 3.0, things became even better when *lambda expressions* were added. Lambda expressions are the preferred way to go when writing new code.

Listing 1-79 shows how you would write the example in Listing 1-73 with newer lambda syntax.

LISTING 1-79 Lambda expression to create a delegate

```
Calculate calc = (x, y) => x + y;
Console.WriteLine(calc(3, 4)); // Displays 7
calc = (x, y) => x * y;
Console.WriteLine(calc(3, 4)); // Displays 12
```

When reading this code, you can say *go* or *goes to* for the special lambda syntax. For example, the first lambda expression in Listing 1-79 is read as *"x and y goes to adding x and y."*

The lambda function has no specific name as the methods in Listing 1-75 have. Because of this, lambda functions are called *anonymous functions*. You also don't have to specify a *return* type explicitly. The compiler infers this automatically from your lambda. And in the case of Listing 1-79, the types of the parameters *x* and *y* are also not specified explicitly.

As you can see, the syntax for writing a lambda can be compact. If a lambda has only one parameter, you can even remove the parentheses around the parameter.

You can create lambdas that span multiple statements. You can do this by adding curly braces around the statements that form the lambda as Listing 1-80 shows.

**LISTING 1-80** Creating a lambda expression with multiple statements

```
Calculate calc =
    (x, y) =>
    {
        Console.WriteLine("Adding numbers");
        return x + y;
    };

int result = calc(3, 4);
// Displays
// Adding numbers
```

Sometimes declaring a delegate for an *event* feels a bit cumbersome. Because of this, the .NET Framework has a couple of built-in *delegate* types that you can use when declaring *delegates*. For the *Calculate* examples, you have used the following *delegate*:

```
public delegate int Calculate(int x, int y);
```

You can replace this *delegate* with one of the built-in types namely *Func<int,int,int>*. The *Func<...>* types can be found in the *System* namespace and they represent *delegates* that return a type and take 0 to 16 parameters. All those types inherit from *System.MulticastDelegate* so you can add multiple methods to the invocation list.

If you want a *delegate* type that doesn't return a value, you can use the *System.Action* types. They can also take 0 to 16 parameters, but they don't return a value. Listing 1-81 shows an example of using the *Action* type.

**LISTING 1-81** Using the *Action* delegate

```
Action<int, int> calc = (x, y) =>
{
    Console.WriteLine(x + y);
};

calc(3, 4); // Displays 7
```

Things start to become more complex when your *lambda* function starts referring to variables declared outside of the *lambda* expression (or to the *this* reference). Normally, when control leaves the scope of a variable, the variable is no longer valid. But what if a delegate refers to a *local* variable and is then returned to the calling method? Now, the delegate has a longer life than the variable. To fix this, the compiler generates code that makes the life of the captured variable at least as long as the longest-living delegate. This is called a *closure*.

## Using events

A popular *design pattern* (a reusable solution for a recurring problem) in application development is that of *publish-subscribe*. You can subscribe to an *event* and then you are notified when the publisher of the *event* raises a new *event*. This is used to establish loose coupling between components in an application.

*Delegates* form the basis for the event system in C#. Listing 1-82 shows how a class can expose a public *delegate* and raise it.

**LISTING 1-82** Using an *Action* to expose an event

```
public class Pub
{
    public Action OnChange { get; set; }

    public void Raise()
    {
        if (OnChange != null)
        {
            OnChange();
        }
    }
}

public void CreateAndRaise()
{
    Pub p = new Pub();
    p.OnChange += () => Console.WriteLine("Event raised to method 1");
    p.OnChange += () => Console.WriteLine("Event raised to method 2");
    p.Raise();
}
```

When calling *CreateAndRaise*, your code creates a new instance of *Pub*, subscribes to the event with two different methods and then raises the event by calling *p.Raise*. The *Pub* class is completely unaware of any subscribers. It just raises the *event*.

If there would be no subscribers to an *event*, the *OnChange* property would be *null*. This is why the *Raise* method checks to see whether *OnChange* is not *null*.

Although this system works, there are a couple of weaknesses. If you change the subscribe line for method 2 to the following, you would effectively remove the first subscriber by using = instead of +=:

```
p.OnChange = () => Console.WriteLine("Event raised to method 2");
```

In the example from Listing 1-82, the *Pub* class raises the *event*. However, nothing prevents outside users of the class from raising the *event*. By just calling *p.OnChange()* every user of the class can raise the *event* to all subscribers.

To overcome these weaknesses, the C# language uses the special *event* keyword. Listing 1-83 shows a modified example of the *Pub* class that uses the *event* syntax.

**LISTING 1-83** Using the *event* keyword

```
public class Pub
{
    public event Action OnChange = delegate { };

    public void Raise()
    {
        OnChange();
    }
}
```

By using the *event* syntax, there are a couple of interesting changes. First, you are no longer using a public property but a public field. Normally, this would be a step back. However, with the *event* syntax, the compiler protects your field from unwanted access.

An *event* cannot be directly assigned to (with the = instead of +=) operator. So you don't have the risk of someone removing all previous subscriptions, as with the delegate syntax.

Another change is that no outside users can raise your *event*. It can be raised only by code that's part of the class that defined the *event*.

Listing 1-83 also uses some special syntax to initialize the *event* to an empty *delegate*. This way, you can remove the *null* check around raising the *event* because you can be certain that the *event* is never *null*. Outside users of your class can't set the *event* to null; only members of your class can. As long as none of your other class members sets the *event* to *null*, you can safely assume that it will always have a value.

There is, however, one change you still have to make to follow the coding conventions in the .NET Framework. Instead of using the *Action* type for your event, you should use the *EventHandler* or *EventHandler<T>*. *EventHandler* is declared as the following delegate:

```
public delegate void EventHandler(object sender, EventArgs e);
```

By default, it takes a *sender object* and some *event arguments*. The *sender* is by convention the object that raised the *event* (or *null* if it comes from a static method). By using *EventHandler<T>*, you can specify the type of *event* arguments you want to use. Listing 1-84 shows an example.

**LISTING 1-84** Custom *event* arguments

```csharp
public class MyArgs : EventArgs
{
    public MyArgs(int value)
    {
        Value = value;
    }

    public int Value { get; set; }
}

public class Pub
{
    public event EventHandler<MyArgs> OnChange = delegate { };

    public void Raise()
    {
        OnChange(this, new MyArgs(42));
    }
}

public void CreateAndRaise()
{
    Pub p = new Pub();

    p.OnChange += (sender, e)
        => Console.WriteLine("Event raised: {0}", e.Value);

    p.Raise();
}
```

The *Pub* class uses an *EventHandler<MyArgs>*, which specifies the type of the *event* arguments. When raising this *event*, you are required to pass an instance of *MyArgs*. Subscribers to the *event* can access the arguments and use it.

Although the *event* implementation uses a public field, you can still customize addition and removal of subscribers. This is called a *custom event accessor.* Listing 1-85 shows an example of creating a *custom event accessor* for an event.

**LISTING 1-85** Custom event accessor

```csharp
public class Pub
{
    private event EventHandler<MyArgs> onChange = delegate { };
    public event EventHandler<MyArgs> OnChange
    {
        add
        {
            lock (onChange)
            {
                onChange += value;
            }
        }
        remove
        {
            lock (onChange)
            {
                onChange -= value;
            }
        }
    }

    public void Raise()
    {
        onChange(this, new MyArgs(42));
    }
}
```

A *custom event accessor* looks a lot like a property with a *get* and *set accessor*. Instead of *get* and *set* you use *add* and *remove*. It's important to put a *lock* around adding and removing subscribers to make sure that the operation is thread safe.

> **MORE INFO**  **USING LOCK**
>
> For more info on when and how to use locking, see the section titled "Objective 1.2: Manage multithreading," earlier in this chapter.

If you use the regular *event* syntax, the compiler generates the accessor for you. This makes it clear that *events* are not *delegates*; instead they are a convenient wrapper around *delegates*.

*Delegates* are executed in a sequential order. Generally, *delegates* are executed in the order in which they were added, although this is not something that is specified within the Common Language Infrastructure (CLI), so you shouldn't depend on it.

One thing that is a direct result of the sequential order is how to handle exceptions. Listing 1-86 shows an example in which one of the *event* subscribers throws an error.

**LISTING 1-86** Exception when raising an *event*

```
public class Pub
{
    public event EventHandler OnChange = delegate { };
    public void Raise()
    {
        OnChange(this, EventArgs.Empty);
    }
}

public void CreateAndRaise()
{
    Pub p = new Pub();

    p.OnChange += (sender,e )
        => Console.WriteLine("Subscriber 1 called");

    p.OnChange += (sender, e)
        => { throw new Exception(); };

    p.OnChange += (sender,e )
        => Console.WriteLine("Subscriber 3 called");


    p.Raise();
}

// Displays
// Subscriber 1 called
```

As you can see, the first subscriber is executed successfully, the second one throws an exception, and the third one is never called.

If this is not the behavior you want, you need to manually raise the *events* and handle any exceptions that occur. You can do this by using the *GetInvocationList* method that is declared on the *System.Delegate* base class. Listing 1-87 shows an example of retrieving the subscribers and enumerating them manually.

**LISTING 1-87** Manually raising *events* with exception handling

```csharp
public class Pub
{
    public event EventHandler OnChange = delegate { };
    public void Raise()
    {
        var exceptions = new List<Exception>();

        foreach (Delegate handler in OnChange.GetInvocationList())
        {
            try
            {
                handler.DynamicInvoke(this, EventArgs.Empty);
            }
            catch (Exception ex)
            {
                exceptions.Add(ex);
            }
        }

        if (exceptions.Any())
        {
            throw new AggregateException(exceptions);
        }
    }
}

public void CreateAndRaise()
{
    Pub p = new Pub();

    p.OnChange += (sender, e)
        => Console.WriteLine("Subscriber 1 called");

    p.OnChange += (sender, e)
        => { throw new Exception(); };

    p.OnChange += (sender, e)
        => Console.WriteLine("Subscriber 3 called");

    try
    {
        p.Raise();
    }
    catch (AggregateException ex)
    {
        Console.WriteLine(ex.InnerExceptions.Count);
    }
}

// Displays
// Subscriber 1 called
// Subscriber 3 called
// 1
```

**MORE INFO** EXCEPTION HANDLING

For more information on how to work with exceptions, see the section titled "Objective 1.5: Implement exception handling" later in this chapter.

## Thought experiment

### Building a loosely coupled system

In this thought experiment, apply what you've learned about this objective. You can find answers to these questions in the "Answers" section at the end of this chapter.

You are working on a desktop application that consists of multiple forms. Those forms show different views of the same data and they should update in real time. Your application is extensible, and third parties can add plug-ins that contain their own views of the data.

1. Should you use delegates or events in this system?

2. How can this help you?

## Objective summary

- Delegates are a type that defines a method signature and can contain a reference to a method.

- Delegates can be instantiated, passed around, and invoked.

- Lambda expressions, also known as anonymous methods, use the => operator and form a compact way of creating inline methods.

- Events are a layer of syntactic sugar on top of delegates to easily implement the publish-subscribe pattern.

- Events can be raised only from the declaring class. Users of events can only remove and add methods the invocation list.

- You can customize events by adding a custom event accessor and by directly using the underlying delegate type.

## Objective review

Answer the following questions to test your knowledge of the information in this objective. You can find the answers to these questions and explanations of why each answer choice is correct or incorrect in the "Answers" section at the end of this chapter.

1. You have a private method in your class and you want to make invocation of the method possible by certain callers. What do you do?

   **A.** Make the method public.

   **B.** Use an event so outside users can be notified when the method is executed.

   **C.** Use a method that returns a delegate to authorized callers.

   **D.** Declare the private method as a lambda.

2. You have declared an event on your class, and you want outside users of your class to raise this event. What do you do?

   **A.** Make the event public.

   **B.** Add a public method to your class that raises the event.

   **C.** Use a public delegate instead of an event.

   **D.** Use a custom event accessor to give access to outside users.

3. You are using a multicast delegate with multiple subscribers. You want to make sure that all subscribers are notified, even if an exception is thrown. What do you do?

   **A.** Manually raise the events by using *GetInvocationList*.

   **B.** Wrap the raising of the event in a *try/catch*.

   **C.** Nothing. This is the default behavior.

   **D.** Let subscribers return *true* or *false* instead of throwing an exception.

# Objective 1.5: Implement exception handling

When you build your applications, sometimes errors occur. Maybe you want to write a file to disk, and the disk is full. You try to connect to a database, but the database server is unavailable or another unexpected condition exists. Instead of working with error codes, the .NET Framework uses exceptions to signal errors. You can also use these exceptions to signal errors that happen in your own applications and you can even create custom exception types to signal specific errors.

It's important to know how to work with exceptions so you can implement a well-designed strategy for dealing with or raising errors.

> **This objective covers how to:**
> - Handle exceptions.
> - Throw exceptions.
> - Create custom exceptions.

# Handling exceptions

When an error occurs somewhere in an application, an *exception* is raised. *Exceptions* have a couple of advantages compared with error codes. An *exception* is an object in itself that contains data about the error that happened. It not only has a user-friendly message but it also contains the location in which the error happened and it can even store extra data, such as an address to a page that offers some help.

If an *exception* goes unhandled, it will cause the current process to terminate. Listing 1-88 shows an example of an application that throws an error and shuts down.

**LISTING 1-88** Parsing an invalid number

```
namespace ExceptionHandling
{
    public static class Program
    {
        public static void Main()
        {
            string s = "NaN";
            int i = int.Parse(s);
        }
    }
}
// Displays
// Unhandled Exception: System.FormatException: Input string was not in a correct format.
//    at System.Number.StringToNumber(String str, NumberStyles options,
//        NumberBuffer& number, NumberFormatInfo info, Boolean parseDecimal)
//    at System.Number.ParseInt32(String s, NumberStyles style,
//        NumberFormatInfo info)
//    at System.Int32.Parse(String s)
//    at ExceptionHandling.Program.Main() in c:\Users\Wouter\Documents\
//    Visual Studio 2012\Projects\ExamRefProgrammingInCSharp\Chapter1\Program.cs:line 9
```

The *int.Parse* method *throws* an *exception* of type *FormatException* when the string is not a valid number. *Throwing* an *exception* halts the execution of your application. Instead of continuing to the following line, the runtime starts searching for a location in which you handle the *exception*. If such a location cannot be found, the *exception* is unhandled and will terminate the application.

To handle an *exception*, you can use a *try/catch statement*. Listing 1-89 shows an example of catching the *FormatException*.

**LISTING 1-89** Catching a *FormatException*

```
using System;
namespace ExceptionHandling
{
    public static class Program
    {
        public static void Main()
        {
            while (true)
            {
                string s = Console.ReadLine();

                if (string.IsNullOrWhiteSpace(s)) break;

                try
                {
                    int i = int.Parse(s);
                    break;
                }
                catch (FormatException)
                {
                    Console.WriteLine("{0} is not a valid number. Please try again", s);
                }
            }
        }
    }
}
```

You need to surround the code that can potentially throw an exception with a *try* statement. Following the *try* statement, you can add several different *catch blocks*. How much code you put inside each *try block* depends on the situation. If you have multiple statements that can throw the same exceptions that need to be handled differently, they should be in different *try blocks*.

A *catch block* can specify the type of the exception it wants to catch. Because all exceptions in the .NET Framework inherit from *System.Exception*, you can catch every possible *exception* by catching this base type. You can catch more specific *exception* types by adding extra *catch blocks*.

The *catch blocks* should be specified as most-specific to least-specific because this is the order in which the runtime will examine them. When an *exception* is thrown, the first matching *catch block* will be executed. If no matching *catch block* can be found, the exception will fall through. Listing 1-90 shows an example of catching two different *exception* types.

If the *string s* is *null*, an *ArgumentNullException* will be thrown. If the *string* is not a number, a *FormatException* will be thrown. By using different *catch blocks*, you can handle those exceptions each in their own way.

**LISTING 1-90** Catching different *exception* types

```
try
{
    int i = int.Parse(s);
}
catch (ArgumentNullException)
{

    Console.WriteLine("You need to enter a value");
}
catch (FormatException)
{
    Console.WriteLine("{0} is not a valid number. Please try again", s);
}
```

In C# 1, you could also use a *catch block* without an *exception* type. This could be used to catch exceptions that were thrown from other languages like C++ that don't inherit from *System.Exception* (in C++ you can throw exceptions of any type). Nowadays, each exception that doesn't inherit from *System.Exception* is automatically wrapped in a *System.Runtime.CompilerServices.RuntimeWrappedException*. Since this exception inherits from *System.Exception*, there is no need for the empty catch block anymore.

It's important to make sure that your application is in the correct state when the *catch block* finishes. This could mean that you need to revert changes that your *try block* made before the exception was thrown.

Another important feature of exception handling is the ability to specify that certain code should always run in case of an exception. This can be done by using the *finally block* together with a *try* or *try/catch* statement. The *finally block* will execute whether an exception happens or not. Listing 1-91 shows an example of a *finally block*.

**LISTING 1-91** Using a finally block

```
using System;

namespace ExceptionHandling
{
    public static class Program
    {
        public static void Main()
        {
            string s = Console.ReadLine();

            try
            {
                int i = int.Parse(s);
            }
            catch (ArgumentNullException)
            {
                Console.WriteLine("You need to enter a value");
            }
            catch (FormatException)

            {
                Console.WriteLine("{0} is not a valid number. Please try again", s);
            }
            finally
            {

                Console.WriteLine("Program complete.");
            }
        }
    }
}

// Displays
// a
// a is not a valid number. Please try again
// Program complete.
```

Of course, there are still situations in which a *finally block* won't run. For example, when the *try block* goes into an infinite loop, it will never exit the *try block and never enter the finally block*. And in situations such as a power outage, no other code will run. The whole operating system will just terminate.

There is one other situation that you can use to prevent a *finally block* from running. Of course, this isn't something you want to use on a regular basis, but you may have a situation in which just shutting down the application is safer than running *finally blocks*.

Preventing the finally block from running can be achieved by using *Environment.FailFast*. This method has two different overloads, one that only takes a *string* and another one that also takes an *exception*. When this method is called, the message (and optionally the exception) are written to the Windows application event log, and the application is terminated. Listing 1-92 shows how you can use this method. When you run this application without a debugger attached, a message is written to the event log.

**LISTING 1-92** Using *Environment.FailFast*

```
using System;
namespace ExceptionHandling
{
    public static class Program
    {
        public static void Main()
        {
            string s = Console.ReadLine();

            try
            {
                int i = int.Parse(s);
                if (i == 42) Environment.FailFast("Special number entered");
            }
            finally
            {
                Console.WriteLine("Program complete.");
            }
        }
    }
}
```

The line *Program Complete* won't be executed if *42* is entered. Instead the application shuts down immediately.

When you catch an exception, you can use a couple of properties to inspect what's happened. Table 1-3 lists the properties of the base *System.Exception* class.

**TABLE 1-3** *System.Exception* properties

| Name | Description |
|------|-------------|
| *StackTrace* | A string that describes all the methods that are currently in execution. This gives you a way of tracking which method threw the exception and how that method was reached. |
| *InnerException* | When a new exception is thrown because another exception happened, the two are linked together with the InnerException property. |
| *Message* | A (hopefully) human friendly message that describes the exception. |
| *HelpLink* | A Uniform Resource Name (URN) or uniform resource locater (URL) that points to a help file. |
| *HResult* | A 32-bit value that describes the severity of an error, the area in which the exception happened and a unique number for the exception This value is used only when crossing managed and native boundaries. |
| *Source* | The name of the application that caused the error. If the Source is not explicitly set, the name of the assembly is used. |
| *TargetSite* | Contains the name of the method that caused the exception. If this data is not available, the property will be null. |
| *Data* | A dictionary of key/value pairs that you can use to store extra data for your exception. This data can be read by other catch blocks and can be used to control the processing of the exception. |

When using a catch block, you can use both an exception type and a named identifier. This way, you effectively create a variable that will hold the exception for you so you can inspect its properties. Listing 1-93 shows how to do this.

**LISTING 1-93** Inspecting an exception

```
using System;

namespace ExceptionHandling
{
    public static class Program
    {
        public static void Main()
        {
            try
            {
                int i = ReadAndParse();
                Console.WriteLine("Parsed: {0}", i);
            }
            catch (FormatException e)
            {
                Console.WriteLine("Message: {0}",e.Message);
                Console.WriteLine("StackTrace: {0}", e.StackTrace);
                Console.WriteLine("HelpLink: {0}", e.HelpLink);
                Console.WriteLine("InnerException: {0}", e.InnerException);
                Console.WriteLine("TargetSite: {0}", e.TargetSite);
                Console.WriteLine("Source: {0}", e.Source);
            }

        }

        private static int ReadAndParse()
        {
            string s = Console.ReadLine();
            int i = int.Parse(s);
            return i;
        }
    }
}


//Displays
//Message: Input string was not in a correct format.
//StackTrace:    at System.Number.StringToNumber(String str, NumberStyles options,
// NumberBuffer& number, NumberFormatInfo info, Boolean parseDecimal)
//    at System.Number.ParseInt32(String s, NumberStyles style,
//        NumberFormatInfo info)
//    at System.Int32.Parse(String s)
//    at ExceptionHandling.Program.ReadAndParse() in
//      c:\Users\Wouter\Documents\Visual Studio 2012\Projects\
//        ExamRefProgrammingInCSharp\Chapter1\Program.cs:line 27
//    at ExceptionHandling.Program.Main() in c:\Users\Wouter\Documents\
//        Visual Studio 2012\Projects\ExamRefProgrammingInCSharp\
//        Chapter1\Program.cs:line 10
// HelpLink:
// InnerException:
```

```
// TargetSite: Void StringToNumber(System.String, System.Globalization.NumberStyles
// , NumberBuffer ByRef, System.Globalization.NumberFormatInfo, Boolean)
// Source: mscorlib
```

It's important to make sure that your *finally block* does not cause any exceptions. When this happens, control immediately leaves the *finally block* and moves to the next outer *try block*, if any. The original exception is lost and you can't access it anymore.

You should only catch an exception when you can resolve the issue or when you want to log the error. Because of this, it's important to avoid general catch blocks at the lower layers of your application. This way, you could accidentally swallow an important exception without even knowing that it happened. Logging should also be done somewhere higher up in your application. That way, you can avoid logging duplicate errors at multiple layers in your application.

## Throwing exceptions

When you want to throw an error, you first need to create a new instance of an exception. You can then use the special *throw* keyword to throw the exception. After this, the runtime will start looking for *catch* and *finally blocks*.

Listing 1-94 shows how you can throw an exception.

**LISTING 1-94** Throwing an *ArgumentNullException*

```
public static string OpenAndParse(string fileName)
{
    if (string.IsNullOrWhiteSpace(fileName))
        throw new ArgumentNullException("fileName", "Filename is required");

    return File.ReadAllText(fileName);
}
```

You should not try to reuse exception objects. Each time you throw an exception, you should create a new one, especially when working in a multithreaded environment, the stack trace of your exception can be changed by another thread.

When catching an exception, you can choose to *rethrow* the exception. You have three ways of doing this:

- Use the *throw* keyword without an identifier.
- Use the *throw* keyword with the original exception.
- Use the *throw* keyword with a new exception.

The first option rethrows the exception without modifying the call stack. This option should be used when you don't want any modifications to the exception. Listing 1-95 shows an example of using this mechanism.

LISTING 1-95 Rethrowing an exception

```
try
{
    SomeOperation();
}
catch (Exception logEx)
{
    Log(logEx);
    throw; // rethrow the original exception
}
```

When you choose the second option, you reset the call stack to the current location in code. So you can't see where the exception originally came from, and it is harder to debug the error.

Using the third option can be useful when you want to raise another exception to the caller of your code.

Say, for example, that you are working on an order application. When a user places an order, you immediately put this order in a message queue so another application can process it.

When an internal error happens in the message queue, an exception of type *Message-QueueException* is raised. To users of your ordering application, this exception won't make any sense. They don't know the internal workings of your module and they don't understand where the message queue error is coming from.

Instead, you can throw another exception, something like a custom *OrderProcessingException*, and set the *InnerException* to the original exception. In your *OrderProcessingException* you can put extra information for the user of your code to place the error in context and help them solve it. Listing 1-96 shows an example. The original exception is preserved, including the stack trace, and a new exception with extra information is added.

LISTING 1-96 Throwing a new exception that points to the original one

```
try
{
    ProcessOrder();
}
catch (MessageQueueException ex)
{
    throw new OrderProcessingException("Error while processing order", ex);
}
```

---

### EXAM TIP

Make sure that you don't swallow any exception details when rethrowing an exception. Throw a new exception that points to the original one when you want to add extra information; otherwise, use the *throw* keyword without an identifier to preserve the original exception details.

---

In C# 5, a new option is added for rethrowing an exception. You can use the *Exception-DispatchInfo.Throw* method, which can be found in the *System.Runtime.ExceptionServices* namespace. This method can be used to throw an exception and preserve the original stack trace. You can use this method even outside of a catch block, as shown in Listing 1-97.

**LISTING 1-97** Using *ExceptionDispatchInfo.Throw*

```
ExceptionDispatchInfo possibleException = null;

try
{
    string s = Console.ReadLine();
    int.Parse(s);
}
catch (FormatException ex)
{
    possibleException = ExceptionDispatchInfo.Capture(ex);
}

if (possibleException != null)
{
    possibleException.Throw();
}


// Displays
// Unhandled Exception: System.FormatException:
// Input string was not in a correct format.
//    at System.Number.StringToNumber(String str, NumberStyles options,
//         NumberBuffer& number, NumberFormatInfo info, Boolean parseDecimal)
//    at System.Number.ParseInt32(String s, NumberStyles style,
//         NumberFormatInfo info)
//    at System.Int32.Parse(String s)
//    at ExceptionHandling.Program.Main() in c:\Users\Wouter\Documents\
//       Visual Studio 2012\Projects\ExamRefProgrammingInCSharp\Chapter1\
//          Program.cs:line 17
//--- End of stack trace from previous location where exception was thrown ---
//    at System.Runtime.ExceptionServices.ExceptionDispatchInfo.Throw()
//    at ExceptionHandling.Program.Main() in c:\Users\Wouter\Documents\
//       Visual Studio 2012\Projects\ExamRefProgrammingInCSharp\Chapter1\
//          Program.cs:line 6
```

When looking at the stack trace, you see this line, which shows where the original exception stack trace ends and the *ExceptionDispatchInfo.Throw* is used:

```
--- End of stack trace from previous location where exception was thrown ---
```

This feature can be used when you want to catch an exception in one thread and throw it on another thread. By using the *ExceptionDispatchInfo* class, you can move the exception data between threads and throw it. The .NET Framework uses this when dealing with *the async/await* feature added in C# 5. An exception that's thrown on an *async* thread will be captured and rethrown on the executing thread.

**MORE INFO**  **THREADS AND** *ASYNC/AWAIT*

For more information on working with threads and the new *async/await* feature, see the section titled "Objective 1.1: Implement multithreading and asynchronous processing" earlier in this chapter.

You shouldn't throw exceptions when dealing with expected situations. You know that when users start entering information into your application, they will make mistakes. Maybe they enter a number in the wrong format or forget to enter a required field. Raising an exception for these kinds of expected situations is not recommended.

Exception handling changes the normal expected flow of your program. This makes it harder to read and maintain code that uses exceptions, especially when they are used in normal situations.

Using exceptions also incurs a slight performance hit. Because the runtime has to search all outer catch blocks until it finds a matching block, and when it doesn't, has to look if a debugger is attached, it takes slightly more time to handle. When a real unexpected situation occurs that will terminate the application, this won't be a problem. But for regular program flow, it should be avoided. Instead you should have proper validation and not rely solely on exceptions.

When you need to throw an exception of your own, it's important to know which exceptions are already defined in the .NET Framework. Because developers will be familiar with these exceptions, they should be used whenever possible.

Some exceptions are thrown only by the runtime. You shouldn't use those exceptions from your own code. Table 1-4 lists those exceptions.

**TABLE 1-4** Runtime exceptions in the .NET Framework

| Name | Description |
| --- | --- |
| *ArithmeticException* | A base class for other exceptions that occur during arithmetic operations. |
| *ArrayTypeMismatchException* | Thrown when you want to store an incompatible element inside an array. |
| *DivideByZeroException* | Thrown when you try to divide a value by zero. |
| *IndexOutOfRangeException* | Thrown when you try to access an array with an index that's less than zero or greater than the size of the array. |
| *InvalidCastException* | Thrown when you try to cast an element to an incompatible type. |
| *NullReferenceException* | Thrown when you try to reference an element that's null. |
| *OutOfMemoryException* | Thrown when creating a new object fails because the CLR doesn't have enough memory available. |
| *OverflowException* | Thrown when an arithmetic operation overflows in a checked context. |

| Name | Description |
|---|---|
| StackOverflowException | Thrown when the execution stack is full. This can happen in a recursive operation that doesn't exit. |
| TypeInitializationException | Thrown when a static constructor throws an exception that's goes unhandled. |

You shouldn't throw these exceptions in your own applications. Table 1-5 shows popular exceptions in the .NET Framework that you can use.

TABLE 1-5 Popular exceptions in the .NET Framework

| Name | Description |
|---|---|
| Exception | The base class for all exceptions. Try avoiding throwing and catching this exception because it's too generic. |
| ArgumentException | Throw this exception when an argument to your method is invalid. |
| ArgumentNullException | A specialized form of ArgumentException that you can throw when one of your arguments is null and this isn't allowed. |
| ArgumentOutOfRangeException | A specialized form of ArgumentException that you can throw when an argument is outside the allowable range of values. |
| FormatException | Throw this exception when an argument does not have a valid format. |
| InvalidOperationException | Throw this exception when a method is called that's invalid for the object's current state. |
| NotImplementedException | This exception is often used in generated code where a method has not been implemented yet. |
| NotSupportedException | Throw this exception when a method is invoked that you don't support. |
| ObjectDisposedException | Throw when a user of your class tries to access methods when Dispose has already been called. |

You should avoid directly using the *Exception* base class both when catching and throwing exceptions. Instead you should try to use the most specific exception available.

## Creating custom exceptions

Once throwing an exception becomes necessary, it's best to use the exceptions defined in the .NET Framework. But there are situations in which you want to use a *custom exception*. This is especially useful when developers working with your code are aware of those exceptions and can handle them in a more specific way than the framework exceptions.

A custom exception should inherit from *System.Exception*. You need to provide at least a parameterless constructor. It's also a best practice to add a few other constructors: one that takes a *string*, one that takes both a *string* and an *exception*, and one for *serialization*. Listing 1-98 shows an example of a custom exception.

LISTING 1-98 Creating a custom exception

```csharp
[Serializable]
public class OrderProcessingException : Exception, ISerializable
{
    public OrderProcessingException(int orderId)
    {
        OrderId = orderId;
        this.HelpLink = "http://www.mydomain.com/infoaboutexception";
    }
    public OrderProcessingException(int orderId, string message)
        : base(message)
    {
        OrderId = orderId;
        this.HelpLink = "http://www.mydomain.com/infoaboutexception";
    }

    public OrderProcessingException(int orderId, string message,
                                    Exception innerException)
        : base(message, innerException)
    {
        OrderId = orderId;
        this.HelpLink = "http://www.mydomain.com/infoaboutexception";
    }

    protected OrderProcessingException(SerializationInfo info, StreamingContext context)
    {
        OrderId = (int)info.GetValue("OrderId", typeof(int));
    }

    public int OrderId { get; private set; }

    public void GetObjectData(SerializationInfo info, StreamingContext context)
    {
        info.AddValue("OrderId", OrderId, typeof(int));
    }
}
```

By convention, you should use the *Exception* suffix in naming all your custom exceptions. It's also important to add the *Serializable* attribute, which makes sure that your exception can be serialized and works correctly across application domains (for example, when a web service returns an exception).

When creating your custom exception, you can decide which extra data you want to store. Exposing this data through properties can help users of your exception inspect what has gone wrong.

You should never inherit from *System.ApplicationException*. The original idea was that all C# runtime exceptions should inherit from *System.Exception* and all custom exceptions from *System.ApplicationException*. However, because the .NET Framework doesn't follow this pattern, the class became useless and lost its meaning.

## Objective summary

- In the .NET Framework, you should use exceptions to report errors instead of error codes.

- Exceptions are objects that contain data about the reason for the exception.

- You can use a try block with one or more catch blocks to handle different types of exceptions.

- You can use a finally block to specify code that should always run after, whether or not an exception occurred.

- You can use the *throw* keyword to raise an exception.

- You can define your own custom exceptions when you are sure that users of your code will handle it in a different way. Otherwise, you should use the standard .NET Framework exceptions.

## Objective review

Answer the following questions to test your knowledge of the information in this objective. You can find the answers to these questions and explanations of why each answer choice is correct or incorrect in the "Answers" section at the end of this chapter.

1. You are checking the arguments of your method for illegal *null* values. If you encounter a *null* value, which exception do you throw?

A. *ArgumentException.*

B. *InvalidOperationException.*

C. *NullReferenceException.*

D. *ArgumentNullException.*

2. Your code catches an *IOException* when a file cannot be accessed. You want to give more information to the caller of your code. What do you do?

A. Change the message of the exception and rethrow the exception.

B. Throw a new exception with extra information that has the *IOException* as *InnerException*.

C. Throw a new exception with more detailed info.

D. Use throw to rethrow the exception and save the call stack.

3. You are creating a custom exception called *LogonFailedException*. Which constructors should you at least add? (Choose all that apply.)

A. *LogonFailed()*

B. *LogonFailed(string message)*

C. *LogonFailed(string message, Exception innerException)*

D. *LogonFailed(Exception innerException)*

## Chapter summary

- Multithreading can help you create programs that are responsive and scalable. You can use the TPL, the Parallel class, and PLINQ for this. The new *async/await* keywords help you write asynchronous code.

- In a multithreaded environment, it's important to manage synchronization of shared data. You can do this by using the *lock* statement.

- C# offers statements for making decisions—*if*, switch, conditional operator (*?*) and null-coalescing operator (*??*)—iterating (*for, foreach, while, do-while*), and *jump* statements (*break, continue, goto, return* and *throw*).

- Delegates are objects that point to a method and can be used to invoke the method. Lambda expressions are a shorthand syntax for creating anonymous methods inline.

- Events are a layer on top of delegates that help you with creating a publish-subscribe architecture.

- Exceptions are the preferred way to work with errors in the .NET Framework. You can throw exceptions, catch them, and run code in a finally block.

# Answers

This section contains the solutions to the thought experiments and answers to the lesson review questions in this chapter.

## Objective 1.1: Thought experiment

1.  Multithreading can improve the responsiveness in a client application. The UI thread can process requests from the user while background threads execute other operations.

2.  A CPU-bound operation needs a thread to execute. In a client application, it can make sense to execute a CPU-bound operation on another thread to improve responsiveness. In a server application, you don't want an extra thread for a CPU-bound operation. Asynchronous I/O operations don't require a thread while executing. Using asynchronous I/O frees the current thread to do other work and improves scalability.

3.  Using multithreading in a server environment can help you distribute operations over multiple CPUs. This way, you can improve performance. Using the TPL to create another thread to execute a CPU-bound operation while the originating thread has to wait for it won't help you with increasing performance.

## Objective 1.1: Review

1.  **Correct answer:** B

    A.  **Incorrect:** Manually creating and managing tasks is not necessary. The Parallel class takes care of this and uses the optimal configuration options.

    B.  **Correct:** *Parallel.For* is ideal for executing parallel operations on a large set of items that have to do a lot of work.

    C.  **Incorrect:** *async/await* does not process items concurrently. Instead it waits until the current task has finished and then continues executing the code.

    D.  **Incorrect:** The *BlockingCollection* can be used to share data between multiple threads. Using one producer and one consumer thread, however, won't improve scalability. The *Parallel* class is designed for this scenario and should be used.

2.  **Correct answer:** A

    A.  **Correct:** *AsParallel* makes a sequential query parallel if the runtime thinks this will improve performance.

    B.  **Incorrect:** *AsSequential* is used to make a parallel query sequential again.

    C.  **Incorrect:** *AsOrdered* is used to make sure that the results of a parallel query are returned in order.

    D.  **Incorrect:** *WithDegreeOfParallelism* is used to specify how many threads the parallel query should use.

3. **Correct answer:** C

   A. **Incorrect:** Because you have to wait for external factors (the database and web response), you should use async/await to free your thread. That way your thread can do some other work while waiting for the external responses to come back.

   B. **Incorrect:** Async/await can be used to improve responsiveness on the client but it can also be used in server scenarios. Especially when waiting for an I/O-bound operation, you can use asynchronous code to free the thread from waiting.

   C. **Correct:** The operating system waits for the I/O request to complete and then activates a thread that can process the response. In the meantime, the thread can do other work.

   D. **Incorrect:** Async/await does not put your thread to sleep in an I/O-bound situation. Instead, your thread can process other work while the operating system monitors the status of the request. When the request finishes, a thread is used to process the response. With a CPU-bound operation, your thread waits for the operation to finish on another thread.

## Objective 1.2: Thought experiment

1. It's important to make sure that all locking follows the same order when locking multiple objects. As soon as you start locking dependent objects in different orders, you start getting deadlocks.

2. The *Interlocked* class can help you to execute small, atomic operations without the need for locking. When you use locking a lot for these kind of operations, you can replace them with the *Interlocked* statement.

## Objective 1.2: Review

1. **Correct answer:** D

   A. **Incorrect:** You should never lock on this. Another part of your code may already be using your object to execute a lock.

   B. **Incorrect:** You shouldn't use a string for locking. With string-interning, one object can be used for multiple strings, so you would be locking on an object that is also in use in other locations.

   C. **Incorrect:** Locking on a value type will generate a compile error. The value type will be boxed each time you lock on it, resulting in a unique lock each time.

   D. **Correct:** A private lock of type object is the best choice.

2. **Correct answer:** B

   A. **Incorrect:** The *CancellationTokenSource* is used to generate a *CancellationToken*. The token should be passed to the task, and the *CancellationTokenSource* can then be used to request cancellation on the token.

   B. **Correct:** A *CancellationToken* generated by a *CancellationTokenSource* should be passed to the task.

   C. **Incorrect:** A Boolean variable can be used to cancel a task, but it's not the preferred way. A *CancellationToken* offers more flexibility and should be used.

   D. **Incorrect:** The *volatile* keyword should be used to signal to the compiler that the order of reads and writes on a field is important and that the compiler shouldn't change it.

3. **Correct answer:** B

   A. **Incorrect:** *Volatile.Write* is used to signal to the compiler that writing the value to a field should happen at that exact location.

   B. **Correct:** *CompareExchange* will see whether the current state is correct and it will then change it to the new state in one atomic operation.

   C. **Incorrect:** Exchange only changes the value; it doesn't check to see whether the current state is correct.

   D. **Incorrect:** Decrement is used to subtract one off the value in an atomic operation.

# Objective 1.3: Thought experiment

1. Using the *goto* statement makes your code much harder to read because the application flow jumps around. *goto* is mostly used in looping statements. You can then replace *goto* with *while* or *do-while*.

2. The *switch* statement can be used to improve long *if* statements.

3. The *for* statement can be used to iterate over a collection by using an *index*. You can modify the collection while iterating. You need to use the *index* to retrieve each item. *foreach* is syntactic sugar over the iterator pattern. You don't use an *index*; instead the compiler gives you a variable that points to each iteration item.

## Objective 1.3: Review

1.  **Correct answer:** C

    A.  **Incorrect:** *switch* is used as a decision statement. You map a value to certain labels to execute specific code; it doesn't iterate over collections.

    B.  **Incorrect:** Although the *foreach* statement can be used to iterate over a collection; it doesn't allow changes to the collection while iterating.

    C.  **Correct:** With *for*, you can iterate over the collection while modifying it. It's your own job to make sure that the *index* stays correct.

    D.  **Incorrect:** *goto* is a *jump* statement that should be avoided.

2.  **Correct answer:** D

    A.  **Incorrect:** *for* is an iteration statement that can't be used to check for *null* values.

    B.  **Incorrect:** The conditional operator can be used to shorten *if* statements. It's not useful to conditionally call a method.

    C.  **Incorrect:** The null-coalescing operator does check for *null* values but it's used to provide a default value. It's not useful when calling a method if the value is not *null*.

    D.  **Correct:** Short-circuiting enables you to see whether a value is *null* and call a member on it in one *and* statement. If the left value is *null*, the right operand won't be executed.

3.  **Correct answer:** C

    A.  **Incorrect:** A *for* statement is most useful when iterating over a collection in which you know the number of items beforehand.

    B.  **Incorrect:** *foreach* can be used only on types that implement *IEnumerable*. It can't be easily used with your two custom methods.

    C.  **Correct:** You can use *while (o.HasNext) { var i = o.Read(); }* to process the items. When *o.HasNext* returns *false*, you automatically end the loop.

    D.  **Incorrect:** *Do-while* will run the code at least once. If there are no items on the network, the code doesn't have to run.

## Objective 1.4: Thought experiment

1.  Events are a nice layer on top of delegates that make them easier and safer to use. In this case, you should use events to make sure that other users won't be able to clear all subscriptions. It also makes sure that they can't raise the event on their own. They can only listen to changes.

2. The advantage of using an event system in an application like this is that you can achieve loose coupling. Your forms don't have to know anything about each other. The class that monitors data changes and raises the event doesn't have to know how many forms are listening and how they look. Third-party plug-ins can easily subscribe to the events at runtime to be able to respond to changes without tightly coupling to the existing system.

## Objective 1.4: Review

1.  **Correct answer:** C

    A.  **Incorrect:** Making the method public gives access to all users of your class.

    B.  **Incorrect:** This doesn't give users of your class the ability to execute the method.

    C.  **Correct:** The method can see whether the caller is authorized and then return a delegate to the private method that can be invoked at will.

    D.  **Incorrect:** Changing the method to a lambda doesn't change the fact that outside users can't access the method.

2.  **Correct answer:** B

    A.  **Incorrect:** The compiler restricts the use of events outside of the class where it's defined. They can only add and remove subscribers. Only the class itself can raise the event.

    B.  **Correct:** The public method can be called by outside users of your class. Internally it can raise the event.

    C.  **Incorrect:** Using a delegate does allow it to be invoked from outside the class. However, you lose the protection that an event gives you. A public delegate can be completely modified by outside users without any restrictions.

    D.  **Incorrect:** Canonical name (CNAME) records map an alias or nickname to the real or canonical name that might lie outside the current zone.

3.  **Correct answer:** A

    A.  **Correct:** You can handle each individual error and make sure that all subscribers are called.

    B.  **Incorrect:** Wrapping the raising of the event in one *try/catch* will still cause the invocation to stop at the first exception. Later subscribers won't be notified.

    C.  **Incorrect:** By default, the invocation of subscribers stops when the first unhandled exception happens in one of the subscribers.

    D.  **Incorrect:** Exceptions are the preferred way of dealing with errors. Returning a value from each event still requires you to invoke them manually one by one to check the return value.

# Objective 1.5: Thought experiment

1. Exceptions are objects, so they can store extra information that can't be done with only an error code. The .NET Framework also offers special support for dealing with exceptions. For example, you can use catch blocks to handle certain types of exceptions and you can use a finally block to make sure that certain code will always run.

2. You should create a custom exception only if you expect developers to handle it or perform custom logging. If a developer won't be able to fix the specific error, it won't make any sense to create a more specific exception. Custom logging can happen when you throw more detailed exceptions, so developers can differentiate between the errors that happen.

# Objective 1.5: Review

1. **Correct answer:** D

   A. **Incorrect:** Although the exception has to do with an argument to your method, you should throw the more specialized *ArgumentNullException*.

   B. **Incorrect:** *InvalidOperationException* should be used when your class is not in the correct state to handle a request.

   C. **Incorrect:** *NullReferenceException* is thrown by the runtime when you try to reference a *null* value.

   D. **Correct:** *ArgumentNullException* is the most specialized exception that you can use to tell which argument was *null* and what you expect.

2. **Correct answer:** B

   A. **Incorrect:** The *Message* property of an exception is read-only. You can't change it after the exception is created.

   B. **Correct:** The new exception can contain extra info. Setting the *InnerException* makes sure that the original exception stays available.

   C. **Incorrect:** Throwing a brand-new exception loses the original exception and the information that it had.

   D. **Incorrect:** Using throw without an identifier will rethrow the original exception while maintaining the stack trace, but it won't add any extra information.

3. **Correct answers:** A, B, C

   A. **Correct:** You should always add a default empty constructor.

   B. **Correct:** A second constructor should take a descriptive message of why the error occurred.

   C. **Correct:** An *InnerException* can be set to correlate two exceptions and show what the original *error* was.

   D. **Incorrect:** You don't have to define a constructor that only takes an *InnerException* without a message.

# CHAPTER 2

# Create and use types

As a craftsman, knowing your tools is important to get the work done. When building object-oriented software, types are your tools. Being skilled in creating useful types can make the difference between a successful project and a disaster. C# offers all the basic building blocks you need to create types that can be the foundation of any software project.

In this chapter, you learn what C# has to offer when it comes to creating types. You learn how to create types that can be easily used by you and your coworkers, types that encapsulate their inner workings so that you can focus on using them in the best way possible.

After learning how to create types, you examine what it means for C# to be a managed environment and how you can play nicely when using unmanaged, external resources. Finally, you look at how to use some of the types that the .NET Framework offers, and you work with the built-in string type.

### Objectives in this chapter:

- Objective 2.1: Create types
- Objective 2.2: Consume types
- Objective 2.3: Enforce encapsulation
- Objective 2.4: Create and implement a class hierarchy
- Objective 2.5: Find, execute, and create types at runtime by using reflection
- Objective 2.6: Manage the object life cycle
- Objective 2.7: Manipulate strings

## Objective 2.1: Create types

Writing an application consists of using and creating types. In C#, there are a lot of options for creating a type. Knowing your options will enable you to choose and use those options wisely. For example, using *enums* can make your code a lot more readable. Using *generics* can make your code much more flexible and save you a lot of time.

But with great power comes great responsibility. The power that C# offers you when you create types makes it easy to make mistakes. In this section, you will learn what C# has to offer and when you should use a particular feature to create meaningful types.

# Choosing a type to create

In an object-oriented language such as C#, objects and types are the fundamental building blocks. A type can be seen as a blueprint for constructing an object. It shows what data can be used and what behavior is present. Creating these blueprints and then using them to construct new objects enables you to build complex, maintainable applications with a lot of functionality. C# enables you to choose which type to create depending on your situation.

## Types in C#

The C# typing system contains three different categories:

- Value types
- Reference types
- Pointer types

Pointer types are rarely used. You use them only when working with unsafe code and when you need to use pointer arithmetic.

> **MORE INFO** **POINTERS AND UNSAFE CODE**
>
> For more information, read "unsafe (C# Reference)" at *http://msdn.microsoft.com/en-us/library/chfa2zb8.aspx*.

## Creating enums

One basic type in C# is the *enum*. An enum (short for *enumeration*) offers you a nice way to create a list of possible options.

```
public enum Gender { Male, Female }
```

Of course, you can use a *Boolean* value such as *IsMale* that is *true or false* to represent the gender. But when reading and working with code that uses this Boolean value, you have to map the true and false values to the actual meaning of gender. Using an enum improves the readability and maintainability of your code.

By default, the first element has the value 0, and each successive element is increased by 1, but you can change the starting index and the underlying type. In the following example, you declare an enum that has a byte type that starts with the value 1. Of course this is something that you should communicate to your team so they know that you changed the default behavior:

```
enum Days : byte { Sat = 1, Sun, Mon, Tue, Wed, Thu, Fri };
```

If you want to compare the Days enum to the underlying *byte* value, you have to cast it to a *byte*:

```
Days day = Days.Sat;
if ((byte)day == 1) { }
```

Enumerations can also be used with a special *Flags* attribute; you can use one enum to set multiple combinations of values. Listing 2-1 shows how to do this.

**LISTING 2-1** Using the *FlagAttribute* for an enum

```
[Flags]
enum Days
{
    None = 0x0,
    Sunday = 0x1,
    Monday = 0x2,
    Tuesday = 0x4,
    Wednesday = 0x8,
    Thursday = 0x10,
    Friday = 0x20,
    Saturday = 0x40
}
Days readingDays = Days.Monday | Days.Saturday;
```

> **MORE INFO**  **USING AND CREATING ATTRIBUTES**
>
> For more information on how to use attributes, see "Objective 2.5: Find, execute, and create types at runtime by reflection" later in this chapter.

## Value and reference types

Enums are only the beginning. An enum is a special kind of *value type*. C# has value and reference types. Both are used extensively in the C# programming language and the .NET Framework. When creating a new type, it's important to know the differences so you can make an informed decision.

You may have been programming for a while and are comfortable with using reference types, but still haven't created a custom value type. As such, there is a lot of misinformation when it comes to value versus reference types. A reference type, as the name suggests, contains a reference to the real value; a value type contains the value directly. An example of a reference type is a uniform resource locator (*URL*). If you read something interesting on the web, you can send the URL to a friend and point to the correct location where the information is stored. A value type is different. If you read an interesting article in a magazine and you want to give it to your friend, you need to make a copy of the article and give it directly.

This same behavior can be seen with value and reference types. In the common language runtime (CLR) that underpins C#, there are two locations in which a type can be stored in memory: the *heap* and the *stack*. The value of a reference type is stored on the heap, and the address to this value is stored on the stack. Although a value type is normally stored on the stack, there are exceptions (for example, a class that contains a value type as one of its fields, a lambda expression that closes over a value type, or a value type that is boxed), but this is the general idea. The benefit of storing data on the stack is that it's faster, smaller, and doesn't need the attention of the garbage collector.

> **MORE INFO**  **THE GARBAGE COLLECTOR AND THE HEAP**
>
> For more information, read "Objective 2.6: Manage the object life cycle" section later in this chapter.

Value types are useful when it comes to small data structures that belong together. For example, a point with an x and y coordinate is a candidate for a value type. As a rule of thumb, you can check the following three criteria to determine whether you want to create a value type:

- The object is small.
- The object is logically immutable.
- There are a lot of objects.

Of course, these are still vague requirements. The only one who can determine whether you need a value type is you. If you're optimizing for speed or for memory usage, the only way to determine whether a value type can improve performance is by measuring.

All objects in C# inherit from *System.Object*. Value types, however, inherit from *System.ValueType* (which inherits from *System.Object*). *System.ValueType* overrides some of the default functions (such as *GetHashCode*, *Equals*, and *ToString*) to give them a more meaningful implementation for a value type.

In C#, you cannot directly inherit from *System.ValueType*. Instead, you can use the *struct* keyword to create a new value type. Listing 2-2 shows how you can create a *struct* that contains the coordinates for a point.

**LISTING 2-2** Creating a custom struct

```
public struct Point
{
    public int x, y;

    public Point(int p1, int p2)
    {
        x = p1;
        y = p2;
    }
}
```

Structs and classes can have methods, fields, properties, constructors, and other function-alities. You cannot, however, declare your own empty constructor for a struct. Also, structs cannot be used in an inheritance hierarchy (which saves you some memory bytes!).

**EXAM TIP**

It's important to know the different types that are available in C#. A value type should be used for small, immutable objects that are used a lot. In all other situations, use a reference type.

# Giving your types some body

After you have decided whether you want to create a value or a reference type, you can start thinking about the body of your type. You probably didn't start out creating an empty struct or class, which isn't that interesting. The goal of your new type should be to encapsulate both related data and behavior so that it can be used by other parts of your program.

The type you create is like a blueprint. You specify which data and behaviors it contains. After you have created your blueprint you can then use it to instantiate objects that follow the blueprint.

## Adding behaviors

The actions that your class exposes should be the core reason for its existence. You should think of your new class in terms of what it can do, not of what data it stores. In C#, you add behavior to classes by using *methods*.

> **NOTE** "FUNCTION" VERSUS "METHOD"
>
> Sometimes the term "function" is used, and sometimes the term "method" is used. A function's meaning implies that it returns a value and doesn't modify anything in the system. You can say a function is the "read" part of the system. This is what is still used in functional languages such as F#, in which immutable data structures are popular.
>
> A method does enable data modification and doesn't return any data. This is the "write" part of the system.
>
> You can see this distinction in the *Func<T>* and *Action* types that were added to the .NET Framework. *Func<T>* always has a return type, whereas *Action* returns nothing.
>
> In C#, this distinction is not used. The preferred term is "method."

Methods can be called by other parts of your code to execute behaviors. For example, a basic Hello World console application shows how this works, as you can see in Listing 2-3.

**LISTING 2-3** Calling a method

```
namespace CallingAMethod
{
    class Program
    {
        static void Main(string[] args)
        {
            System.Console.WriteLine("I'm calling a method!");
        }
    }
}
```

The call to *Console.WriteLine* executes the function named *WriteLine* on the *Console* class and passes it a string argument.

The important steps when adding a method to your own type are the following:

1. Choose a name for your method.

2. Decide which data should be passed to your method.

3. Decide which data you want to return to the caller.

4. Decide on the visibility of your method.

If you want to create a *Calculator* class that needs to be able to add two numbers together, what would your method signature look like? Listing 2-4 shows a basic implementation of the *Calculator*.

**LISTING 2-4** Creating a method

```
class Calculator
{
    public int Add(int x, int y)
    {
        return x + y;
    }
}
```

The name *Add* clearly states what the method does. When reading the method name of a class, you should be able to understand what it does without looking at the implementation.

This improves the quality of your code. When writing code in a procedural style, you can fall into the trap of creating one big method that runs all kinds of actions. This results in code that's less readable and maintainable. Object-oriented software is a paradigm shift from procedural coding. By using objects, you can create code that's more meaningful and should be easier to maintain. But it can still happen that you write object-oriented applications as if they are procedural. Breaking large, complex methods into their individual parts and naming those methods wisely is one of the steps you can take to avoid procedural methods in an object-oriented system. Make sure your method name is focused on one thing. If your method starts growing and you have difficulty naming it, think about simplifying your method by splitting it into multiple methods that each has its own specific goal.

The *Add* method has two *arguments*: *x* and *y*. Naming your parameters is also important. When using Visual Studio, a user of your method (that could be you in a couple of days, weeks, or months!) often relies on IntelliSense to check which arguments your method expects. A good parameter name helps others use your method because it's clear to them what you expect.

When deciding on which arguments to take, it's important to think about what you will do with the data. Look at the examples shown in Listing 2-5 and Listing 2-6.

**LISTING 2-5** Passing a complete customer to a method

```
public Distance CalculateDistanceTo(Customer customer)
{
    Distance result =  … // Some difficult calculation that uses customer.Address
    return result;
}
```

**LISTING 2-6** Passing only an address to a method

```
public Distance CalculateDistanceTo(Address address)
{
    Distance result = … // Some difficult calculation that uses address
    return result;
}
```

Which method should you choose? The problem with the one in Listing 2-5 is that the *Customer* object is only used to retrieve the address. Suddenly the distance calculation algorithm is coupled to a *Customer*. Changes in the *Customer* class, such as adding a shipping address and a billing address, will ripple through to this class.

Listing 2-6 asks for only the data it needs. This is a clearer and simpler design that improves maintainability.

> **MORE INFO**  **LAW OF DEMETER**
>
> This pattern is called the Law of Demeter. For more information on choosing your arguments read "Law of Demeter" at *http://msdn.microsoft.com/en-us/magazine/cc947917. aspx#id0070040.*

## Named arguments, optional arguments, and overloading visibility

A new feature in C# 4 is the use of *named* and *optional* arguments. Optional arguments enable you to omit arguments for some parameters. Named arguments are useful to specify which arguments you want to pass a value. Named and optional arguments can be used with methods, indexers, constructors, and delegates. Optional arguments can be useful when you want to specify default values for certain parameters. Listing 2-7 shows how to use named and optional arguments.

LISTING 2-7 Using named and optional arguments

```
void MyMethod(int firstArgument, string secondArgument = "default value",
    bool thirdArgument = false) { }

void CallingMethod()
{
    MyMethod(1, thirdArgument: true);
}
```

It's also possible to create methods with the same name that differ in the arguments they take, which is called *overloading*. An example in the .NET Framework is *Console.WriteLine*. This method has 19 different overloads that take different parameters. You create an overload for a method by using the exact same name and return type, but by differing in the arguments you expect.

When creating a method, you can choose whether you want to return a value to the caller. If you don't want to return a value, you can declare the return type of a method as void. If you do want to return a value, you need to specify the type that you want to return. Listing 2-8 shows how to create a void method and a method that returns data.

LISTING 2-8 Returning data from a method

```
public void MethodWithoutAnyReturnValue()
{ /* Don't return any value to the caller */ }

public int MethodWithReturnValue()
{
    return 42;
}
```

When creating a method, it's important to decide on the visibility of the method. When you don't declare an access modifier, your method is private by default. The other options you can use are public, internal, protected, and internal protected (for a class you can use public or internal). The default is internal.

> **MORE INFO   ACCESS MODIFIERS**
>
> For more information on access modifiers, read "Objective 2.3: Enforce encapsulation" later in this chapter.

## Adding some data

A method such as *Add* in the *Calculator* class uses only data that's passed into the method. A class can contain both behavior and data, however. The easiest way to store data inside a class is to use a *field, which* offers direct access to the value it stores. Listing 2-9 shows how to use a field.

LISTING 2-9 Declaring and using a field

```
public class MyClass
{
    public string MyInstanceField;

    public string Concatenate(string valueToAppend)
    {
        return MyInstanceField + valueToAppend;
    }
}

MyClass instance = new MyClass();
instance.MyInstanceField = "Some New Value";
```

Just as with methods, fields can have an access modifier, a type, and a name. Choosing the name is as important as the name of a method. Clear, descriptive names improve code quality and readability.

A field can be marked as read-only, which allows the field to be set only once during construction of the object. You can do this in the constructor or as a part of declaring your variable. After this, the field's value cannot be changed.

If the fields value is set at compile time, you can also mark it as const. That way, the compiler knows for sure that the value will never change and it can perform some optimization. This also ensures that you don't accidentally overwrite the value of the field. All assignments to the field in your code will result in a compile error.

Another way to access data in a class is with an *indexer*, which enables instances of your class or struct to be used like arrays. This is useful when your object contains data that resembles a collection.

For example, imagine that you are creating a class to play a card game. You have a *Deck* class that contains a collection of cards. Listing 2-10 shows an example implementation.

LISTING 2-10 Creating a collection such as a *Deck* class

```
class Card {}

class Deck
{
    public ICollection<Card> Cards { get; private set; }
}
```

If you want to access a specific card, you can go through the *Cards* property to access it, but this is not always convenient. That's why C# has *indexer properties*. An indexer property allows your class to be accessed with an index, just like a regular array. An example of an indexer property in the .NET Framework can be found in the *List<T>* collection type. You can declare a new *List<int>*, initialize it with some values, and access the first item in the following way:

```
List<int> myList = new List<int>() { 1, 3, 5 };
myList[0] = 1;
```

You can access the elements inside the list by using the [] notations. You can also implement this on your own classes. For the Deck class, use the following:

```
public Card this[int index]
{
    get { return Cards.ElementAt(index); }
}
```

Until now, all properties are declared as instance fields. Each object instance has its own properties, and the values of each one are independent of other instances. When you want to store data that's not specific for an instance, you can make it static, like so:

```
class MyClass
{
    public static int MyStaticField = 42;
}
```

The *MyStaticField* is not coupled to one specific instance of *MyClass*. To access the field, you don't have to create a new instance. Instead, you can directly access it:

```
MyClass.MyStaticField = 43;
```

A static field or property is shared with all code that has access to it. This can have some dangerous side effects because if you change a static value in one place, it will change for all code that has access to the field.

Static can also be used for methods. The same idea applies that you don't have to create an instance of a class to access a static method. If all methods in a class are static, the whole class can be declared static.

## Using a blueprint

After you have created your type with all its properties and methods, you can start using it. Creating an instance of a class is done with the *new* operator. Calling *new* on an object executes that object's *constructor*. By default, each class has an empty constructor that can be called. You can also define your own constructors. You do this for two reasons:

- To initialize the type with data
- To run some initialization code

Look at the card example in Listing 2-11.

LISTING 2-11 Adding a constructor to your type

```
class Deck
{
    private int _maximumNumberOfCards;

    public List<Card> Cards { get; set; }

    public Deck(int maximumNumberOfCards)
    {
        this.maximumNumberOfCards = maximumNumberOfCards;
        Cards = new List<Card>();
```

```
    }

    // Rest of the class
}
```

As you can see in Listing 2-11, the constructor takes an argument of *int*. When you want to instantiate a new instance of this class, you need to pass a value to the constructor:

```
Deck deck = new Deck(5);
```

The constructor also runs some code to make sure that the object is in a usable state. Some good practices when designing your constructors are these:

- Explicitly declare the public default construct in classes if such a constructor is required.
- Ensure that your constructor takes as few parameters as possible.
- Map constructor parameters to properties in your class.
- Throw exceptions from instance constructors if appropriate.
- Do not call virtual members from an object inside its constructor.

> *MORE INFO*  **BEST PRACTICES FOR DESIGNING CONSTRUCTORS**
>
> If you want to know more best practices for designing your constructors, see *http://msdn. microsoft.com/en-us/library/vstudio/ms229060(v=vs.100).aspx.*

A class can also have multiple constructors, which can be chained to each other so you can avoid duplicate code. Listing 2-12 shows how you can chain multiple constructors.

**LISTING 2-12** Chaining constructors

```
class ConstructorChaining
{
    private int _p;

    public ConstructorChaining() : this(3) { }
    public ConstructorChaining(int p)
    {
        this._p = p;
    }
}
```

In production code it's important that you make clear which constructor users of your class should use. You can do this by picking meaningful parameter names and by adding comments that explain the use of each constructor.

## Designing classes

When designing a new class, you should keep in mind a couple of key design principles. These principles help you design classes that can be easily used, maintained, and extended. Not adhering to these principles can lead to a code base that starts to *rot* and eventually becomes a *big ball of mud*—a system that lacks a perceivable architecture.

All the principles come down to making sure that your code has two characteristics:

- High cohesion
- Low coupling

These principles mean that code shouldn't depend on other code when it's not absolutely necessary. This enables you to make changes to code without worrying that your changes will ripple through code and affect other subsystems.

An important list of principles is represented by the acronym SOLID. Table 2-1 explains what each initial stands for.

**TABLE 2-1** SOLID design principles

| Initial | Stands for | Description |
|---------|-----------|-------------|
| S | Single responsibility principle | A class should have only one responsibility. For example, a class shouldn't be both responsible for saving itself to the database and for displaying to the user. |
| O | Open/closed principle | An object should be open for extension but closed for modification. For example, by using a common interface, new objects can integrate with existing code without modifying the existing code. |
| L | Liskov substitution principle | A base type should be replaceable with subtypes in each and every situation. For example, a Duck that can swim and an inherited ElectricDuck that can swim only if the batteries are full. Suddenly, code needs to check whether the Duck is an ElectricDuck to replace empty batteries. |
| I | Interface segregation principle | Use client-specific interfaces instead of one general interface. A user of an interface should not have to implement all kinds of methods that he doesn't use. |
| D | Dependency Inversion principle | Depend upon abstractions, not concretions. For example, when you use *SomeServiceType* inside your class, you shouldn't depend on the actual implementation of *SomeServiceType*. Instead you should depend on an interface or abstract class. This way, you are less coupled to the actual implementation. |

> *MORE INFO*  **DESIGN PRINCIPLES**
>
> If you want to know more about the big ball of mud principle, see *http://www.codinghor-ror.com/blog/2007/11/the-big-ball-of-mud-and-other-architectural-disasters.html*.
>
> Other information about designing systems with high cohesion and low coupling can be found at *http://msdn.microsoft.com/en-us/magazine/cc947917.aspx*.
>
> Uncle Bob, a prominent figure in the software industry, has an excellent website on the SOLID principles; see *http://butunclebob.com/ArticleS.UncleBob.PrinciplesOfOod*.

# Using generic types

A new feature added in C# 2.0 is *generics*. A *generic type* uses a *Type parameter* instead of hard-coding all the types.

One area in the .NET Framework in which you can see the use of generics is in the support for *Nullables*. A reference type can have an actual value of null, meaning it has no value. A value type can't have a value of null, however. For example, how would you express that some Boolean value is true, false, or unknown? A regular Boolean can be only true or false.

This is why Nullables were added to the .NET Framework. A Nullable is a wrapper around a value type with a Boolean flag that it stores if the Nullable has a value set.

Listing 2-13 is a simplified version of the support for Nullables in the .NET Framework.

**LISTING 2-13** Generic *Nullable<T>* implementation

```
struct Nullable<T> where T : struct
{
  private bool hasValue;
  private T value;

  public Nullable(T value)
  {
    this.hasValue = true;
    this.value = value;
  }

  public bool HasValue { get { return this.hasValue; } }

  public T Value
  {
    get
    {
      if (!this.HasValue) throw new ArgumentFxception();
        return this.value;
    }
  }

  public T GetValueOrDefault()
  {
    return this.value;
  }
}
```

Instead of creating a Nullable type for each possible value type, there is now only one implementation that uses a generic type parameter to make it more flexible. This way, generics can be used to promote code reuse.

Normally, a value type would need to be boxed to be used in a nongeneric collection. By using generics, you can avoid the performance penalty for boxing and unboxing.

**MORE INFO**  BOXING AND UNBOXING

For more information, see "Objective 2.2: Consume types" later in this chapter.

The .NET Framework has several generic implementations of collection classes in the *System.Collections.Generic* namespace. Whenever possible, those generic collections should be used in favor of their nongeneric counterparts.

C# has a lot of possibilities when using generics. They can be used on structs, classes, interfaces, methods, properties, and delegates. You can even specify multiple generic type parameters when necessary.

As you can see in the example of *Nullable<T>*, a generic type parameter can also be *constrained*. In the case of *Nullable<T>*, it wouldn't make any sense if *T* could be a reference type. Reference types by their nature already have the option of being null.

C# lets you add a simple *where clause* that constrains a type parameter. In Table 2-2, you can see the different constraints you can use.

**TABLE 2-2** Possible constraints for a generic type parameter

| Constraint | Description |
|---|---|
| where T: struct | The type argument must be a value type (only Nullable is not allowed). |
| where T : class | The type argument must be a reference type: for example, a class, interface, delegate, or array. |
| where T : new() | The type must have a public default constructor. |
| where T : <base class name> | The type argument must be or derive from the specified base class. |
| where T : <interface name> | The type argument must be or implement the specified interface. Multiple interface constraints can be specified. The constraining interface can also be generic. |
| where T : U | The type argument supplied for *T* must be or derive from the argument supplied for *U*. |

Listing 2-14 shows how to add such a clause to your class definition.

**LISTING 2-14** Using a *where* clause on a class definition

```
class MyClass<T>
    where T : class, new()
{
    public MyClass()
    {
        MyProperty = new T();
    }

    T MyProperty { get; set; }
}
```

When working with a reference type, the default value is *null*; with a value type such as int, it is *0*. But what is the default value when working with a generic type parameter? In this case, you can use the special *default(T)* keyword. This gives you the default value for the specific type of T. Listing 2-15 shows how to use this.

**LISTING 2-15** Using *default(T)* with a generic type parameter

```
public void MyGenericMethod<T>()
{
    T defaultValue = default(T);
}
```

# Extending existing types

C# offers several ways to extend existing types without having to modify the existing code. In this section, you look at two different ways: extension methods and overriding.

## Extension methods

In .NET 4.0, a new capability was added called *extension methods*, which enable you to add new capabilities to an existing type. You don't need to make any modifications to the existing type; just bring the extension method into scope and you can call it like a regular instance method.

Extension methods need to be declared in a nongeneric, non-nested, static class. Listing 2-16 shows the creation of an extension method.

**LISTING 2-16** Creating an extension method

```
public class Product
{
    public decimal Price { get; set; }
}

public static class MyExtensions
{
    public static decimal Discount(this Product product)
    {
        return product.Price * .9M;
    }
}

public class Calculator
{
    public decimal CalculateDiscount(Product p)
    {
        return p.Discount();
    }
}
```

Notice that the *Discount* method has *this Product* as its first argument. The special *this* keyword makes this method an extension method.

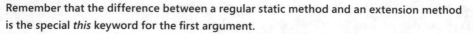

**EXAM TIP**

Remember that the difference between a regular static method and an extension method is the special *this* keyword for the first argument.

The nice thing is that an extension method cannot only be declared on a class or struct. It can also be declared on an *interface* (such as *IEnumerable<T>*). Normally, an interface wouldn't have any implementation. With extension methods, however, you can add methods that will be available on every concrete implementation of the interface.

Language Integrated Query (LINQ) is one of the best examples of how you can use this technique to enhance existing code. Instead of having to add all the LINQ operators to each and every class, they are created as extension methods on the base interfaces of each collection type. This way, all collections can suddenly use LINQ.

**MORE INFO**   LINQ

For more information on LINQ, see Chapter 4, "Implement data access."

## Overriding Methods

Another way to extend an existing type is to use inheritance and overriding. When a method in a class is declared as virtual, you can override the method in a derived class. You can completely replace the existing functionality or you can add to the behavior of the base class. Listing 2-17 shows how to override a method in a derived class to change some functionality.

**LISTING 2-17** Overriding a virtual method

```
class Base
{
    public virtual int MyMethod()
    {
        return 42;
    }
}

class Derived : Base
{
    public override int MyMethod()
    {
        return base.MyMethod() * 2;
    }
}
```

Now you can extend classes without modifying the original code. When designing your classes, it's important to plan for extension points such as these. You can disable inheritance by using the *sealed* keyword on a class or a method. When used on a class, you can't derive other classes from it. When used on a method, derived classes can't override the method. Listing 2-18 shows how this works.

**LISTING 2-18** Using the *sealed* keyword on a method

```
class Base
{
    public virtual int MyMethod()
    {
        return 42;
    }
}

class Derived : Base
{
    public sealed override int MyMethod()
    {
        return base.MyMethod() * 2;
    }
}

class Derived2 : Derived
{
    // This line would give a compile error
    // public override int MyMethod() { return 1;}
}
```

> **MORE INFO  INHERITANCE AND OVERRIDING**
>
> For more information on using inheritance, see "Objective 2.4: Create and implement a class hierarchy" later in this chapter.

## *Thought experiment*
### Creating a new web shop

In this thought experiment, apply what you've learned about this objective. You can find answers to these questions in the "Answers" section at the end of this chapter.

You are tasked with creating the basic types for a new web shop. As a customer, you can search through the existing product database and compare different items by reviewing specifications and reviews from other users. The system should keep track of popular products and make recommendations to the customer. Of course, the customer can then select the products he wants and place an order. There are also some business rules that you need to be aware of. A new customer is not allowed to place an order that exceeds $500. An order should be at least $10 to qualify for free shipping. More business rules will be added, but are not clear at the moment. Answer the following questions for your manager:

1. Which basic types are you going to use to build your web shop?

2. How can you make sure that your types contain both behavior and data?

3. How can you improve the usability of your types?

## Objective summary

- Types in C# can be a value or a reference type.
- Generic types use a type parameter to make the code more flexible.
- Constructors, methods, properties, fields, and indexer properties can be used to create a type.
- Optional and named parameters can be used when creating and calling methods.
- Overloading methods enable a method to accept different parameters.
- Extension methods can be used to add new functionality to an existing type.
- Overriding enables you to redefine functionality from a base class in a derived class.

## Objective review

Answer the following questions to test your knowledge of the information in this objective. You can find the answers to these questions and explanations of why each answer choice is correct or incorrect in the "Answers" section at the end of this chapter.

1. You are creating a new collection type and you want to make sure the elements in it can be easily accessed. What should you add to the type?

   A. Constructor

   B. Indexer property

   C. Generic type parameter

   D. Static property

2. You are creating a generic class that should work only with reference types. Which type constraint should you add?

   A. *where T : class*

   B. *where T : struct*

   C. *where T : new()*

   D. *where T : IDisposable*

3. You pass a struct variable into a method as an argument. The method changes the variable; however, when the method returns, the variable has not changed. What happened?

   A. The variable was not initialized before it was passed in.

   B. A value type cannot be changed inside a method.

   C. Passing a value type makes a copy of the data. The original wasn't changed.

   D. The method didn't return the changes.

# Objective 2.2: Consume types

C# is for the most part a *statically typed language*. This means that the C# compiler will check the type of every expression. This helps you in finding errors like trying to store one type into another type (such as a string in an int). It could be that you know that a type can be used as another type and you want to tell it to the compiler. Because of this, you sometimes have to convert between types. But parts of C# aren't statically typed. The new *dynamic* keyword in C# 4.0 enables you to override the compile-time checking and work with C# as a *weakly typed* language.

> **This objective covers how to:**
> - Box and unbox a value type.
> - Convert between different types.
> - Use the *dynamic* keyword.

## Boxing and unboxing

When working with value types in C#, sometimes you'll want to store a value type inside a reference type. For example, the .NET library contains a *string.Concat* method that adds the arguments it receives together and returns them as a string.

Assume that you call *string.Concat* with the following arguments:

```
string.Concat("To box or not box", 42, true);
```

If you put this code in Visual Studio and hover your mouse over the *Concat* function, you see that it takes three arguments, all of type *object*.

You might notice that you are dealing with a string, an int, and a Boolean value. This is where boxing comes in.

The example in Listing 2-19 puts an int inside an object and then gets it back again.

LISTING 2-19 Boxing an integer value

```
int i = 42;
object o = i;
int x = (int)o;
```

The important difference between a value type and a reference type is that the value type stores its value directly. A reference type stores a reference that points to an object on the heap that contains the value.

So *boxing* is the process of taking a value type, putting it inside a new object on the heap, and storing a reference to it on the stack. *Unboxing* is the exact opposite: It takes the item from the heap and returns a value type that contains the value from the heap.

If you execute an invalid unbox operation, the runtime will throw an *InvalidCastException*. You won't see the error at compile time because the compiler trusts you in making the right call. At runtime, however, the conversion fails, and an exception is thrown.

The only other important thing to know is that when boxing and unboxing happen (as shown in the example, unboxing is clear), you need to explicitly cast your object from a reference to a value type. Boxing, on the other hand, is not that obvious. For example, calling *GetType* always boxes your value type because *GetType* is defined only on an object and can't be overridden. Boxing occurs in other situations, too. One that can come as a surprise is that a value type is boxed when you use it as an interface. This snippet boxes the value *3* so you can use it as an interface.

```
IFormattable x = 3;
```

There are some performance implications with each box and unbox operation. When using the nongeneric collections to store a value type, you have a lot of those operations. The boxing and unboxing operations can hurt performance; however, now that you have generic support in the .NET Framework, this is less of an issue because you can store value types in a collection without boxing them.

# Converting between different types

Because C# is mostly a statically typed language, you can't change the type of a variable after it is declared. Unless an explicit conversion exists, it's not possible to convert one item to another. For example, converting an int to a double is allowed, but changing an *Address* into a *Person* isn't allowed.

The process of converting one type to another is called *type conversion*. There are several different types of conversions:

- Implicit conversions
- Explicit conversions
- User-defined conversions
- Conversion with a helper class

## Implicit conversions

An implicit conversion doesn't need any special syntax. It can be executed because the compiler knows that the conversion is allowed and that it's safe to convert.

A value type such as int can be stored as a double because an int can fit inside a double without losing any precision. The other way around is not implicitly possible. When converting a double to an int, you have to truncate or round the double, which might lead to some data loss. Listing 2-20 shows an implicit conversion from int to double.

**LISTING 2-20** Implicitly converting an integer to a double

```
int i = 42;
double d = i;
```

Another implicit conversion is that from a reference type to one of its base types. For example, each reference type can be stored inside an object because ultimately each reference type inherits from an object. If an object implements an interface, it can also be implicitly converted to the interface. Listing 2-21 shows the implicit conversion from an object to one of its base types.

**LISTING 2-21** Implicitly converting an object to a base type

```
HttpClient client = new HttpClient();
object o = client;
IDisposable d = client;
```

## Explicit conversions

Because of the type safety of the C# language, the compiler protects you from all implicit conversions that are not safe, such as converting a double to an int. If you do want to make this conversion, you need to do it explicitly. This is called *casting*. Listing 2-22 shows how to cast a double to an int explicitly.

**LISTING 2-22** Casting a double to an int

```
double x = 1234.7;
int a;
// Cast double to int
a = (int)x; // a = 1234
```

As with implicit conversion, explicit conversions also exist for reference types. Where you can go implicitly from a derived type to a base type, you need to cast from a base type to a derived type, as Listing 2-23 shows.

**LISTING 2-23** Explicitly casting a base type to a derived type

```
Object stream = new MemoryStream();
MemoryStream memoryStream = (MemoryStream)stream;
```

**EXAM TIP**

Make sure that you know the difference between an implicit and explicit conversion. An explicit conversion is called *casting* and always needs some special syntax.

## User-defined conversions

When creating your own types, you can add support for both implicit and explicit conversions.

Suppose you are working on a *Money* class that encapsulates all kinds of rounding algorithms for working with different currencies. Listing 2-24 shows some of the implicit and explicit conversion you can add.

LISTING 2-24 Implementing an implicit and explicit conversion operator

```
class Money
{
    public Money(decimal amount)
    {
        Amount = amount;
    }

    public decimal Amount { get; set; }


    public static implicit operator decimal(Money money)
    {
        return money.Amount;
    }

    public static explicit operator int(Money money)
    {
        return (int)money.Amount;
    }
}
```

Now, when working with the *Money* class, you can use an implicit conversion to decimal and an explicit conversion to int, as Listing 2-25 shows.

**LISTING 2-25** Using an implicit and explicit cast operator on a custom type

```
Money m = new Money(42.42M);
decimal amount = m;
int truncatedAmount = (int)m;
```

Adding these kinds of conversion can really improve the usability of your type. As you can see, the implicit and explicit operator should be declared as a public static method on your class. You need to specify the return type (the type you are casting to) and the type you are casting from (an instance of your class).

## Conversions with a helper class

The .NET Framework also offers helper classes for conversions between types. For converting between noncompatible types, you can use *System.BitConverter*. For conversion between compatible types, you can use *System.Convert* and the *Parse* or *TryParse* methods on various types. Listing 2-26 shows how to use *Parse* and *TryParse*.

**LISTING 2-26** Using the built-in *Convert* and *Parse* methods

```
int value = Convert.ToInt32("42");
value = int.Parse("42");
bool success = int.TryParse("42", out value);
```

When creating your own types, you can override *ToString* to return a string representation of your object. If necessary, you can then create a *Parse* and *TryParse* method that converts the string back to the original object. Implementing the *IFormattable* interface is required so that your object can be used by the *Convert* class.

> **MORE INFO   IFORMATTABLE INTERFACE**
>
> For more information on using the *IFormattable* interface, see "Objective 2.7: Manipulate strings" later in this chapter.

## Confirming that a conversion is valid

Sometimes you get passed a type and you want to check whether you can convert it to some other type. This can happen when you are given a base type and you want to determine whether you can convert it to a derived type. Of course, you can always wrap it in a *try/catch statement* and catch the *InvalidCastException*, but that would decrease both the performance and the readability of your code.

C# has both, the *is* operator and the *as* operator that can be used to check whether a type can be converted to another type and to do so in a safe way. The *is* operator returns *true* or *false*, depending on whether the conversion is allowed. The *as* operator returns the converted value or *null* if the conversion is not possible. Listing 2-27 shows how to use these operators.

**LISTING 2-27** Using the *is* and *as* operators

```
void OpenConnection(DbConnection connection)
{
    if (connection is SqlConnection)
    {
        // run some special code
    }
}

void LogStream(Stream stream)
{
    MemoryStream memoryStream = stream as MemoryStream;
    if (memoryStream != null)
    {
      // ....
    }
}
```

Using the *as* operator is more efficient when you want to use the value afterward. If you only want to check whether your type is of a certain type, you can use the *is* operator. The *is* and *as* operators can also be used on *Nullable* types.

# Using dynamic types

As stated before, C# is a partially static typed language. The *dynamic* keyword, added in C# 4.0, is where you enter the world of weakly typed languages. Working in a weakly typed system is helpful when communicating with external resources (such as COM Interop, Iron-Python, JavaScript Object Notation (JSON) result sets, or the HTML Document Object Model [DOM]) or when working with reflection inside C#.

When the C# compiler encounters the *dynamic* keyword, it stops with statically type checking (for example, checking whether a method exists on a type or if it has certain arguments). Instead, the compiler saves the intent of the code so that it can be later executed at runtime. This is why using dynamic types won't generate any compile-time errors, although it can certainly generate runtime errors.

## Office automation APIs

When integrating with Component Object Model (COM) applications, you use a Primary Interop Assembly (PIA). PIAs are .NET assemblies that bridge the gap between .NET and COM. For example, Microsoft Office has the kinds of assemblies that enable you to integrate with Word, Excel, and other Office applications from your .NET application.

Before the *dynamic* keyword was added, doing some Office automation was not something you wanted to do as a hobby. But with the new *dynamic* keyword, accessing Office is a lot easier. Listing 2-28 shows how the *dynamic* keyword enables you to export some data to Excel.

**LISTING 2-28** Exporting some data to Excel

```
static void DisplayInExcel(IEnumerable<dynamic> entities)
{
    var excelApp = new Excel.Application();
    excelApp.Visible = true;

    excelApp.Workbooks.Add();

    dynamic workSheet = excelApp.ActiveSheet;

    workSheet.Cells[1, "A"] = "Header A";
    workSheet.Cells[1, "B"] = "Header B";

    var row = 1;
    foreach (var entity in entities)
    {
        row++;
        workSheet.Cells[row, "A"] = entity.ColumnA;
        workSheet.Cells[row, "B"] = entity.ColumnB;
    }

    workSheet.Columns[1].AutoFit();
    workSheet.Columns[2].AutoFit();
}
```

```
var entities = new List<dynamic> {
            new
            {
                ColumnA = 1,
                ColumnB = "Foo"
            },
            new
            {
                ColumnA= 2,
                ColumnB= "Bar"
            }
    };

DisplayInExcel(entities);
```

In this example, the type of *workSheet* is dynamic. The statements that use the worksheet variable are evaluated at runtime and dispatched to the Office application programming interfaces (APIs). All the type checking and necessary conversions take place at runtime.

## *DynamicObject* and *ExpandoObject*

The .NET Framework offers two special classes when working with dynamic types: *DynamicObject* and *ExpandoObject*. *DynamicObject* is the most flexible. When inheriting from *DynamicObject*, you can override members that enable you to override operations such as getting or setting a member, calling a method, or performing conversions. By using *DynamicObject*, you can create truly dynamic objects and have full control over how they operate at runtime. Listing 2-29 shows how to inherit from *DynamicObject*.

**LISTING 2-29** Creating a custom *DynamicObject*

```
public class SampleObject : DynamicObject
{
    public override bool TryGetMember(GetMemberBinder binder, out object result)
    {
        result = binder.Name;
        return true;
    }
}

dynamic obj = new SampleObject();
Console.WriteLine(obj.SomeProperty); // Displays 'SomeProperty'
```

*ExpandoObject* is a sealed implementation that enables you to get and set properties on a type. In ASP.NET Model-View-Controller (MVC), for example, there is a *ViewBag* that can be used to pass data from the *Controller* to the *View*. *ViewBag* is an *ExpandoObject*. Instead of creating a new, statically typed property for each data element you want to pass, you can use the *ViewBag*, as Listing 2-30 shows.

LISTING 2-30 The *dynamic* keyword in ASP.NET MVC

```
public ActionResult Index()
{
    ViewBag.MyDynamicValue = "This property is not statically typed";
    return View();
}
```

The *dynamic* keyword should be used carefully. It gives you great flexibility, but because you lose static typing it can also easily lead to errors that can only be found at runtime. But when integrating with other languages or to replace reflection, the dynamic support is a nice addition to the .NET Framework.

### Thought experiment
### Optimizing your code

In this thought experiment, apply what you've learned about this objective. You can find answers to these questions in the "Answers" section at the end of this chapter.

You are developing a reusable library for doing complex calculations. Your application is gaining popularity, but you are starting to hear some negative responses. Some say that your types cannot be used easily. When displaying the end results of calculations to the end user, there is a lot of manual work involved. Others experience performance problems and want you to do something about it. You started developing your application with C# 1.0, and your application uses *ArrayList*s to keep track of all the parameters needed for the calculations. Your parameters are implemented as a struct. Your algorithms are implemented in a class hierarchy, and you often need to cast a base type to a derived type. Because this isn't always possible, you have added a lot of *try/catch* statements to recover from errors. Answer the following questions:

1. How can a generic collection improve performance?

2. Is there anything you can do to avoid the exceptions when converting between types?

3. How can you ensure your type is better converted to the basic CLR types?

## Objective summary

- Boxing occurs when a value type is treated as a reference type.
- When converting between types, you can have an implicit or an explicit conversion.
- An explicit conversion is called casting and requires special syntax.

- You can create your own implicit and explicit user-defined conversions.

- The .NET Framework offers several helper methods for converting types.

- The *dynamic* keyword can be used to ease the static typing of C# and to improve interoperability with other languages.

# Objective review

Answer the following questions to test your knowledge of the information in this objective. You can find the answers to these questions and explanations of why each answer choice is correct or incorrect in the "Answers" section at the end of this chapter.

1.  You are creating a custom *Distance* class. You want to ease the conversion from your *Distance* class to a double. What should you add?

    **A.** Nothing; this is already possible.

    **B.** An implicit cast operator.

    **C.** An explicit cast operator.

    **D.** A static *Parse* method.

2.  You want to determine whether the value of an object reference is derived from a particular type. Which C# language feature can you use? (Choose all that apply.)

    **A.** An *as* operator

    **B.** An implicit cast

    **C.** An *is* operator

    **D.** A *dynamic* keyword

3.  You are using an *ArrayList* as a collection for a list of *Points*, which are a custom struct. You are experiencing performance problems when working with a large amount of *Points*. What do you have to do?

    **A.** Use a generic collection instead of *ArrayList*.

    **B.** Change *Point* to be a reference type.

    **C.** Add an implicit conversion from *Point* to *object*.

    **D.** Make the collection of type *dynamic*.

# Objective 2.3: Enforce encapsulation

Encapsulation is one of the pillars of object-oriented development. Hiding the private elements from other objects inside an object-oriented system makes better software. When you want something done, ask another object to perform this action. The only thing you have to know is the external interface. The implementation is hidden from you, and you don't have to understand how it works as long as it complies with the interface. C# helps with encapsulating the inner workings of an object by providing properties, access modifiers, and interfaces.

**This objective covers how to:**

- Use access modifiers.
- Use properties.
- Use explicit interface implementation.

## Using access modifiers

One of the key concepts of encapsulation is hiding information. This is where *the access modifiers* of C# can be used. Access modifiers enable you to restrict access to all types and type members. Listing 2-31 shows how to use the public access modifier on a class and a method.

LISTING 2-31 Using access modifiers

```
public class Dog
{
    public void Bark() { }
}
```

Because of the public access modifier of the class *Dog*, everyone can create new instances of it. The *Bark* method is also public, which means everyone can call it. There are other access modifiers in C# that are more restrictive. Table 2-3 shows which access modifiers you can use in C#.

TABLE 2-3 Access modifiers in C#

| Access modifier | Description |
| --- | --- |
| public | None; restricted access |
| internal | Limited to the current assembly |
| protected | Limited to the containing class and derived classes |
| protected internal | Limited to the current assembly *or* derived types |
| private | Limited to the containing type |

# Hiding with private

A *private* member can be accessed only by members within the same type. This is the most restricted access modifier. For nested members such as properties and methods, private is the default access modifier. However, mentioning it explicitly in your code can help other developers understand your intentions. Listing 2-32 shows how to use the private access modifier on a field.

**LISTING 2-32** Using the private access modifier

```
public class Accessibility
{
    private string _myField;

    public string MyProperty
    {
        get { return _myField;  }
        set{ _myField = value;  }
    }
}
```

The field *_myField* has an accessibility of private. This means that it can be accessed only inside the class. The public property *MyProperty* wraps access to the field.

This helps you to enforce business rules when users of your class try to change the value of your property. In your set accessor, you can see whether the new value is allowed and make sure that no one can change it to an illegal value.

Users of this class are also encapsulated from changes to the inner workings of the class. For example, when the implementation changes to a lookup for the value of *MyProperty*, outside users wouldn't notice, as Listing 2-33 shows.

**LISTING 2-33** Changing a private field without outside users noticing

```
public class Accessibility
{
    // initialization code and error checking omitted
    private string[] _myField;

    public string MyProperty
    {
        get { return _myField[0]; }
        set { _myField[0] = value; }
    }
}
```

Users of your class can still access *MyProperty* without even knowing that the implementation has changed.

## Protecting accessibility in inheritance hierarchies

When working with a hierarchy of objects, there is another access modifier that can be used: *protected*. Protected restricts accessibility to members of the type and all classes that derive from it. It can be used on all members of a class. A member marked with private is not accessible by derived types. Listing 2-34 shows the difference between private and protected in an inheritance hierarchy.

LISTING 2-34 Using the protected access modifier with inheritance

```
public class Base
{
    private int _privateField = 42;
    protected int _protectedField = 42;

    private void MyPrivateMethod() { }
    protected void MyProtectedMethod() { }
}

public class Derived : Base
{
    public void MyDerivedMethod()
    {
        // _privateField = 41; // Not OK, this will generate a compile error
        _protectedField = 43; // OK, protected fields can be accessed


        // MyPrivateMethod(); // Not OK, this will generate a compile error
        MyProtectedMethod(); // OK, protected methods can be accessed
    }
}
```

> **MORE INFO** **INHERITANCE**
>
> For more information on using inheritance, see "Objective 2.4: Create and implement a class hierarchy" later in this chapter.

## Keeping types internal to your assembly

Code in C# is contained in *assemblies*. Inside Visual Studio, you can think of an assembly as a project. This is where another access modifier can be used: *internal*. Internal restricts access to a type or a type member to the same assembly. It is more restrictive than public, but less than private. Internal is useful when you have a type, such as a helper class or an implementation detail, that shouldn't be accessible outside of the assembly you're building. Listing 2-35 shows how to use the internal access modifier.

LISTING 2-35 Using the internal access modifier

```
internal class MyInternalClass
{
    public void MyMethod() { }
}
```

The class *MyInternalClass* can be used only inside the assembly where it's declared. The public method inside the class is restricted by its enclosing type. So only users who have access to the internal class can call the public method.

You can also combine the protected and internal access modifier. When using the *protected internal access modifier*, keep in mind that it is or, not and. In practice, this means that access is limited to the current assembly or types derived from the class, even if those types are in another assembly.

When you want to expose internal types or type members to another assembly, you can use a special attribute: *InternalsVisibleToAttribute*. You can use this attribute to specify another assembly that can also access the internal types. One situation where this can be useful is when you write unit tests. Maybe you have an internal class that encapsulates a difficult algorithm and you want to write unit tests for it. Normally, you include this attribute inside the *AssemblyInfo.cs* file that's stored in the *Properties* folder of your project:

```
[assembly:InternalsVisibleTo("Friend1a")]
[assembly:InternalsVisibleTo("Friend1b")]
```

You can use as many attributes as you need. In this example, the assemblies *Friend1a* and *Friend1b* are now allowed to access the internal types and members of your assembly.

Table 2-4 summarizes which access modifiers can be used in specific situations.

**TABLE 2-4** Allowed access modifiers on nested types

| Members of | Default member accessibility | Allowed declared accessibility of the member |
|---|---|---|
| enum | public | None |
| class | private | public<br>protected<br>internal<br>private<br>protected internal |
| interface | public | None |
| struct | private | public<br>internal<br>private |

*MORE INFO*  **ATTRIBUTES**

For more information on using attributes, see "Objective 2.5: Find, execute, and create types at runtime by using reflection" later in this chapter.

Something to keep in mind is that the access modifier of the enclosing type is always taken into account. For example, a public method inside an internal class has an accessibility of internal. There are exceptions to this (for example, when an internal class implements a public interface or when a class overrides a public virtual member of a base class), so you need to keep track of those things when determining the accessibility of a type you need.

It's a good practice to always explicitly choose for the lowest visibility possible because you want to hide as much information as possible. If you don't declare any access modifier, C# assigns a default member accessibility as defined in Table 2-4.

## Using properties

A field offers direct access to the data it contains. In object-oriented development, however, you often prefer to have some control over your data. In some languages, this leads to the pattern shown in Listing 2-36.

**LISTING 2-36** Encapsulating a field with custom methods

```
private int _field;
public void SetValue(int value) { _field = value; }
public int GetValue() { return _field; }
```

In this way, you can run custom code when setting and getting a value. For example, you can see whether the new value is allowed or you can calculate the result on the fly.

C# offers a nice compact way to use this pattern: *properties*. A property looks like a regular field. It has a type, a name, and an access modifier. The difference is that it adds *accessors*.

Listing 2-37 shows how to create a property.

**LISTING 2-37** Creating a property

```
class Person
{
    private string _firstName;

    public string FirstName
    {
        get { return _firstName; }
        set
        {
            if (string.IsNullOrWhiteSpace(value))
                throw new ArgumentException();
            _firstName = value;
        }
    }
}
```

As you can see, the *get* and *set* methods are part of the property definition. The field that contains the real data is private and can be accessed only through the property (except when inside the class).

Using a property with the default *get* and *set* methods is so common that C# added a shorthand notation for it:

```
public int Value { get; set; }
```

This is called an *auto-implemented property*. The compiler translates this into a property with a private, anonymous backing field. This can save you some time when you type a lot of properties. When you need some additional code to execute, the code is easily changed to use a *get* and *set* method.

The get and set accessor can have different access modifiers. You can, for example, have a *public get* and a *private set* method. For outside users, this creates the illusion of a read-only field. You can also have properties with only a get or only a set accessor. A single get accessor can come in handy when creating a true read-only property or when creating a property that calculates its value on the fly. A property with only a set accessor is a little uncommon, but you can use it in a "fire-and-forget" scenario where the user sets a value and never checks it.

**EXAM TIP**

Always favor properties over fields for public members. An automatically implemented property looks like a field to the outside world, but you can always add extra behavior when necessary.

## Using explicit interface implementations

Interfaces are useful when using encapsulation. In the next objective, you look at how you can design and use interfaces. But regarding the topic of encapsulation, you need to know about *explicit interface implementation*.

As an example of explicit interface implementation, look at the Entity Framework (an object-relational mapper that's part of the .NET Framework). When working with the Entity Framework, you work with a class *DbContext*, which is a wrapper around *ObjectContext* and exposes an easier-to-use interface.

*DbContext* implements the following interface (see Listing 2-38).

**LISTING 2-38** The *IObjectContextAdapter* interface

```
public interface IObjectContextAdapter
{
    ObjectContext ObjectContext { get; }
}
```

Although the interface shows an *ObjectContext* property, the following code won't compile:

```
DbContext ctx = ...; // create a new context
var context = ctx.ObjectContext;
```

The following will compile:

```
var adaptedContext = ((IObjectContextAdapter)ctx).ObjectContext;
```

How is this possible? It's possible because *DbContext* implements the interface *IObjectContextAdapter* explicitly. *Explicit interface implementation* means that an interface type element can be accessed only when using the interface directly. You can create an explicit interface implementation by adding the interface name and a period to the implementation.

**LISTING 2-39** Implementing an interface explicitly

```
interface IInterfaceA
{
    void MyMethod();
}

class Implementation : IInterfaceA
{
    void IInterfaceA.MyMethod() { }
}
```

The *Implementation* class implements the interface *IInterfaceA* explicitly. When you have an instance of *Implementation*, you can't access *MyMethod*. But when you cast *Implementation* to *IInterfaceA*, you have access to *MyMethod*. In such a way, explicit interface implementation can be used to hide members of a class to outside users.

There is another situation in which explicit interface implementation is necessary: when a class implements two interfaces that contain duplicate method signatures but wants a different implementation for both. When implicitly implementing those two interfaces, only one method exists in the implementation. With explicit interface implementation, both interfaces have their own implementation. Listing 2-40 shows how to implement an interface explicitly.

**LISTING 2-40** Implementing an interface explicitly

```
interface ILeft
{
    void Move();
}

interface IRight
{
    void Move();
}

class MoveableOject : ILeft, IRight
{
    void ILeft.Move() { }
    void IRight.Move() { }
}
```

## Objective summary

- Encapsulation is important in object-oriented software. It hides internal details and improves the usability of a type.
- Data can be encapsulated with a property.
- Properties can have both a get and a set accessor that can run additional code, commonly known as getters and setters.
- Types and type elements can have access modifiers to restrict accessibility.
- The access modifiers are public, internal, protected, protected, internal, and private.
- Explicit interface implementation can be used to hide information or to implement interfaces with duplicate member signatures.

# Objective review

Answer the following questions to test your knowledge of the information in this objective. You can find the answers to these questions and explanations of why each answer choice is correct or incorrect in the "Answers" section at the end of this chapter.

1. What access modifier should you use to make sure that a method in a class can only be accessed inside the same assembly by derived types?

   **A.** Make the class public and its members public.

   **B.** Make the class public and its members protected.

   **C.** Make the class internal and its members internal.

   **D.** Make the class internal and its members protected.

2. You need to expose some data from a class. The data can be read by other types but can be changed only by derived types. What should you use?

   **A.** A protected field

   **B.** A public property with a protected set modifier

   **C.** A protected property

   **D.** A protected property with a public get modifier

3. You have a class that implements two interfaces that both have a method with the same name. Interface IA should be the default implementation. Interface IB should be used only in special situations. How do you implement those interfaces?

   **A.** Implement IA implicitly and IB explicitly.

   **B.** Implement both IA and IB explicitly.

   **C.** Implement both IA and IB implicitly.

   **D.** Implement IA explicitly and IB implicitly.

# Objective 2.4: Create and implement a class hierarchy

Inheritance is another pillar of object-oriented development. *Inheritance* is the process of letting one class derive from another class. Inheritance between a base and a derived class establishes an "is-a-kind-of" relationship. For example, a child is a human, and a *SqlConnection* is a *DbConnection*. This enables you to create hierarchies of objects that can be used to better model real-world scenarios. It also encourages code reuse. C# is a typical object-oriented language in that it offers all the support you need to create your own class hierarchies and to use them in the most efficient way. You will look at how using interfaces and base classes can help you create generic code that can work with multiple implementations, and you will look at how a base class can help with code reuse and some of the standard interfaces the .NET Framework offers.

> **This objective covers how to:**
> - Design and implement interfaces.
> - Create and use base classes.
> - Use some of the standard .NET Framework interfaces.

# Designing and implementing interfaces

Interfaces are a key concept inside C#. An *interface* contains the public signature of methods, properties, events, and indexers. A type (both a class and a struct) can *implement an interface*. Listing 2-41 shows how to implement a custom interface.

**LISTING 2-41** Creating and implementing an interface

```
interface IExample
{
    string GetResult();
    int Value { get; set; }
    event EventHandler ResultRetrieved;
    int this[string index] { get; set; }
}

class ExampleImplementation : IExample
{
    public string GetResult()
    {
        return "result";
    }

    public int Value { get; set; }

    public event EventHandler CalculationPerformed;

    public event EventHandler ResultRetrieved;

    public int this[string index]
    {
        get
        {
            return 42;
        }
        set { }
    }
}
```

The convention in C# is to let the name of an interface start with a capital I. This helps you when using IntelliSense to see if a type is an interface. As you can see in the example, no access modifiers are mentioned for the elements of the interface because all interface members are public by default. It's not possible to implement an interface and change the access modifier to anything other than public.

One thing to note is that an interface might define a property with only a get accessor while the implementing type also has a set accessor (see Listing 2-42).

LISTING 2-42 Adding a set accessor to an implemented interface property

```
interface IReadOnlyInterface
{
    int Value { get; }
}

struct ReadAndWriteImplementation:IReadOnlyInterface
{
    public int Value { get;  set; }
}
```

In this case, the implementing class adds an extra set accessor. The advantage of using this pattern is that if a user accesses your class through its interface, it will see only the get accessor. Direct users of the class will see both the get and the set accessor.

Interfaces can also inherit from other interfaces. This way, you can have a chain of interfaces that each adds to the public signature of a type. A class that inherits from one of the derived interfaces has to implement all signatures in the whole hierarchy.

You can also use generics when defining interfaces. For example, if you are implementing the repository pattern (a repository offers access to objects stored in a database or some other storage type), you can use a generic type parameter so you don't have to create different interfaces for each entity that you want to store, as Listing 2-43 shows.

LISTING 2-43 Creating an interface with a generic type parameter

```
interface IRepository<T>
{
    T FindById(int id);
    IEnumerable<T> All();
}
```

Now you can create concrete implementations of your *Repository<T>* for different classes. For example, you can have an *IRepository<Product>* and an *IRepository<Order>*. Generic interfaces can have multiple type parameters and type constraints.

## Using interfaces

Because an interface has no implementation, you can't instantiate an interface directly. You can instantiate only a concrete type that implements an interface, as Listing 2-44 shows.

```
interface IAnimal
{
    void Move();
}

class Dog : IAnimal
{
    public void Move() {}
    public void Bark() {}
}

IAnimal animal = new Dog();
```

Your code now holds a reference to some implementation of the interface *IAnimal*. Although you know that it actually points to a *Dog*, you can't call the method *Bark* on it. If you want to go from the interface *IAnimal* to the type Dog, you will have to cast it.

> **MORE INFO   CASTING AND CONVERTING**
>
> For more information on casting an interface to another type, see "Objective 2.2: Consume types" later in this chapter.

Interfaces can also be used as parameters in a method. This way you can create generic code that can work against all kinds of different implementations:

```
void MoveAnimimal(IAnimal animal)
{
    animal.Move();
}
```

One of the important concepts of object-oriented development is programming against a contract, not an implementation. The interface guarantees you that certain functionality is available (the contract). You shouldn't care how this is implemented, only that it works. This helps with writing code that's loosely coupled and can be better maintained.

> **NOTE   NO MULTIPLE INHERITANCE**
>
> Some languages such as C++ offer the concept of multiple inheritance. This means that a single class can have multiple base classes. This way, a *Bat* can be both a *Mammal* (which inherits from *Animal*) and a *DrawableObject*. Multiple inheritance is not supported in C#. The creators of C# decided against implementing multiple inheritance because of the associated difficulties it can have. When using multiple inheritance, you can get conflicts when both base classes have a method with the same signature. C# does offer multiple interface inheritance with the option of explicitly implementing an interface to separate the different implementations. Multiple class inheritance is not supported.

# Creating and using base classes

An interface defines only the public signature of a type. Deriving from an interface doesn't inherit any implementation code. The derived type is completely free in how to implement the interface. When you do want to inherit implementation code, you can inherit from another class. Listing 2-45 shows how to create a base class.

**LISTING 2-45** Creating a base class

```
interface IEntity
{
    int Id { get; }
}

class Repository<T>
    where T : IEntity
{
    protected IEnumerable<T> _elements;

    public Repository(IEnumerable<T> elements)
    {
        _elements = elements;
    }

    public T FindById(int id)
    {
        return _elements.SingleOrDefault(e => e.Id == id);
    }
}
```

The *Repository* base class offers a method for finding entities by ID. This code is generic and can be used by all entities. What if you want to add a specific query that would filter orders on date and amount? That wouldn't be something that applied to all entities; only to the order entity. Using inheritance can help you reuse your code while adding some extra behavior. Listing 2-46 shows how to inherit from a class.

**LISTING 2-46** Inheriting from a base class

```
class Order : IEntity
{
    public int Id { get; }
    // Other implementation details omitted
    // …
}

class OrderRepository : Repository<Order>
{
    public OrderRepository(IEnumerable<Order> orders)
        : base(orders) { }

    public IEnumerable<Order> FilterOrdersOnAmount(decimal amount)
    {
        List<Order> result = null;
```

```
        // Some filtering code
        return result;
    }
}
```

The *OrderRepository* now has both a method for finding an order by ID and a specific method for filtering orders on their amount. You can use inheritance in a similar manner to add members to an existing type. As you can see, you can use the *base* keyword to call the constructor of the base class. The *base* keyword can also be used when you want to call methods or other members on a base class.

> ### *NOTE*  CHILD AND PARENT OR BASE AND DERIVED
> When talking about inheritance, the terms *parent* and *child* classes are often used. But is that the correct terminology when thinking about inheritance? For example, a Dog is a kind of Animal. This can be modeled by using an inheritance relation. However, would you say that a Dog is a Child of an Animal? A Child is not a kind of Parent. In languages that support multiple inheritance things get even messier. Instead of using Parent and Child when defining an inheritance relation, you can better use the terms *base* and *derived class* to avoid any confusion with inheritance in the real world.

## Changing behavior

When building a class hierarchy, you sometimes want to replace or extend the behavior of a base class. Assume that you want to add some logging capabilities to the repository you created. You don't want to rewrite all filtering code; instead you just want to add some extra behavior.

This is where the *virtual* and *override* keywords come into play. Marking a method virtual allows derived classes to override the method. The derived class can choose to completely replace or to extend the behavior of the base class. Listing 2-47 shows how to override a method to extend the base class.

**LISTING 2-47** Overriding a virtual method

```
class Base
{
    protected virtual void Execute()
    {}
}

class Derived : Base
{
    protected override void Execute()
    {
        Log("Before executing");
        base.Execute();
        Log("After executing");
    }
    private void Log(string message) { /* some logging code */ }
}
```

By marking the method in the base class as virtual, the derived class can override it. By prefixing a method name with base, a derived class can execute the method on the base class. By skipping the call to base, the derived class completely replaces the functionality.

If a base class doesn't declare a method as virtual, a derived class can't override the method. It can, however, use the *new* keyword, which explicitly hides the member from a base class (this is different from using the *new* keyword to create a new instance of an object). This can cause some tricky situations, as Listing 2-48 shows.

**LISTING 2-48** Hiding a method with the *new* keyword

```
class Base
{
    public void Execute() { Console.WriteLine("Base.Execute"); }
}

class Derived : Base
{
    public new void Execute() { Console.WriteLine("Derived.Execute"); }
}
class Program
{
    static void Main(string[] args)
    {
        Base b = new Base();
        b.Execute();
        b = new Derived();
        b.Execute();
    }
}
```

Running this code will output *Base.Execute* twice. If you change the base execute method to be virtual and the derived class to override instead of hide the *Execute* method, the code will display *Base.Execute* and *Derived.Execute*. You should try to avoid hiding methods with the *new* keyword.

## Abstract and sealed base classes

If you don't want to allow a base class to be instantiated, you can declare it as an *abstract* class. An abstract class can have implementation code for its members, but it's not required. Because the class is abstract, you can't use the new operator on it to create a new instance. Listing 2-49 shows how to declare an abstract class.

LISTING 2-49 Creating an abstract class

```
abstract class Base
{
    public virtual void MethodWithImplementation() {/*Method with implementation*/}

    public abstract void AbstractMethod();
}

class Derived : Base
{
    public override void AbstractMethod() { }
}
```

As you can see, an abstract class can have both fully implemented members and abstract members. A concrete derived type is required to implement all abstract members (just as with an interface). Abstract classes can be a nice way to share both an interface and some implementation details, especially when only derived types should be instantiable.

Listing 2-49 uses the *override* keyword to implement the abstract method that's defined in the base class. It can also be used on abstract or virtual methods, properties, indexers, and events to extend or modify the implementation.

The opposite of an abstract class is a *sealed* class, which cannot be derived from. As such, it can't be marked as abstract, and all members should have an implementation. Structs are implicitly sealed in C#. It's never possible to inherit from a struct. Marking a class as sealed is a good practice. If you don't do this, others can start inheriting from your class without you having thought about this. If inheritance is necessary, you can remove the sealed keyword and think about the implications.

---

**EXAM TIP**

Make sure that you know the difference between an interface and an abstract class. An interface has no implementation code. An abstract class can choose to implement methods or leave it to the derived class.

---

## Liskov substitution principle

Inheritance is a powerful technique, but it should be used with caution. As already mentioned, inheritance should be used only when you are dealing with a "is-a-kind-of" relationship. The *Liskov substitution principle* states that a subclass should be usable in each place you can use one of the base classes. They shouldn't suddenly change behavior that users would depend on.

It's easy to violate this principle. Consider the code in Listing 2-50.

LISTING 2-50 A *Rectangle* class with an *Area* calculation

```
class Rectangle
{
    public Rectangle(int width, int height)
    {
        Width = width;
        Height = height;
    }

    public int Height { get; set; }

    public int Width { get; set; }

    public int Area
    {
        get
        {
            return Height * Width;
        }
    }
}
```

When looking at this *Rectangle* class, would you say that a *Square* is a kind of *Rectangle*? In mathematics, this would be true. We know that a square is a special type of rectangle. You can model this using an inheritance relation, as shown in Listing 2-51.

LISTING 2-51 A *Square* class that inherits from *Rectangle*

```
class Square : Rectangle
{
    public override int Width
    {
        get
        {
            return base.Width;
        }
        set
        {
            base.Width = value;
            base.Height= value;
        }
    }

    public override int Height
    {
        get
        {
            return base.Height;
        }
        set
        {
            base.Height = value;
            base.Width = value;
        }
    }
}
```

Because you know that you are dealing with a square, you help the user of the class by modifying both the *Width* and *Height* properties together. This way, the rectangle will always be a square.

Suppose you want to use the class as shown in Listing 2-52.

**LISTING 2-52** Using the *Square* class

```
Rectangle rectangle = new Square();
rectangle.Width = 10;
rectangle.Height = 5;

Console.WriteLine(rectangle.Area);
```

This code will output *25*. The user thinks he's dealing with a *Rectangle* with a calculated *Area*, but because the *Rectangle* is pointing to a *Square*, only the latest value of *Height* is stored.

This is a typical example of violating the Liskov substitution principle. The *Square* class cannot be used in all places where you would normally use a *Rectangle*.

# Implementing standard .NET Framework interfaces

The .NET Framework has a few standard interfaces that can you can use on your own types. When implementing those interfaces, your classes can be used in the infrastructure that the .NET Framework offers.

## *IComparable*

The *IComparable* interface features a single method, as shown in Listing 2-53.

**LISTING 2-53** *IComparable* interface

```
public interface IComparable
{
    int CompareTo(object obj);
}
```

This interface is used to sort elements. The *CompareTo* method returns an int value that shows how two elements are related. Table 2-5 shows the possible values the *CompareTo* method returns.

**TABLE 2-5** Return values of *CompareTo*

| Value | Meaning |
| --- | --- |
| Less than zero | The current instance precedes the object specified by the *CompareTo* method in the sort order. |
| Zero | This current instance occurs in the same position in the sort order as the object specified by the *CompareTo* method. |
| Greater than zero | This current instance follows the object specified by the *CompareTo* method in the sort order. |

For example, if you are creating an *Order* class that has a *DateTime Created* property that you want to sort on, you can implement *IComparable* on the *Order* class and compare the *Created* dates of both orders. Listing 2-54 shows how to do this.

**LISTING 2-54** Implementing the *IComparable* interface

```csharp
class Order : IComparable
{
    public DateTime Created { get; set; }

    public int CompareTo(object obj)
    {
        if (obj == null) return 1;

        Order o = obj as Order;

        if (o == null)
        {
            throw new ArgumentException("Object is not an Order");
        }


        return this.Created.CompareTo(o.Created);
    }
}

List<Order> orders = new List<Order>
{
    new Order { Created = new DateTime(2012, 12, 1 )},
    new Order { Created = new DateTime(2012, 1, 6 )},
    new Order { Created = new DateTime(2012, 7, 8 )},
    new Order { Created = new DateTime(2012, 2, 20 )},
};

orders.Sort();
```

The call to *orders.Sort()* calls the *CompareTo* method to sort the items. After sorting, the list contains the ordered *Orders*.

*IComparable* also has a generic version: *IComparable<T>*. Especially when dealing with methods from the .NET Framework, it's a good idea to implement both *IComparable* and *IComparable<T>*. Of course, you can share some code between those two implementations.

## IEnumerable

The *IEnumerable* and *IEnumerator* interface in .NET helps you to implement *the iterator pattern*, which enables you to access all elements in a collection without caring about how it's exactly implemented. You can find these interfaces in the *System.Collection* and *System.Collections. Generic* namespaces. When using the iterator pattern, you can just as easily iterate over the elements in an array, a list, or a custom collection. It is heavily used in LINQ, which can access all kinds of collections in a generic way without actually caring about the type of collection.

The *IEnumerable* interface exposes a *GetEnumerator* method that returns an *enumerator*. The enumerator has a *MoveNext* method that returns the next item in the collection.

The *foreach* statement in C# is some nice syntactic sugar that hides from you that you are using the *GetEnumerator* and *MoveNext* methods. Listing 2-55 shows how to iterate over a collection without using *foreach*.

**LISTING 2-55** Syntactic sugar of the *foreach* statement

```
List<int> numbers = new List<int> { 1, 2, 3, 5, 7, 9 };
using (List<int>.Enumerator enumerator = numbers.GetEnumerator())
{
    while (enumerator.MoveNext()) Console.WriteLine(enumerator.Current);
}
```

The *GetEnumerator* function on an *IEnumerable* returns an *IEnumerator*. You can think of this in the way it's used on a database: *IEnumerable<T>* is your table and *IEnumerator* is a cursor that keeps track of where you are in the table. It can only move to the next row. You can have multiple database cursors around that all keep track of their own state.

Before C# 2 implementing *IEnumerable* on your own types was quite a hassle. You need to keep track of the current state and implement other functionality such as checking whether the collection was modified while you were enumerating over it. C# 2 made this a lot easier, as Listing 2-56 shows.

**LISTING 2-56** Implementing *IEnumerable<T>* on a custom type

```
class Person
{
    public Person(string firstName, string lastName)
    {
        FirstName = firstName;
        LastName = lastName;
    }

    public string FirstName { get; set; }
    public string LastName { get; set; }

    public override string ToString()
    {
        return FirstName + " " + LastName;
    }
}

class People : IEnumerable<Person>
{
    public People(Person[] people)
    {
        this.people = people;
    }

    Person[] people;
```

```
    public IEnumerator<Person> GetEnumerator()
    {
        for (int index = 0; index < people.Length; index++)
        {
            yield return people[index];
        }
    }
    IEnumerator IEnumerable.GetEnumerator()
    {
        return GetEnumerator();
    }
}
```

Notice the *yield* return in the *GetEnumerator* function. *Yield* is a special keyword that can be used only in the context of iterators. It instructs the compiler to convert this regular code to a state machine. The generated code keeps track of where you are in the collection and it implements methods such as *MoveNext* and *Current*.

Because creating iterators is so easy now, it has suddenly become a feature that you can use in your own code quite easily. Whenever you do a lot of manual loops through the same data structure, think about the iterator pattern and how it can help you create way nicer code.

## IDisposable

Another useful interface in the .NET Framework is *IDisposable*. This interface is used to facilitate working with external, unmanaged resources. As Objective 2.6 discusses, C# is a managed language that uses a garbage collector to clean up memory. However, you will still access external, unmanaged resources like database connections or file handles. This is where *IDisposable* comes into play. Listing 2-57 shows the definition of the *IDisposable* interface.

**LISTING 2-57** The *IDisposable* interface

```
public interface IDisposable
{
        void Dispose();
}
```

The only method the *IDisposable* interface has is *Dispose()*. This method is used to free any unmanaged resources.

> **MORE INFO**  **IMPLEMENTING *IDISPOSABLE***
>
> For more information implementing *IDisposable*, see "Objective 2.6: Manage the object life cycle" later in this chapter.

## IUnknown

Before .NET existed, the first generation of the Windows API was based on a library of functions contained in a dynamic-link library (DLL). Later generations collected these functions into a Component Object Model (COM) interface. The .NET Framework provides classes that wrap much of these APIs in a managed version so that in normal life you almost never touch any COM components directly.

Normally, you just add a reference to a COM object and the compiler generates the necessary wrapper classes called *COM Interop* classes. If this fails for some reason, you have to create the wrapper class; this is where the *IUnknown* interface is used.

> **MORE INFO**   **IMPLEMENTING *IUNKNOWN***
>
> For more information about implementing *IUnknown*, see *http://msdn.microsoft.com/en-us/library/aa645712(v=vs.71).aspx*.

### Thought experiment
### Optimizing your code

In this thought experiment, apply what you've learned about this objective. You can find answers to these questions in the "Answers" section at the end of this chapter.

You are working on a brand-new web application for a real estate agent. The agent wants to display his property on a website and ensure that users can easily search for it. For example, a user will be able to filter the results on location, size, property type, and price. You need to create the infrastructure that uses all the selected criteria to filter the list of available houses.

You want to see whether you can use some of the standard interfaces from the .NET Framework to implement your infrastructure.

1. Why does the .NET Framework offer some interfaces without any implementation? Wouldn't it be easier if the .NET Framework used abstract base classes?

2. Would you use interface or class inheritance to create your search criteria?

3. Which of the following interfaces would you use?

- *IComparable*
- *IEnumerable*
- *IDisposable*
- *IUnknown*

# Objective summary

- Inheritance is the process in which a class is derived from another class or from an interface.
- An interface specifies the public elements that a type must implement.
- A class can implement multiple interfaces.
- A base class can mark methods as virtual; a derived class can then override those methods to add or replace behavior.
- A class can be marked as abstract so it can't be instantiated and can function only as a base class.
- A class can be marked as sealed so it can't be inherited.
- The .NET Framework offers default interfaces such as *IComparable, IEnumerable, IDisposable* and *IUnknown*.

# Objective review

Answer the following questions to test your knowledge of the information in this objective. You can find the answers to these questions and explanations of why each answer choice is correct or incorrect in the "Answers" section at the end of this chapter.

1. You want to create a hierarchy of types because you have some implementation code you want to share between all types. You also have some method signatures you want to share. What should you use?

    **A.** An interface

    **B.** A class with virtual methods

    **C.** An abstract class

    **D.** A sealed class

2. You want to create a type that can be easily sorted. Which interface should you implement?

    **A.** *IEnumerable*

    **B.** *IComparable*

    **C.** *IDisposable*

    **D.** *IUnknown*

3. You want to inherit from an existing class and add some behavior to a method. Which steps do you have to take? (Choose all that apply.)

    **A.** Use the *abstract* keyword on the base type.

    **B.** Use the *virtual* keyword on the base method.

    **C.** Use the *new* keyword on the derived method.

    **D.** Use the *override* keyword on the derived method.

# Objective 2.5: Find, execute, and create types at runtime by using reflection

A .NET application doesn't just contain code and data; it also contains *metadata*, which is information about data. In .NET, this means that an application contains the code that defines the application and data that describes the code. An *attribute* is one type of metadata that can be stored in a .NET application. Other types of metadata contain information about the types, code, assembly, and all other elements stored in your application. *Reflection* is the process of retrieving this metadata at runtime. The data can be inspected and used to make decisions. In this section, you will learn how to use attributes in your own code and how to use reflection. You will also look at generating code at runtime by using both *CodeDom* and *expression trees*.

---

**This objective covers how to:**

- Create and use attributes.
- Use reflection to inspect and execute code at runtime.
- Generate code at runtime.

---

## Creating and using attributes

*Using attributes* is a powerful way to add metadata to an application. Attributes can be added to all kinds of types: assemblies, types, methods, parameters, and properties. At runtime, you can query for the existence of an attribute and its settings and then take appropriate action.

Attributes are used for a variety of reasons. They can be used to describe the author information of an assembly or to give specific hints to the compiler on how to optimize your code. Custom attributes can store all types of data that you want.

### Applying attributes

In C#, you apply an attribute by placing the attribute name in square brackets ([]) above the declaration that you want the attribute to apply to.

One example of an attribute in the .NET Framework is *System.SerializableAttribute*. This attribute indicates that a type can be serialized. The .NET Framework checks for the existence of this attribute when serializing a type, and it makes sure that all members of the type can also be serialized. Listing 2-58 shows how to apply the *Serializable* attribute.

**LISTING 2-58** Applying an attribute

```
[Serializable]
class Person
{
    public string FirstName { get; set; }
    public string LastName { get; set; }
}
```

As you can see, the actual class in the .NET Framework is called *SerializableAttribute*. By convention, the name is suffixed with *Attribute* so you can easily distinguish between attributes and other types in the .NET Framework. When using the attribute, however, you can skip the *Attribute* suffix.

A type can have as many attributes applied to it as necessary. Some attributes can even be applied multiple times. For example, you can use the *ConditionalAttribute* to indicate to the compiler that a method call should be ignored unless a specific compiler option is specified. Listing 2-59 shows how to apply this attribute.

**LISTING 2-59** Using multiple attributes

```
[Conditional("CONDITION1"), Conditional("CONDITION2")]
static void MyMethod(){ }
```

As shown in the listing, an attribute can have parameters. Just as with regular types, those parameters can be named an optional. The values set to an attribute can later be inspected at runtime.

An attribute also has a specific target to which it applies. It can be an attribute applied to a whole assembly, a class, a specific method, or even a parameter of a method.

If you look at the AssemblyInfo.cs of a new class library, you can see how the target is explicitly specified (see Listing 2-60).

**LISTING 2-60** Specifying the target of an attribute explicitly

```
[assembly: AssemblyTitle("ClassLibrary1")]
[assembly: AssemblyDescription("")]
[assembly: AssemblyConfiguration("")]
[assembly: AssemblyCompany("")]
[assembly: AssemblyProduct("ClassLibrary1")]
[assembly: AssemblyCopyright("Copyright ©  2013")]
[assembly: AssemblyTrademark("")]
[assembly: AssemblyCulture("")]
```

These attributes are all applied to the current assembly and describe some metadata about the assembly.

## Reading attributes

Applying an attribute isn't that useful if you can't retrieve it. Luckily, the .NET Framework offers support for reading attributes through a process called *reflection*. The *System.Attribute* class, from which all other attributes inherit, defines some static methods that can be used to see whether an attribute is applied and to get the current instance of an attribute so you can further inspect it.

Suppose that you want to check that a class has the *Serializable* attribute applied. You can do this by calling the static *IsDefined* method on *Attribute*, as Listing 2-61 shows.

**LISTING 2-61** Seeing whether an attribute is defined

```
[Serializable]
class Person { }
if (Attribute.IsDefined(typeof(Person), typeof(SerializableAttribute))) { }
```

You can also retrieve the specific instance of an attribute so that you can look at its properties. Listing 2-62 shows how you can get the *ConditionalAttribute* from Listing 2-59.

**LISTING 2-62** Getting a specific attribute instance

```
ConditionalAttribute conditionalAttribute =
    (ConditionalAttribute)Attribute.GetCustomAttribute(
    typeof(ConditionalClass),
    typeof(ConditionalAttribute));
string condition = conditionalAttribute.ConditionString; // returns CONDITION1
```

The *GetAttribute* and *GetAttributes* methods have several overloads so you can inspect attributes for an assembly, method, module, or a parameter.

## Creating custom attributes

Next to the built-in attributes of the .NET Framework, you can also create your own attributes. A custom attribute class has to derive from *System.Attribute* (directly or indirectly). For example, xUnit (a popular unit testing framework) enables you to categorize your unit tests by applying an attribute to them.

**LISTING 2-63** Using a category attribute in xUnit

```
[Fact]
[Trait("Category", "Unit Test")]
public void MyUnitTest()
{ }

[Fact]
[Trait("Category", "Integration Test")]
public void MyIntegrationTest()
{ }
```

Using the *Trait* attribute works perfect except that that you have to type the *Category* and *Value* by hand each time. This is error-prone and repetitive work that you want to avoid as much as possible. Luckily, xUnit gives you the option to create your own custom attributes that inherit from *Trait*. Listing 2-64 shows how to create a derived attribute that you can use more easily.

LISTING 2-64 Creating a custom attribute

```
public class CategoryAttribute : TraitAttribute
{
    public CategoryAttribute(string value)
        : base("Category", value)
    { }
}

public class UnitTestAttribute : CategoryAttribute
{
    public UnitTestAttribute()
        : base("Unit Test")
    { }
}
```

As you can see in Listing 2-65, the new *UnitTestAttribute* can be easily applied to methods and mark them as being in the *Unit Test* category.

LISTING 2-65 Using a custom attribute

```
[Fact]
[UnitTest]
public void MySecondUnitTest()
{}
```

When creating your own custom attribute from scratch, you also have to define the targets on which an attribute can be used. For example, you may want your attribute to be used only on methods and parameters. Listing 2-66 shows how to set the allowed targets of your custom attribute.

LISTING 2-66 Defining the targets for a custom attribute

```
[AttributeUsage(AttributeTargets.Method | AttributeTargets.Class)]
public class MyMethodAndParameterAttribute : Attribute { }
```

Defining the usage of an attribute is done by applying an attribute. You can combine as many targets as you want. You can also use the *AllowMultiple* parameter to enable multiple instances of one attribute to a single type (see Listing 2-67).

LISTING 2-67 Setting the *AllowMultiple* parameter for a custom attribute

```
[AttributeUsage(AttributeTargets.Class, AllowMultiple = true)]
class MyMultipleUsageAttribute : Attribute{ }
```

After having declared your custom attribute, you can add properties to it and a constructor to initialize your attribute. Be aware, however, that attributes require all properties to be read-write. Listing 2-68 shows how to add a custom property.

**LISTING 2-68** Adding properties to a custom attribute

```
[AttributeUsage(AttributeTargets.Class | AttributeTargets.Method, AllowMultiple=true)]
class CompleteCustomAttribute : Attribute
{
    public CompleteCustomAttribute(string description)
    {
        Description = description;
    }
    public string Description { get; set; }
}
```

# Using reflection

When reading attributes, you've already looked at some of the functionality that *reflection* offers. Reflection enables an application to collect information about itself and act on this information. Reflection is slower than normally executing static code. It can, however, give you a flexibility that static code can't provide.

The most basic example of reflection is getting the current type of an object you have:

```
int i = 42;
System.Type type = i.GetType();
```

This returns *System.Int32* as the type of int. *System.Type* is a class in the .NET Framework that you can use to get all kinds of metadata about any given type.

When would you use reflection? Assume that you want to create a plug-in system, and you have a directory in your system that contains all plug-ins. If a new assembly is dropped in this location, you inspect the assembly for the plug-ins it contains and then add them to your application. This is impossible without reflection.

> **MORE INFO**  **MANAGED EXTENSIBILITY FRAMEWORK**
>
> If you are looking into building such a plug-in system, have a look at the Managed Extensibility Framework (MEF) at *http://msdn.microsoft.com/en-us/library/dd460648.aspx*.

When creating a plug-in system, you need some way of finding plug-ins, getting some info, and executing them. One option is to create a custom *IPlugin* interface that exposes members that give you information about the plug-in and the capability to load it (see Listing 2-69).

**LISTING 2-69** Creating an interface that can be found through reflection

```
public interface IPlugin
{
    string Name { get; }
    string Description { get; }
    bool Load(MyApplication application);
}
```

Now that you have a custom base interface, you can create a plug-in by inheriting from this interface with a specific plug-in class, as Listing 2-70 shows.

**LISTING 2-70** Creating a custom plug-in class

```csharp
public class MyPlugin : IPlugin
{
    public string Name
    {
        get { return "MyPlugin"; }
    }

    public string Description
    {
        get { return "My Sample Plugin"; }
    }

    public bool Load(MyApplication application)
    {
        return true;
    }
}
```

Using reflection, you can now inspect an assembly and check it for any available plug-ins. The types you get back can then be used to create an instance of the plug-in and use it. The *System.Reflection* namespace defines the elements you need for reflection.

Listing 2-71 shows how to get all plug-ins from an assembly with a LINQ query and construct them.

**LISTING 2-71** Inspecting an assembly for types that implement a custom interface

```csharp
Assembly pluginAssembly = Assembly.Load("assemblyname");

var plugins = from type in pluginAssembly.GetTypes()
              where typeof(IPlugin).IsAssignableFrom(type) && !type.IsInterface
              select type;

foreach (Type pluginType in plugins)
{
    IPlugin plugin = Activator.CreateInstance(pluginType) as IPlugin;
}
```

The first line loads the assembly by name. One thing to note is that if you call this multiple times, the runtime will load the assembly only once. If you want to reload the assembly you would have to restart your application. After you have the assembly, you can check which plugins are defined in it and then construct your IPlugin objects.

Reflection can also be used to inspect the value of a property or a field. Suppose that you need to create a method that iterates over an object and selects all the private integer fields to display them on-screen. You can easily do this by using reflection (see Listing 2-72). You use the *BindingFlags* enumeration to control how reflection searches for members.

LISTING 2-72 Getting the value of a field through reflection

```
static void DumpObject(object obj)
{
    FieldInfo[] fields = obj.GetType().GetFields(BindingFlags.Instance | BindingFlags.
NonPublic);

    foreach (FieldInfo field in fields)
    {
        if (field.FieldType == typeof(int))
        {
            Console.WriteLine(field.GetValue(obj));
        }
    }
}
```

Reflection can also be used to execute a method on a type. You can specify the parameters the method needs, and at runtime the .NET Framework will see whether the parameters match and it will execute the method (see Listing 2-73).

LISTING 2-73 Executing a method through reflection

```
int i = 42;
MethodInfo compareToMethod = i.GetType().GetMethod("CompareTo",
    new Type[] { typeof(int) });
int result = (int)compareToMethod.Invoke(i, new object[] { 41 });
```

# Using CodeDom and lambda expressions to generate code

Besides inspecting types at runtime through reflection, C# also has support for generating code at runtime. One way this is done is through the *CodeDOM*. You can use the CodeDOM to create an object graph that can be converted to a source file or to a binary assembly that can be executed.

Typical usage scenarios for using the CodeDOM involve generating code for ASP.NET, Web Services, code wizards, or designers. Every time you create the same code over and over with some slight modifications, you can look into the CodeDOM to automate the process. The nice thing about the CodeDOM is that you can represent the logical structure of a piece of code independent of the specific language syntax you use. For example, you can use the CodeDOM to create a source file in both Visual Basic and C# syntax.

The CodeDOM is located in the *System.CodeDom* namespace. You can think of your source file as a tree with containers. You have a topmost container (called a *CodeCompileUnit*) that contains other elements such as namespaces, classes, methods, and individual statements. If you want to output a simple Hello World application, you need to create a *CodeCompileUnit*, a namespace, a class, and the entry *Main* method of your program that will call *Console. WriteLine* (see Listing 2-74).

**LISTING 2-74** Generating "Hello World!" with the CodeDOM

```
CodeCompileUnit compileUnit = new CodeCompileUnit();
CodeNamespace myNamespace= new CodeNamespace("MyNamespace");
myNamespace.Imports.Add(new CodeNamespaceImport("System"));
CodeTypeDeclaration myClass = new CodeTypeDeclaration("MyClass");
CodeEntryPointMethod start = new CodeEntryPointMethod();
CodeMethodInvokeExpression cs1 = new CodeMethodInvokeExpression(
    new CodeTypeReferenceExpression("Console"),
    "WriteLine", new CodePrimitiveExpression("Hello World!"));

compileUnit.Namespaces.Add(myNamespace);
myNamespace.Types.Add(myClass);
myClass.Members.Add(start);
start.Statements.Add(cs1);
```

Now that the compilation unit is complete, you can create a source file from it with the *CSharpCodeProvider* class that you can find in the *Microsoft.CSharp* namespace (see Listing 2-75).

**LISTING 2-75** Generating a source file from a *CodeCompileUnit*

```
CSharpCodeProvider provider = new CSharpCodeProvider();

using (StreamWriter sw = new StreamWriter("HelloWorld.cs", false))
{
    IndentedTextWriter tw = new IndentedTextWriter(sw, "    ");
    provider.GenerateCodeFromCompileUnit(compileUnit, tw,
        new CodeGeneratorOptions());
    tw.Close();
}
```

The generated output in HelloWorld.cs is shown in Listing 2-76.

**LISTING 2-76** The automatically generated source file

```
//------------------------------------------------------------------------------
// <auto-generated>
//     This code was generated by a tool.
//     Runtime Version:4.0.30319.18010
//
//     Changes to this file may cause incorrect behavior and will be lost if
//     the code is regenerated.
// </auto-generated>
//------------------------------------------------------------------------------

namespace MyNamespace {
    using System;

    public class MyClass {
        public static void Main() {
            Console.WriteLine("Hello World!");
        }
    }
}
```

# Lambda expressions

*Lambda functions* were introduced in C# 3.0. You can think of a lambda expression as a compact method to create an anonymous method.

> **MORE INFO**  **ANONYMOUS METHODS**
>
> For more info on anonymous methods, see *http://msdn.microsoft.com/en-us/library/0yw3tz5k.aspx*.

When working with lambdas, you will also need to know about the *Func<..>* and *Action* types. These generic types were added to have some predefined delegate types in the .NET Framework. You use *Action* when you have a delegate that doesn't return a value and Func when you do want to return a value. Both can take up to 16 type arguments in the .NET Framework 4.0.

When combining lambda and the *Func* type, you can easily create a type that returns the sum of two integers, as shown in Listing 2-77.

**LISTING 2-77** Creating a Func type with a lambda

```
Func<int, int, int> addFunc = (x, y) => x + y;
Console.WriteLine(addFunc(2, 3));
```

The lambda is of the *type Func<int, int, int>* which means that it takes two integer arguments and returns an int as result. The strange => notation can be read as "becomes" or "for which." The *addFunc* type can be read as "x, y become x + y".

# Expression trees

When using lambdas, you will come across *expression trees*, which are representations of code in a tree-like data structure. Just as the CodeDom can represent code in a tree-like manner, Expression trees can do the same; they can also be used to generate code.

An expression tree describes code instead of being the code itself. Expression trees are heavily used in LINQ. When using *Linq To Entities* to query a database, the query is not executed (as is the case in *Linq To Objects*). Instead, an expression tree describes the query. Later on, this expression tree is translated in a SQL statement that can be sent to the database.

The *System.Linq.Expressions* namespace contains all the types you need to create an expression. You have expressions for calling a method and creating a new object or even basic operations such as addition or subtraction.

The Hello World example from the *CodeDOM* can also be created as an expression tree (see Listing 2-78).

**LISTING 2-78** Creating "Hello World!" with an expression tree

```
BlockExpression blockExpr = Expression.Block(
 Expression.Call(
     null,
     typeof(Console).GetMethod("Write", new Type[] { typeof(String) }),
     Expression.Constant("Hello ")
     ),
  Expression.Call(
     null,
     typeof(Console).GetMethod("WriteLine", new Type[] { typeof(String) }),
     Expression.Constant("World!")
     )
);

Expression.Lambda<Action>(blockExpr).Compile()();
```

The expression is first constructed with a call to *Console.Write* and *Console.WriteLine*. After construction, the expression is compiled to an *Action* (because it doesn't return anything) and executed.

---

> **MORE INFO**  **EXPRESSION TREES**
>
> For more info on expression trees, see *http://msdn.microsoft.com/en-us/library/bb397951.aspx.*

---

### Thought experiment
#### Optimizing your code

In this thought experiment, apply what you've learned about this objective. You can find answers to these questions in the "Answers" section at the end of this chapter.

You are creating your own optimized object-relational mapper. You allow the user to map types one-on-one to a table in the database. You also use special attributes for security reasons. For example, a type can be decorated with an *AuthorizeAttribute* to make sure that only specific users can access a certain table. You use a lot of reflection in your app and you start seeing some performance problems. You are also thinking about a generator that will create types that map exactly to an existing database.

1. Why do you use an attribute instead of inheriting from an interface? Wouldn't that be easier than adding a whole new concept to C#?

2. What can you do about the performance problems with using reflection?

3. Which technique would you use to create your generator?

# Objective summary

- A C# assembly stores both code and metadata.
- Attributes are a type of metadata that can be applied in code and queried at runtime.
- Reflection is the process of inspecting the metadata of a C# application.
- Through reflection you can create types, call methods, read properties, and so forth.
- The CodeDOM can be used to create a compilation unit at runtime. It can be compiled or converted to a source file.
- Expression trees describe a piece of code. They can be translated to something else (for example, SQL) or they can be compiled and executed.

# Objective review

Answer the following questions to test your knowledge of the information in this objective. You can find the answers to these questions and explanations of why each answer choice is correct or incorrect in the "Answers" section at the end of this chapter.

1. You want to read the value of a private field on a class. Which *BindingFlags* do you need? (Choose all that apply.)

   A. *Instance*

   B. *DeclaredOnly*

   C. *Static*

   D. *NonPublic*

2. You need to create an attribute that can be applied multiple times on a method or a parameter. Which syntax should you use?

   A. *[AttributeUsage(AttributeTargets.GenericParameter | AttributeTargets. Method,AllowMultiple = true)]*

   B. *[AttributeUsage(AttributeTargets.Method | AttributeTargets.Parameter, AllowMultiple = true)]*

   C. *[AttributeUsage(AttributeTargets.All)]*

   D. *[AttributeUsage(AttributeTargets.Method | AttributeTargets.Parameter)]*

3. You want to create a delegate that can filter a list of strings on a specific value. Which type should you use?

   A. *Action<bool, IEnumerable<string>>.*

   B. *Func<IEnumerable<string>, IEnumerable<string>>.*

   C. *Func<string, IEnumerable<string>, IEnumerable<string>>.*

   D. *Func<IEnumerable<string>>.*

# Objective 2.6: Manage the object life cycle

In languages such as C++, you have to worry about memory management. Using pointers and managing memory whenever possible is necessary for writing applications. Forgetting to free some memory can result in a memory leak. In C#, things are different. C# is a managed language that uses a garbage collector to free memory whenever necessary. As long as you use only managed objects, the garbage collector frees you from worrying about memory management. However, when writing applications, you will often cross the boundaries and use unmanaged resources such as database connections or file handles. When dealing with these kinds of situations, you need to free those resources as soon as possible. In this objective, you learn how you can work with unmanaged resources and how you can influence the garbage collection when you need it.

> **This objective covers how to:**
> - Manage unmanaged resources.
> - Implement and use *IDisposable*.
> - Manage finalization and garbage collection.

## Understanding garbage collection

When building an application in C#, you rely on the fact that C# manages all memory for you. When you create a new object—whether a string, an int, or a custom type—you know that somehow the .NET Framework allocates memory and puts your object in it. Most of the time, this process happens completely behind the scenes (by the CLR), and you don't ever have to know about it. But having a basic understanding of how things work helps you understand why things are happening and enables you to optimize your code when it's necessary.

There are two places in memory where the CLR stores items while your code executes. One is the *stack;* the other is the *heap*. The stack keeps track of what's executing in your code, and the heap keeps track of your objects.

Of course, this is an oversimplification. Value types can be stored on both the stack and the heap. For an object on the heap, there is always a reference on the stack that points to it. Large objects go on a special part of the heap. But basically, this is the distinction between the two types of memory.

The stack is automatically cleared at the end of a method. The CLR takes care of this and you don't have to worry about it.

The heap is another story—it is managed by the *garbage collector*. In unmanaged environments without a garbage collector, you have to keep track of which objects were allocated on the heap and you need to free them explicitly. In the .NET Framework, this is done by the garbage collector.

The garbage collector works with a *mark and compact algorithm*. The mark phase of a collection checks which items on the heap are still being referenced by a *root item*. A root can be a static field, a method parameter, a local variable, or a CPU register. If the garbage collector finds a "living" item on the heap, it marks the item. After checking the whole heap, the compact operation starts. The garbage collector then moves all living heap objects close together and frees the memory for all other objects.

For doing this, the garbage collector has to make sure that no state is changing while performing all the marking and compacting. Because of this, all threads are frozen while doing a collect operation. It also has to make sure that all references to living objects are correct. After moving objects around, the garbage collector will fix all existing references to objects.

This can have a huge performance impact. When you are executing a complex important operation that should return to the user as fast as possible and suddenly the garbage collector kicks in, you have to wait till it finishes before you can continue.

But luckily for us, the garbage collector is quite clever. The garbage collector starts cleaning up only when there is not enough room on the heap to construct a new object (or when Windows signals that it's low on memory). So as long as there is enough room in memory, you won't ever notice anything about garbage collection. And when it does, it tries to do this on a moment that the usage of the application is low.

When garbage collection does start, it collects only Generation 0. What does this mean? Well, when executing a cleanup, items that survive (because they are still being referenced) are promoted to a higher *generation*. They are longer-living objects and the garbage collector makes the assumption that longer-living objects will probably stay around for some time. Because of this, the garbage collector focuses on the objects in Generation 0. They are just created and will probably be unnecessary in a small amount of time. The other generations will be touched only when the garbage collector cannot free enough memory by cleaning Generation 0.

In short, that's how garbage collection works: It removes items from the heap that are no longer necessary and makes sure that no object can stay alive and occupy memory if it's not in use.

## Managing unmanaged resources

All of this would be enough if you were only working with managed resources. Keeping objects such as strings, numbers, and other managed types around is completely handled by the garbage collector. But when you start accessing *unmanaged resources,* things change.

Unmanaged resources can be a network connection, file handle, window handle, and so on. You have to explicitly release those items. If not, you will get errors such as *"This File is in use"* or you won't be able to connect to your database because all connections are in use.

Because of this, C# supports the concept of *finalization*. This mechanism allows a type to clean up prior to garbage collection. It's important to understand that a C# finalizer is not the same as a C++ destructor. C++ destructors can be called deterministic. You know when they will execute. In C#, however, you can't be sure when a finalizer is called. It will happen only when the garbage collector determines that your object is ready for being cleaned up.

A *finalizer* in C# requires some special syntax, just as a constructor. You need to prefix the class name with a tilde (~) to create a finalizer. Listing 2-79 shows how to declare a finalizer.

**LISTING 2-79** Adding a finalizer

```
public class SomeType
{
    ~SomeType()
    {
        // This code is called when the finalize method executes
    }
}
```

Inside the finalizer, you can clean up other resources and make sure that all memory is freed. For example, when working with a *File* inside C# you will have to free any unmanaged resources before you can delete the file, as Listing 2-80 shows.

**LISTING 2-80** Not closing a file will throw an error

```
StreamWriter stream = File.CreateText("temp.dat");
stream.Write("some data");

File.Delete("temp.dat"); // Throws an IOException because the file is already open.
```

As already mentioned, the finalizer is called only when a garbage collection occurs. You can force this by adding a call to *GC.Collect*, as shown in Listing 2-81. The line *WaitForPendingFinalizers* makes sure that all finalizers have run before the code continues. The garbage collector is pretty smart in managing memory, and it's not recommended that you call *GC.Collect* yourself.

**LISTING 2-81** Forcing a garbage collection

```
StreamWriter stream = File.CreateText("temp.dat");
stream.Write("some data");
GC.Collect();
GC.WaitForPendingFinalizers();
File.Delete("temp.dat");
```

When running this piece of code in *Release* mode, the garbage collector will see that there are no more references to stream, and it will free any memory associated with the *StreamWriter* instance. This will run the finalizer, which in turn will release any file handles to the *temp.dat* file (in debug mode, the compiler will make sure that the reference isn't garbage collected till the end of the method).

What's important to understand is that a finalizer increases the life of an object. Because the finalization code also has to run, the .NET Framework keeps a reference to the object in a special finalization queue. An additional thread runs all the finalizers at a time deemed appropriate based on the execution context. This delays garbage collection for types that have a finalizer.

This is not an ideal situation. You shouldn't depend on the garbage collector to run a finalizer at some point in time to close your file. Instead, you should do this yourself. To offer you the opportunity of explicitly freeing unmanaged resources, C# offers the idea of the *IDisposable* interface that you can see in Listing 2-82.

**LISTING 2-82** The *IDisposable* interface

```
public interface IDisposable
{
    void Dispose();
}
```

The *IDiposable* interface offers one method: *Dispose*, which will free any unmanaged resources immediately. The example from Listing 2-82 could also have been written as in Listing 2-83.

**LISTING 2-83** Calling *Dispose* to free unmanaged resources

```
StreamWriter stream = File.CreateText("temp.dat");
stream.Write("some data");
stream.Dispose();
File.Delete("temp.dat");
```

But what if an exception would occur before *stream.Dispose()* is called? To make sure that your resources are always cleaned up, you need to wrap all types that implement *IDisposable* in a *try/finally statement*. Because this is so common, C# has a special statement for this: the *using statement*. The *using* statement is translated by the compiler in a *try/finally* statement that calls *Dispose* on the object. Because of this, the *using* statement can be used only with types that implement *IDisposable*.

```
using (StreamWriter sw = File.CreateText("temp.dat"))
{ }
```

The *using* statement ensures that *Dispose* is always called. Every type that implements *IDisposable* should be used in a *using* statement whenever possible. This way you make sure that you clean up all unmanaged resources.

After disposing an item, you can't use it any more. Using a disposed item will result in an *ObjectDisposedException*.

If you also want to use a *catch* statement when working with an *IDisposable* object, you need to do this manually by writing a *try/catch/finally* statement where you call *Dispose* in the *finally* clause.

---

**MORE INFO    EXCEPTION HANDLING**

For more information on how to use exception handling, see "Objective 1.5: Implement exception handling."

---

## Implementing *IDisposable* and a finalizer

Creating your own custom type that implements *IDisposable* and a finalizer correctly is not a trivial task.

For example, suppose you have a wrapper class around a file resource and an unmanaged buffer. You implement *IDisposable* so users of your class can immediately clean up if they want. You also implement a finalizer in case they forget to call *Dispose*. Listing 2-84 shows how to do this.

**LISTING 2-84** Implementing *IDisposable* and a finalizer

```
using System;
using System.IO;
using System.Runtime.InteropServices;

class UnmanagedWrapper : IDisposable
{
    private IntPtr unmanagedBuffer;
    public FileStream Stream { get; private set; }

    public UnmanagedWrapper()
    {
        CreateBuffer();
        this.Stream = File.Open("temp.dat", FileMode.Create);
    }

    private void CreateBuffer()
    {
        byte[] data = new byte[1024];
        new Random().NextBytes(data);
        unmanagedBuffer = Marshal.AllocHGlobal(data.Length);
        Marshal.Copy(data, 0, unmanagedBuffer, data.Length);
    }

    ~UnmanagedWrapper()
    {
        Dispose(false);
    }

    public void Close()
    {
        Dispose();
    }

    public void Dispose()
    {
        Dispose(true);
        System.GC.SuppressFinalize(this);
    }
```

```
    protected virtual void Dispose(bool disposing)
    {
        Marshal.FreeHGlobal(unmanagedBuffer);
        if (disposing)
        {
            if (Stream != null)
            {
                Stream.Close();
            }
        }
    }
}
```

There are a couple of things to notice about this implementation:

- The finalizer only calls *Dispose* passing *false* for *disposing*.

- The extra *Dispose* method with the Boolean argument does the real work. This method checks if it's being called in an explicit *Dispose* or if it's being called from the finalizer:

  - If the finalizer calls *Dispose*, you only release the unmanaged buffer. The *Stream* object also implements a finalizer and the garbage collector will take care of calling the finalizer of the *FileStream* instance. Because the order in which the garbage collector calls the finalizers is unpredictable, you can't call any methods on the *FileStream*.

  - If *Dispose* is called explicitly, you also close the underlying *FlleStream*. It's important to be defensive in coding this method and always check for any source of possible exceptions. It could be that *Dispose* is called multiple times and that shouldn't cause any errors.

- The regular *Dispose* method calls *GC.SuppressFinalize(this)* to make sure that the object is removed from the finalization list that the garbage collector is keeping track of. The instance has already cleaned up after itself, so it's not necessary that the garbage collector call the finalizer.

---

**EXAM TIP**

It's important to know the difference between implementing *IDisposable* and a finalizer. Both clean up your object, but a finalizer is called by the garbage collector, and the *Dispose* method can be called from code.

---

**MORE INFO**   IMPLEMENTING *IDISPOSABLE* AND A FINALIZER

For more information on how to implement *IDisposable* and a finalizer, see: *http://msdn.microsoft.com/en-us/library/b1yfkh5e.aspx.*

## Weak references

Sometimes you have to work with large objects that require a lot of time to create. For example, a list of objects that has to be retrieved from a database. It would be nice if you can just keep the items in memory; however, that increases the memory load of your application, and maybe the list won't be needed any more. But if garbage collection hasn't occurred yet, it would be nice if you could just reuse the list you created.

This is where the type *WeakReference* can be used. A *WeakReference*, as the name suggests, doesn't hold a real reference to an item on the heap, so that it can't be garbage collected. But when garbage collection hasn't occurred yet, you can still access the item through the *WeakReference*. Listing 2-85 shows how to use a *WeakReference*.

LISTING 2-85 Using *WeakReference*

```
static WeakReference data;
public static void Run()
{
    object result = GetData();
    // GC.Collect(); Uncommenting this line will make data.Target null
    result = GetData();
}

private static object GetData()
{
    if (data == null)
    {
        data = new WeakReference(LoadLargeList());
    }

    if (data.Target == null)
    {
        data.Target = LoadLargeList();
    }
    return data.Target;
}
```

The *GetData* function checks that the *WeakReference* still contains data. If not, the data is loaded again and saved in the *WeakReference*. The interesting thing is that uncommenting the line *GC.Collect()* frees the memory that the *WeakReference* points to. If garbage collection has not occurred, the data inside *WeakReference.Target* can be accessed and returned to the caller.

Using *WeakReference* is not a complete solution for a caching scenario. If you want to implement a cache, you should define an algorithm that decides which items should be removed from the cache. Upon removing, you turn a reference into a *WeakReference* and leave it up to the garbage collector.

> **Thought experiment**
>
> **Cleaning up your stuff**
>
> In this thought experiment, apply what you've learned about this objective. You can find answers to these questions in the "Answers" section at the end of this chapter.
>
> You have created your first Windows 8 app. It's a nice game that enables users to take a video of themselves describing a word. Others have to guess; that way, they can earn points that enable them to create a longer video.
>
> One day you wake up and you suddenly realize that Microsoft chose your app as its app of the week. Your web server that's running all the logic of the game is trembling under the user load because of the sudden popularity. Both memory and CPU pressure are a lot higher than you expected. You have some types that are qualified to be a value type but at the time of creating your app, you just used classes.
>
> 1. How can using value types when possible improve your performance? Or could it be that your performance will deteriorate more?
>
> 2. Why is implementing *IDisposable* important to reduce memory pressure? Is it always the best to call *Dispose* on an element as soon as you are done with it?
>
> 3. Should you implement a finalizer on all your types that implement *IDisposable*?
>
> 4. You have some items that are used a lot. Would it be wise to put them in a static field so you don't have to re-create them each time?

## Objective summary

- Memory in C# consists of both the stack and the heap.

- The heap is managed by the garbage collector.

- The garbage collector frees any memory that is not referenced any more.

- A finalizer is a special piece of code that's run by the garbage collector when it removes an object.

- *IDisposable* can be implemented to free any unmanaged resources in a deterministic way.

- Objects implementing *IDisposable* can be used with a *using* statement to make sure they are always freed.

- A *WeakReference* can be used to maintain a reference to items that can be garbage collected when necessary.

# Objective review

Answer the following questions to test your knowledge of the information in this objective. You can find the answers to these questions and explanations of why each answer choice is correct or incorrect in the "Answers" section at the end of this chapter.

1. You are about to execute a piece of code that is performance-sensitive. You are afraid that a garbage collection will occur during the execution of this code. Which method should you call before executing your code?

   A. *GC.RemoveMemoryPressure()*

   B. *GC. SuppressFinalize()*

   C. *GC.Collect()*

   D. *GC.WaitForPendingFinalizers()*

2. An object that is implementing *IDisposable* is passed to your class as an argument. Should you wrap the element in a *using* statement?

   A. Yes, otherwise a memory leak could happen.

   B. No, you should call *Close* on the object.

   C. No, you should use a *try/finally* statement and call *Dispose* yourself.

   D. No, the calling method should use a *using* statement.

3. Your application is using a lot of memory. Which solution should you use?

   A. Turn all references into *WeakReferences*.

   B. Set all references to null when you are done with them.

   C. Use a caching algorithm to decide which objects can be freed.

   D. Use a background thread to call *GC.Collect()* on a scheduled interval.

# Objective 2.7: Manipulate strings

Text is one of the most important concepts in almost every application, so C# offers quite a lot of support when working with text. All this support revolves around the built-in type *System.String*. When creating your applications, you often manipulate strings. For example, adding strings together, searching for a certain string or character within another string, iterating over a string, and then finally formatting them for display is a common practice. You will learn how to perform all those steps while keeping an eye on both usability and performance.

# Using strings in the .NET Framework

A *string* in C# is an object of type *String* whose value is text. The *string* object contains an array of *Char* objects internally. A *string* has a *Length* property that shows the number of *Char* objects it contains. *String* is a *reference type* that looks like value type (for example, the equality operators == and != are overloaded to compare on value, not on reference).

In C#, you can refer to a *string* both as *String* and *string*. You can use whichever naming convention suits you. The *string* keyword is just an alias for the .NET Framework's *String*.

One of the special characteristics of a string is that it is *immutable*, so it cannot be changed after it has been created. Every change to a string will create a new string. This is why all of the *String* manipulation methods return a *string*.

Immutability is useful in many scenarios. Reasoning about a structure if you know it will never change is easier. It cannot be modified so it is inherently thread-safe. It is more secure because no one can mess with it. Suddenly something like creating undo-redo is much easier, your data structure is immutable and you maintain only snapshots of your state.

But immutable data structures also have a negative side. The code in Listing 2-86 looks innocent, but it will create a new string for each iteration in your loop. It uses a lot of unnecessary memory and shows why you have to use caution when working with strings.

**LISTING 2-86** Creating a large number of strings

```
string s = string.Empty;

for (int i = 0; i < 10000; i++)
{
    s += "x";
}
```

This code will run 10,000 times, and each time it will create a new string. The reference *s* will point only to the last item, so all other strings are immediately ready for garbage collection.

Because C# is aware of this problem, the compiler tries to optimize working with strings for you. When creating two identical string literals in one compilation unit, the compiler ensures that only one string object is created by the CLR. This is called *string interning*, which is done only at compile time. Doing it at runtime would incur too much of a performance penalty (searching through all strings every time you create a new one is too costly).

When working with such a large number of string operations, you have to keep in mind that string is immutable and that the .NET Framework offers some special helper classes when dealing with strings.

**EXAM TIP**

Because of the immutability of the string type, all string operations return a new string. Make sure that you use this value instead of the original string.

## Manipulating strings

Because of the immutability of strings, the .NET Framework offers several classes that can be used when building strings.

### StringBuilder

The *StringBuilder* class can be used when you are working with strings in a tight loop. Instead of creating a new string over and over again, you can use the *StringBuilder*, which uses a string buffer internally to improve performance. The *StringBuilder* class even enables you to change the value of individual characters inside a string (see Listing 2-87).

**LISTING 2-87** Changing a character with a *StringBuilder*

```
System.Text.StringBuilder sb = new System.Text.StringBuilder("A initial value");
sb[0] = 'B';
```

Our previous example of concatenating a string 10,000 times can be rewritten with a *StringBuilder*, as Listing 2-88 shows.

**LISTING 2-88** Using a *StringBuilder* in a loop

```
StringBuilder sb = new StringBuilder(string.Empty);

for (int i = 0; i < 10000; i++)
{
    sb.Append("x");
}
```

One thing to keep in mind is that the *StringBuilder* does not always give better performance. When concatenating a fixed series of strings, the compiler can optimize this and combine individual concatenation operations into a single operation. When you are working with an arbitrary number of strings, such as in the loop example, a *StringBuilder* is a better choice (in this example, you could have also used *new String("x", 10000)* to create the string; when dealing with more varied data, this won't be possible).

## StringWriter and StringReader

Some APIs in the .NET Framework expect a *TextWriter* or *TextReader* to work. Those APIs can't work with a string or *StringBuilder* directly. Because of this, the .NET Framework adds a *StringReader* and *StringWriter* class. These classes *adapt* the interface of the *StringBuilder* so they can be used in places where a *TextWriter* or *TextReader* is expected.

Internally, *StringWriter* and *StringReader* use a *StringBuilder*. The only thing they do is adapt the interface of the *StringBuilder* to that of the *TextWriter* and *TextReader*.

One of the methods in the .NET Framework that expects an instance of *TextWriter* is *XmlWriter.Create*. Normally, you pass an instance of *StreamWriter* so that you can create a new XML file. But when you want the resulting XML only in memory, you can pass a *StringWriter* (see Listing 2-89).

**LISTING 2-89** Using a *StringWriter* as the output for an *XmlWriter*

```
var stringWriter = new StringWriter();
using (XmlWriter writer = XmlWriter.Create(stringWriter))
{
    writer.WriteStartElement("book");
    writer.WriteElementString("price", "19.95");
    writer.WriteEndElement();
    writer.Flush();
}
string xml = stringWriter.ToString();
```

The value of xml is now:

```
<?xml version=\"1.0\" encoding=\"utf-16\"?>
    <book>
        <price>19.95</price>
    </book>
```

When using the *XmlReader*, you can parse some XML and access the individual elements. *XmlReader* expects an instance of *TextWriter*, so you can pass it a *StringReader* (see Listing 2-90).

**LISTING 2-90** Using a *StringReader* as the input for an *XmlReader*

```
var stringReader = new StringReader(xml);
using (XmlReader reader = XmlReader.Create(stringReader))
{
    reader.ReadToFollowing("price");
    decimal price = decimal.Parse(reader.ReadInnerXml(),
        new CultureInfo("en-US")); // Make sure that you read the decimal part correctly
}
```

# Searching for strings

When working with strings, you often look for a *substring* inside another string (to parse some content or to check for valid user input or some other scenario).

The *String* class offers a couple of methods that can help you perform all kinds of search actions. The most common are *IndexOf*, *LastIndexOf*, *StartsWith*, *EndsWith*, and *SubString*.

One thing to keep in mind is that string methods can be *culture sensitive*. This is why most of the methods accept an instance of the *StringComparison* enumeration. When working with strings, always try to avoid the methods that don't use an explicit value of *StringComparison*.

> **MORE INFO**   **BEST PRACTICES WHEN WORKING WITH STRINGS**
>
> For more information on best practices when working with strings, see the MSDN documentation at *http://msdn.microsoft.com/en-us/library/dd465121.aspx*.

*IndexOf* returns the index of the first occurrence of a character or substring within a string. If the value cannot be found, it returns *-1*. The same is true with *LastIndexOf*, except this method begins searching at the end of a string and moves to the beginning. Look at Listing 2-91 for an example of *IndexOf* and *LastIndexOf*.

**LISTING 2-91**  Using *IndexOf* and *LastIndexOf*

```
string value = "My Sample Value";
int indexOfp = value.IndexOf('p'); // returns 6
int lastIndexOfm = value.LastIndexOf('m'); // returns 5
```

*StartsWith* and *EndsWith* see whether a string starts or ends with a certain value, respectively. It returns *true* or *false* depending on the result. Listing 2-92 shows how to use them.

**LISTING 2-92**  Using *StartsWith* and *EndsWith*

```
string value = "<mycustominput>";
if (value.StartsWith("<")) { }
if (value.EndsWith(">")) { }
```

*Substring* can be used to retrieve a partial string from another string. You can pass a start and a length to *Substring*. If necessary, you can calculate these indexes by using *IndexOf* or *LastIndexOf*. Listing 2-93 shows how to use *Substring*.

**LISTING 2-93**  Reading a substring

```
string value = "My Sample Value";
string subString = value.Substring(3, 6); // Returns 'Sample'
```

Another way to search a string is by using a *regular expression*, which uses a pattern-matching notation that can quickly parse large amounts of text looking for a specific format. Regular expressions can be useful when validating user input (such as an e-mail address, ZIP code, or date). The code in Listing 2-94 strips all titles from the names that you pass it. Imagine how much work it would have been to create this when using *IndexOf* and *SubString*.

**LISTING 2-94** Changing a string with a regular expression

```
string pattern = "(Mr\\.? |Mrs\\.? |Miss |Ms\\.? )";
string[] names = { "Mr. Henry Hunt", "Ms. Sara Samuels",
            "Abraham Adams", "Ms. Nicole Norris" };

foreach (string name in names)
    Console.WriteLine(Regex.Replace(name, pattern, String.Empty));
```

## Enumerating strings

A string is an array of characters. You can *enumerate* a string just as if it were a typical collection. Because a string implements *IEnumerable* and *IEnumerable<Char>*, it exposes the *GetEnumerator* method that you can use to iterate over a string.

You can use a string in a *foreach* loop to check all individual characters, as Listing 2-95 shows.

**LISTING 2-95** Iterating over a string

```
string value = "My Custom Value";
foreach (char c in value)
    Console.WriteLine(c);
```

Splitting a string in words and then iterating over them is also possible. The following line splits the sentence on spaces; it returns an *IEnumerable* that can then be iterated:

```
foreach (string word in "My sentence separated by spaces".Split(' ')) { }
```

Of course, this is a simplified version. When dealing with large amounts of text that contain all kinds of punctuation you need to use a regular expression to split the words.

## Formatting strings

When displaying strings to the user, you want to make sure that they are in the right format. Especially when working with culture-sensitive data such as *DateTime* or numbers, it's important to make sure that the string is displayed in a manner that is suitable for current users and their settings.

*Formatting* is the process of converting an instance of a type to a string representation. When converting an instance to a string, the basic way of doing this is to call the *ToString* method that's defined as a virtual member on *System.Object*. Overriding *ToString* is a good practice. If you don't do this, *ToString* will return by default the name of your type. When you override *ToString*, you can give it a more meaningful value, as Listing 2-96 shows.

**LISTING 2-96** Overriding *ToString*

```
class Person
{

    public Person(string firstName, string lastName)
    {
        this.FirstName = firstName;
        this.LastName = lastName;
    }

    public string FirstName { get; set; }
    public string LastName { get; set; }

    public override string ToString()
    {
        return FirstName + LastName;
    }
}

Person p = new Person("John", "Doe");
Console.WriteLine(p); // Displays 'John Doe'
```

When an object has multiple string representations, overriding *ToString* is not enough. For example, a *Temperature* object can display its temperature in degrees Fahrenheit, Celsius, or Kelvin. An integer value can also be displayed in multiple ways. Maybe it represents a phone number or an amount of money.

To enable this kind of behavior, you can use format strings, which are strings that describe how an object should display. The .NET Framework uses them for numeric types, dates, times, and enumerations, as Listing 2-97 shows.

**LISTING 2-97** Displaying a number with a currency format string

```
double cost = 1234.56;
Console.WriteLine(cost.ToString("C",
                new System.Globalization.CultureInfo("en-US")));
// Displays $1,234.56
```

You can use the same approach when displaying a date and time value. Depending on the culture, the formatted output can be completely different. Listing 2-98 shows how to use different format strings with a *DateTime* for an English culture.

**LISTING 2-98** Displaying a *DateTime* with different format strings

```
DateTime d = new DateTime(2013, 4, 22);
CultureInfo provider = new CultureInfo("en-US");
Console.WriteLine(d.ToString("d", provider)); // Displays 4/22/2013
Console.WriteLine(d.ToString("D", provider)); // Displays Monday, April 22, 2013
Console.WriteLine(d.ToString("M", provider)); // Displays April 22
```

Providing the correct *CultureInfo* is important when formatting values. It contains all the necessary information about how a particular type is displayed in that culture. In the same way, it's important to make sure that when you save values to a database; for example, you do this in a culture-insensitive way. If the culture-insensitive data is than loaded, it can be formatted depending on the user who is viewing the data.

You can also implement this custom formatting on your own types. You do this by creating a *ToString(string)* method on your type. When doing this, make sure that you are compliant with the standard format strings in the .NET Framework.

For example, a format string of *G* should represent a common format for your object (the same as calling *ToString()*) and a *null* value for the format string should also display the common format. Listing 2-99 shows how to do this.

**LISTING 2-99** Implementing custom formatting on a type

```
class Person
{
    ...
    public string ToString(string format)
    {
        if (string.IsNullOrWhiteSpace(format) || format = "G") format = "FL";

        format = format.Trim().ToUpperInvariant();

        switch (format)
        {
            case "FL":
                return FirstName + " " + LastName;
            case "LF":
                return LastName + " " + FirstName;
            case "FSL":
                return FirstName + ", " + LastName;
            case "LSF":
                return LastName + ", " + FirstName;
            default:
                throw new FormatException(String.Format(
                    "The '{0}' format string is not supported.", format));
        }
    }
}
```

## IFormatProvider and IFormattable

When formatting strings, you can also use an *IFormatProvider*. The *IFormatProvider* has one method, *GetFormat(Type)*, which returns specific formatting information for formatting a type. All *CultureInfo* objects implement *IFormatProvider*. The *CultureInfo* object returns a culture-specific *NumberFormatInfo* or *DateTimeFormatInfo* if a string or *DateTime* is formatted. That way, you can format a string as culture specific by passing a *CultureInfo* object to the *ToString* method.

When implementing your own *ToString* formatting method on a type, you can also choose to accept an *IFormatProvider*. When doing this, you can implement the *IFormattable* interface. Using *IFormattable* makes sure that you can integrate with the .NET Framework when it comes to formatting strings.

When implementing *IFormattable*, you have support for string conversion by the *Convert* class (which has an overload that accepts an object and *IFormatProvider*). You can also support composite formatting, in which your type is used to create a composite string with other types (see Listing 2-100).

**LISTING 2-100** Creating a composite string formatting

```
int a = 1;
int b = 2;
string result = string.Format("a: {0}, b: {1}", a, b);
Console.WriteLine(result); // Displays 'a: 1, b: 2'
```

Formatting strings is a large area in the .NET Framework. It pays to be familiar with the possible options and to know where you can find more information when you need it. Make sure that you use the correct *CultureInfo* when formatting a string and use format strings to ensure that you get the correct result.

## Thought experiment
### Showing some text

In this thought experiment, apply what you've learned about this objective. You can find answers to these questions in the "Answers" section at the end of this chapter.

You are working on a localized application to be used for time tracking. A team can use it to track time for various projects and tasks, and make sure that all billable time is correct. The application consists of a web front end based on ASP.NET and a desktop application that uses C#. Suddenly, your manager announces that your application is going global. You currently support only the English language; you didn't take globalization into account when first architecting the application. Now you have to support Spanish and German.

1. Make a list of the things you have to keep in mind when updating your application for globalization.

# Objective summary

- A string is an immutable reference type.
- When doing a lot of string manipulations, you should use a *StringBuilder*.
- The String class offers a lot of methods for dealing with strings like *IndexOf*, *LastIndexOf*, *StartsWith*, *EndsWith*, and *Substring*.
- Strings can be enumerated as a collection of characters.
- Formatting is the process of displaying an object as a string.
- You can use format strings to change how an object is converted to a string.
- You can implement formatting for your own types.

# Objective review

Answer the following questions to test your knowledge of the information in this objective. You can find the answers to these questions and explanations of why each answer choice is correct or incorrect in the "Answers" section at the end of this chapter.

1. You want to display only the date portion of a *DateTime* according to the French culture. What method should you use?

    **A.** dt.ToString(new CultureInfo("fr-FR"))

    **B.** dt.ToString("M", new CultureInfo("fr-FR"));

    **C.** dt.ToString("d");

    **D.** dt.ToString("d", new CultureInfo("fr-FR"));

2. You want your type to be able to be converted from string. Which interface should you implement?

    **A.** *IFormattable*

    **B.** *IFormatProvider*

    **C.** *IComparable*

    **D.** *IConvertible*

3. You are parsing a large piece of text to replace values based on some complex algorithm. Which class should you use?

    **A.** *StringReader*

    **B.** *StringBuilder*

    **C.** *StringWriter*

    **D.** *String*

# Chapter summary

- C# uses types such as class, struct, interface, and enum. Types have can have members such as methods, events, fields, properties, indexed properties, and constructors.

- When working with types, you sometimes need to convert between them. This can be done either implicitly or explicitly. When creating your own types, you can add support for these types of conversions.

- You use accessors such as public, private, protected, internal, and protected internal to enforce encapsulation and accessibility. Properties can be used to encapsulate data.

- An object hierarchy can be created by inheritance, and you can have both interface and class inheritance. By marking members as virtual, a derived class can override the member.

- Reflection is the process of inspecting metadata at runtime. Attributes can be used to add metadata to a type.

- C# is a managed language, which means that a garbage collector makes sure that all managed objects are freed from memory whenever they are no longer in use.

- Strings can be used for text. The string type is immutable. The .NET Framework offers a *StringBuilder* for manipulating large amounts of text. Strings can be searched, enumerated, and formatted for display.

# Answers

This section contains the solutions to the thought experiments and answers to the lesson review questions in this chapter.

## Objective 2.1: Thought experiment

1. Some of the types that you can use in building your web shop are: *Order, OrderLine, Product, Customer, Review, SearchCriteria, BusinessRule.*

2. When designing the system, you should focus on the behavior and then make sure that you have the data to support it. For example, instead of publicly exposing the *OrderLines* that an order contains, you should expose a method *AddProduct(*product, amount) that creates an *OrderLine* internally and makes sure that the *Order* follows all business rules.

3. By making sure that you have the correct constructors, users of your types can easily see which data is required. By using enums (for example for the *Order* status and *Customer* status), you can improve readability of your code. By using a base class for your business rules you can make the system more extensible so that other business rules can be easily defined.

## Objective 2.1: Review

1. **Correct answer:** B

   A. **Incorrect:** A constructor is used to create an instance of a new type.

   B. **Correct:** An indexer property enables the user of the type to easily access a type that represents an array-like collection.

   C. **Incorrect:** Making the type generic enables you to store multiple different types inside your collection.

   D. **Incorrect:** A static property cannot access the instance data of the collection.

2. **Correct answer:** A

   A. **Correct:** Constraining your generic type parameter to class allows the class to be used only with a reference type.

   B. **Incorrect:** This will constrain the class to be used with a value type, not a reference type.

   C. **Incorrect:** This will constrain the class to be used with a type that has an empty default constructor. It can be both a value and a reference type.

   D. **Incorrect:** This constrains the class to be used with a type that implements the *IDisposable* interface.

3. **Correct answer:** C

    **A.** **Incorrect:** Passing a noninitialized struct will result in a compile error of using an unassigned local variable.

    **B.** **Incorrect:** A struct can be changed inside a method. It won't change the original struct that was passed in, however.

    **C.** **Correct:** Passing a struct will make a copy of the data. The copy can be changed; the original won't change with it.

    **D.** **Incorrect:** With a reference type, the method can make changes that will reflect on the original. Because a value type is copied, it won't change the original. Returning the changes from the method will again create a new instance that will overwrite the original.

## Objective 2.2: Thought experiment

1. *ArrayLists* are nongeneric; they can only work with items of type object. Because of this, you have to box and unbox your calculation parameters each time you use them. Switching to a generic collection will avoid all the boxing and unboxing and will improve performance.

2. Throwing and catching exceptions is expensive. You can avoid the exceptions when converting items by first making sure that the conversion is allowed by using the *is* and *as* keywords. You can use a simple Boolean check to see whether a conversion is allowed.

3. One thing you can do is make sure to implement implicit conversions to the CLR types that you want to support. You could also add a helper class that aids in converting items.

## Objective 2.2: Review

1. **Correct answer:** B

    **A.** **Incorrect:** A conversion between a custom class and a value type does not exist by default.

    **B.** **Correct:** Adding an implicit operator will enable users of your class to convert between *Distance* and double without any extra work.

    **C.** **Incorrect:** Although adding an explicit cast operator will enable users of the class to convert from *Distance* to double, they will still need to explicitly cast it.

    **D.** **Incorrect:** A *Parse* method is used when converting a string to a type. It doesn't add conversions from your type to another type.

2. **Correct answers:** A, C

  A. **Correct:** The *as* operator will return *null* if the conversion failed. If it succeeds, it will return the converted object. Seeing whether the result is *null* enables you to check for a valid conversion.

  B. **Incorrect:** Implicitly casting something of type object to another type is not possible. It would require an explicit cast.

  C. **Correct:** The *is* keyword will see whether a type is derived from another type.

  D. **Incorrect:** The *dynamic* keyword can be used when you want weakly typing. It will still throw errors at runtime if an action is not possible.

3. **Correct answer:** A

  A. **Correct:** Using a generic collection will eliminate the need to box and unbox values. This will improve performance, especially when working with a large number of items.

  B. **Incorrect:** Changing *Point* to be a reference type could increase memory usage. You will still have to convert from object to *Point* when using the nongeneric *ArrayList*.

  C. **Incorrect:** Point is a struct that inherits from *System.ValueType*, which in turn inherits from *System.Object*. The implicit conversion is already present; adding it won't improve performance.

  D. **Incorrect:** Making the collection dynamic will loosen compile-time checking. It won't improve performance because the runtime has to do extra work.

# Objective 2.3: Thought experiment

1. Making each and every type public will remove all the benefits that encapsulation offers. Encapsulating data means that the internal representation of an object is hidden from the outside world. This prevents users of your type from setting an invalid or inconsistent state, and also hides complexity. This makes your system more robust because you can change implementation details while not changing the public interface of your type.

2. Because a property offers a controlled way of accessing a field, you can run extra code both on reading and changing the value. You can, for example, make sure that only authorized personnel can change specific values that determine who can use a specific chemical.

3. Because a type can implement multiple interfaces, you can use an interface to expose only a subset of the type members. By using explicit interface implementation, you can also hide certain members that should be visible under only certain circumstances. This way, you can enhance the public interface of a type by exposing fewer members at a given time.

# Objective 2.3: Review

1. **Correct answer:** D

   A. **Incorrect:** A public class with public members can be accessed from other assemblies without any restrictions.

   B. **Incorrect:** Types in other assemblies can derive from the class and access the protected methods.

   C. **Incorrect:** Types in other assemblies cannot derive from the class, but other types in the same assembly can access the method.

   D. **Correct:** An internal class cannot be accessed outside of its assembly. The protected methods can be accessed only by derived types.

2. **Correct answer:** B

   A. **Incorrect:** A protected field cannot be read by other types outside of the class.

   B. **Correct:** A public property can be read by all other types. The protected set modifier restricts changes to derived types.

   C. **Incorrect:** A protected property cannot be read by other types outside of the class.

   D. **Incorrect:** This will generate a compile error because the accessibility modifier of the get accessor must be more restrictive than the property. Public is less restrictive than protected.

3. **Correct answer:** A

   A. **Correct:** Implementing IA implicitly will make this the default implementation. When dealing with a reference to the class, this method will be invoked. Implementing IB explicitly will invoke the implementation for IB when dealing with a reference to the IB interface.

   B. **Incorrect:** When both IA and IB are implemented explicitly, you need to cast a reference to the class to one or both interface types to invoke the method.

   C. **Incorrect:** Implementing both IA and IB implicitly won't allow for a different implementation for IB.

   D. **Incorrect:** Implementing IB implicitly makes IB the default implementation instead of IA.

# Objective 2.4: Thought experiment

1. The problem is that C# doesn't have multiple inheritance for classes, but you can have multiple interface inheritance. When types such as *IDisposable* would be implemented as a base class, you would be able to inherit only from that class. Inheriting from other custom types would be impossible.

2. Implementing the search criteria can be best done through using class inheritance. By making an abstract class that accepts an input and then executes a specific filter over the items, you can reuse as much code as possible. The inherited criteria would need to specify only the filter expression (maybe through a lambda) and their exact parameters through the constructor.

3. *IUnknown* is not usable in this scenario; it's only for dealing with unmanaged code. Implementing *IDisposable* should be used when you are dealing with unmanaged resources that you want to free. In this case, that's not necessary. *IComparable* could come in handy when you want to order your criteria (for example, one criterion should execute before any of the others). *IEnumerable* can be used to implement the iterator pattern on your criteria. This could give you a performance benefit. Instead of processing all the houses at once, you can return an iterator and filter the whole set one by one.

# Objective 2.4: Review

1. **Correct answer:** C

    A. **Incorrect:** An interface won't let you share any implementation code, only the public member signatures.

    B. **Incorrect:** A class requires you to have an implementation for every member. It doesn't give you the option to only declare a member signature.

    C. **Correct:** An abstract class enables you to share both implemented methods and method signatures that a derived class needs to implement.

    D. **Incorrect:** A sealed class can't be inherited.

2. **Correct answer:** B

    A. **Incorrect:** *IEnumerable* should be implemented on collection-like types so they can be easily iterated over.

    B. **Correct:** *IComparable* enables objects to be compared to each other. It returns an integer value that represents the relative position as smaller than 0, 0 or larger than 0.

    C. **Incorrect:** *IDisposable* should be implemented on types that access unmanaged resources and that need to release them.

    D. **Incorrect:** *IUnknown* is used only when working with the COM.

3. **Correct answers:** B, D

    **A. Incorrect:** When you mark the base type as abstract, you can't create an instance of it. You can't use both the base and the derived type as concrete types in your code.

    **B. Correct:** Marking the method in the base class as virtual enables it to be overridden by derived classes.

    **C. Incorrect:** The *new* keyword hides the method in the base class. You shouldn't use it when you want to extend the behavior from the base class.

    **D. Correct:** The *override* keyword enables you to override a method marked as virtual in a base class.

## Objective 2.5: Thought experiment

1. Although interface inheritance describes an "is-a-kind-of" relation, but you can't say that your type is "a kind of *AuthorizedObject*." Instead, you use attributes to say something about another type, which is why C# contains metadata. Inheritance should not be used to decorate a type with certain information.

2. Reflection can be a really slow process. You can replace reflection with expression trees. When you are mapping data to a custom type, you can build an expression tree (and cache it!). The expression tree can be compiled to native code. Of course, you will still have the penalty of doing this extra step, but it will be much faster than reflection.

3. For generating code, you can use the CodeDOM. A *CompilationUnit* created by the CodeDOM can be outputted as a source file.

## Objective 2.5: Review

1. **Correct answers:** A, D

    **A. Correct:** The field is a nonstatic instance field.

    **B. Incorrect:** *DeclaredOnly* is used when you don't want to include inherited members.

    **C. Incorrect:** The field is not static; it's a per-instance field.

    **D. Correct:** Nonpublic is necessary because the field is private.

2. **Correct answer:** B

   A. **Incorrect:** The *AttributeTargets.GenericParameter* can be applied to generic parameters. It's not used for regular method arguments.

   B. **Correct:** The *Attribute* targets both *Methods* and *Parameters*. It can also be applied multiple times.

   C. **Incorrect:** With *AttributeTargets.All*, the attribute can be applied to all types. It also can't be applied multiple times.

   D. **Incorrect:** Because *AllowMultiple* is *false* by default, this attribute can't be applied multiple times.

3. **Correct answer:** C

   A. **Incorrect:** An *Action* doesn't return a value. It also takes a Boolean input instead of the list of strings and the filter value.

   B. **Incorrect:** This delegate doesn't have a parameter for the value to filter on.

   C. **Correct:** It takes both the input list and the value to filter on and returns the filtered list.

   D. **Incorrect:** This returns only a list of strings. It doesn't have an argument for the filter parameter or the original list.

# Objective 2.6: Thought experiment

1. Reference types are on the heap and managed by the garbage collector. Value types are on the stack most of the time and are freed when the current method ends. When a value type is on the stack, it takes up less memory than it would on the heap. However, if a value type is enclosed in a reference type, it's still on the heap. Changing the type to a struct is no guarantee that your memory pressure will drop.

2. *IDisposable* gives you a way to explicitly free up unmanaged resources and you won't have to wait for the garbage collector to free memory. However, calling *Dispose* is something that takes up CPU time. When leaving things to the garbage collector, the garbage collector will decide when is the best time to start calling finalizers. There is a compromise to make between explicitly or implicitly freeing your resources.

3. A class that implements *IDisposable* should have some unmanaged resources. A finalizer is important for making sure that an item always frees the unmanaged resources, even when *Dispose* is not called. However, a class with a finalizer is threaded in a special way. The object is added to a finalization queue and is kept in memory until the finalizer has run. It's important to make sure that when *Dispose* is called, the object is explicitly removed from the finalization queue.

4. A static field is a root reference; the garbage collector will never free an object that is referenced by a static field. In this case, it would be better to use a cache that keeps track of which objects should be kept in memory. A caching algorithm that decides on how frequently an object is accessed can make sure that your objects are around. However, when there is a memory shortage, the cache can turn some objects into *WeakReferences* and make sure they can be garbage collected.

## Objective 2.6: Review

1. **Correct answer:** C

   A. **Incorrect:** *RemoveMemoryPressure* should be called only after calling *AddMemoryPressure* to inform the runtime that a managed object uses a large amount of unmanaged memory.

   B. **Incorrect:** *SuppressFinalize* should be called in the *Dispose* method of an object to inform the runtime that the object doesn't need to be finalized any more.

   C. **Correct:** *Collect* will execute a garbage collection, freeing as much memory as possible at that time, which can be a very expensive process. This won't prevent the garbage collector from executing during your time-sensitive code, but it will make it less likely to happen.

   D. **Incorrect:** *WaitForPendingFinalizers* suspends the current thread so all finalizers that are on the finalization queue can run. This will free some memory (for all objects that are waiting for finalization). Normally, however, you call this code after calling *Collect* if you want to make sure that all finalizers have run.

2. **Correct answer:** D

   A. **Incorrect:** A memory leak won't happen because the finalizer of the class will eventually execute and dispose of the element. Disposing of the object in your method will cause an *ObjectDisposedException* to be thrown in other code that uses the object.

   B. **Incorrect:** The *Close* method is sometimes used as a secondary method that internally calls *Dispose*. It's implemented on types such as *File*. The same reasoning applies as with answer A.

   C. **Incorrect:** A *using* statement is equivalent to a *try/finally* statement with a *Dispose* call. However, you don't want to dispose of the item because the calling code could depend on the object being in a usable state.

   D. **Correct:** The calling code knows what the lifetime of the object should be and should decide when to dispose of the object.

3. **Correct answer:** C

  A. **Incorrect:** A *WeakReference* is not an equivalent to an efficient caching strategy. Turning all items into *WeakReferences* will complicate your code (you have to see whether the memory is cleared). It could potentially increase your memory usage because the *WeakReference* itself also takes up memory.

  B. **Incorrect:** Setting references to *null* is optimized away by the compiler. Unlike some other languages, it doesn't explicitly free any memory.

  C. **Correct:** A caching strategy is the best solution. You can decide whether you want to free memory based on usage, a timestamp, or some other criteria.

  D. **Incorrect:** Calling *GC.Collect* on a scheduled interval won't improve your memory usage. Memory is freed only when there are no root references to an object. *GC.Collect* will stall your execution thread, making things slower, while not freeing any more memory than waiting for a regular *Collect* to take place.

## Objective 2.7: Thought experiment

This is not a trivial task to do. Building globalization into an existing application requires more effort than taking it into account from the start.

The areas you will have to focus on are the display of text. Especially because this is a time tracking application there will be a lot of dates and times that are displayed.

There are a few areas you will have to focus on:

- Make sure that all string comparisons use an explicit overload that takes a *StringComparison* object.
- Use *StringComparison.Ordinal* or *StringComparison.OrdinalIgnoreCase* when comparing strings in a culture-agnostic way.
- Use *StringComparison.CurrentCulture* when displaying text to the user.
- Make sure that all persisted text is persisted with the invariant culture.
- Make sure that you are not using *String.Compare* or *CompareTo* for equality testing.
- Implement *IFormattable* for custom types that are displayed to the user to make sure that all culture settings are respected.
- Use the correct format strings when displaying numbers, dates, and times to the user.

## Objective 2.7: Review

1. **Correct answer:** D

  A. **Incorrect:** Only specifying the culture will give you the full date and time.

  B. **Incorrect:** Specifying "M" as the format string results in "22 avril" without the year.

  C. **Incorrect:** This will give the date in the correct format, but not with the French culture.

  D. **Correct:** This will give the date in the correct French format.

2. **Correct answer:** A

   A. **Correct:** *IFormattable* provides the functionality to format the value of an object into a string representation. It is also used by the *Convert* class to do the opposite.

   B. **Incorrect:** *IFormatProvider* is used to retrieve an object that controls formatting, not the actual formatting.

   C. **Incorrect:** *IComparable* is used to sort items.

   D. **Incorrect:** *IConvertible* defines methods to convert a type to an equivalent CLR type.

3. **Correct answer:** B

   A. **Incorrect:** *StringReader* is an adapter of the *StringBuilder* class so that it can be used in places where a *TextReader* is required.

   B. **Correct:** The *StringBuilder* class is most efficient when changing large amounts of strings.

   C. **Incorrect:** The *StringWriter* is used in places where a *TextWriter* is required. It's an adapter of the *StringBuilder*.

   D. **Incorrect:** The regular *String* class is immutable, so it's not efficient to use when changing large amounts of strings.

# CHAPTER 3

# Debug applications and implement security

When you are building your applications, you will always run into unforeseen problems. Maybe you see the error and you start looking for the problem, or a user reports the error while the application is being tested or is already in production.

Debugging is the process of finding errors in your software and removing them. The C# compiler and the .NET Framework help you identify these bugs, whether on your development machine or in a production environment. In this chapter, you learn how to use the compiler to output extra information that can help you find bugs. You also look at implementing diagnostics in your application that output critical information about its health.

When building real-world applications, it's also important to make sure that your applications are secure. You look at validating application input to ensure that the data is correct, but also to avoid malicious actions. Another area of security has to do with the code itself. If a user can change your assemblies and deploy them in a production environment, he can change the way your application behaves without you even knowing it. In this chapter, you look at the options you have to protect yourself against these attacks.

## Objectives in this chapter:

- Objective 3.1: Validate application input
- Objective 3.2: Perform symmetric and asymmetric encryption
- Objective 3.3: Manage assemblies
- Objective 3.4: Debug an application
- Objective 3.5. Implement diagnostics in an application

## Objective 3.1: Validate application input

If your application runs in total isolation and processes only its own data, you can be sure that your application behaves the way it should behave.

But in the real world, you have to deal with external input. This input can come from another system, but most of the time it comes from your users. Validating all input to your application is an area that's sometimes overlooked but that is of critical importance.

# Why validating application input is important

When your application is in production, it has to deal with various types of input. Some of this input comes from other systems that it integrates with, and most input is generated by users. Those users fall into two categories:

- Innocent users
- Malicious users

*Innocent users* are the ones who try to use your application to get some work done. They have no bad intentions when working with your application, but they can still make mistakes. Maybe they forget to input some required data, or they make a typo and insert invalid data.

*Malicious users* are a different species. They actively seek weaknesses in your application and try to exploit them. Maybe they want access to some privileged information, or they try to add or remove information. These are the users who try to insert invalid data, decompile your code to see how it works, or just start looking for hidden areas of your system.

Even when your application integrates with other applications that have no bad intentions, you still have to validate the data you're consuming. Maybe you have developed your application, tested it, and made sure everything was working, but suddenly the other system is upgraded to a new version. The fields you were expecting are gone or moved to another location, and new data is suddenly added. If you don't protect yourself against these kinds of situations, they can crash your application or corrupt the data in your system.

When building real world applications, you will probably use frameworks such as Windows Presentation Foundation (WPF), ASP.NET, or the Entity Framework. Those frameworks have built-in functionality to validate data, but it's still important to make sure that you know how to perform your own validation.

# Managing data integrity

When invalid data enters your application, it can be that your application crashes. Maybe you expect a valid date, but a user makes a typo. When you try to perform some calculations on the date, an exception is thrown, and your application crashes.

Of course, this is inconvenient for the user and definitely something you should avoid. But crashing isn't the worst that can happen. What if the invalid data isn't recognized and is saved to your database? That can lead to corrupt data and jeopardize the integrity of your data.

Let's say, for example, that you have built an online shopping application. One of the administrators decides to do some cleaning and removes a couple of user accounts that he presumes are no longer in use. But he forgets that those accounts have a purchase history. Suddenly your data is in an inconsistent state. You have orphaned orders in your database that can't be linked to a specific user any more.

Another situation can arise when you have a power outage or a hardware failure. Maybe you have developed an application for a bank. You receive a message that a certain amount of money should be removed from one account and added to another one. After removing the money, your application is abruptly terminated, and suddenly the money is gone.

Avoiding these types of problems is the area of *managing data integrity*. There are four different types of data integrity:

- **Entity integrity**    States that each entity (a record in a database) should be uniquely identifiable. In a database, this is achieved by using a primary key column. A primary key uniquely identifies each row of data. It can be generated by the database or by your application.

- **Domain integrity**    Refers to the validity of the data that an entity contains. This can be about the type of data and the possible values that are allowed (a valid postal code, a number within a certain range, or a default value, for example).

- **Referential integrity**    The relationship that entities have with each other, such as the relationship between an order and a customer.

- **User-defined integrity**    Comprises specific business rules that you need to enforce. A business rule for a web shop might involve a new customer who is not allowed to place an order above a certain dollar amount.

Most of these integrity checks are integrated into modern database systems. You can use *primary keys and foreign keys* to let the database perform certain basic checks on your data. A primary key uniquely identifies each row of data. Defining them makes sure that no rows have the same ID. A foreign key is used to point to another record (for example, the manager of a person or the order for an order line). You can configure the database to disallow the removal of an order without also removing the order lines.

When working with a database, you will probably use an object-relational mapper such as the Entity Framework, which enables a couple of different ways to work with your database. One approach is to define your object model in code and then let the Entity Framework generate a database that can store your model. You can annotate your classes with attributes that specify certain validation rules, or you can use a special mapping syntax to configure the way your database schema is generated.

**MORE INFO**  ENTITY FRAMEWORK

For more information on the Entity Framework and the different ways you can use it, see Chapter 4, "Implement data access."

For example, when working with a web shop, you have classes for at least an order, a customer, an order line, and a product.

You need entity integrity to ensure that each entity can be uniquely identified. You do this by adding an ID property to each entity. The database helps you generate unique values for your IDs when you add entities to the database.

Referential integrity is necessary to ensure a relationship is maintained between orders, order lines, customers, and products. Foreign key constraints show which relationships are required and which are optional.

Domain integrity also comes into play. You have specific data types, such as a *DateTime* for your order date and shipping date. Some fields are required, such as the name of the customer and the quantity of products you want to order.

User-defined integrity is another issue. It can't be handled automatically by the Entity Framework. You can define these checks in code or write custom code that will be executed by your database. Another way is to use a *trigger*. Triggers are special methods that run when data in your database is updated, inserted, or removed. Such an action triggers your method to execute. You can also use *stored procedures*, which are subroutines that are stored in your database and can be executed to validate date or control access to data.

Listing 3-1 is a code sample that describes the Customer and Address classes. As you can see, some of the properties are annotated with special attributes. These attributes can be found in the System.ComponentModel.DataAnnotations.dll, which is included in the Entity Framework. You can add the Entity Framework to your application by installing the Entity Framework NuGet package.

**MORE INFO**  NUGET

NuGet is a free and open-source package manager. It's installed as a Visual Studio extension that can be used to easily download software packages and add them to your applications. You can find more information about NuGet at *http://nuget.org/*.

LISTING 3-1 *Customer* and *Address* classes

```
public class Customer
{
    public int Id { get; set; }

    [Required, MaxLength(20)]
    public string FirstName { get; set; }

    [Required, MaxLength(20)]
    public string LastName { get; set; }

    [Required]
    public Address ShippingAddress { get; set; }

    [Required]
    public Address BillingAddress { get; set; }
}

public class Address
{
    public int Id { get; set; }

    [Required, MaxLength(20)]
    public string AddressLine1 { get; set; }

    [Required, MaxLength(20)]
    public string AddressLine2 { get; set; }

    [Required, MaxLength(20)]
    public string City { get; set; }

    [RegularExpression(@"^[1-9][0-9]{3}\s?[a-zA-Z]{2}$")]
    public string ZipCode { get; set; }
}
```

You can use the following predefined attributes:

- *DataTypeAttribute*
- *RangeAttribute*
- *RegularExpressionAttribute*
- *RequiredAttribute*
- *StringLengthAttribute*
- *CustomValidationAttribute*
- *MaxLengthAttribute*
- *MinLengthAttribute*

You can apply these attributes to your class members, and when you save your changes to the database, the validation code runs.

Listing 3-2 shows an example of using an Entity Framework context to save a new customer to the database.

LISTING 3-2 Saving a new customer to the database

```
public class ShopContext : DbContext
{
    public IDbSet<Customer> Customers { get; set; }

    protected override void OnModelCreating(DbModelBuilder modelBuilder)
    {
        // Make sure the database knows how to handle the duplicate address property
        modelBuilder.Entity<Customer>().HasRequired(bm => bm.BillingAddress)
            .WithMany().WillCascadeOnDelete(false);
    }
}

using (ShopContext ctx = new ShopContext())
{
    Address a = new Address
    {
        AddressLine1 = "Somewhere 1",
        AddressLine2 = "At some floor",
        City = "SomeCity",
        ZipCode = "1111AA"
    };

    Customer c = new Customer()
    {
        FirstName = "John",
        LastName = "Doe",
        BillingAddress = a,
        ShippingAddress = a,
    };

    ctx.Customers.Add(c);
    ctx.SaveChanges();
}
```

If you forget to set the *FirstName* property, the Entity Framework throws the following exception:

```
System.Data.Entity.Validation.DbEntityValidationException : Validation failed for one or
more entities. See 'EntityValidationErrors' property for more details.
```

Looking at the *EntityValidationErrors* property tells you that the *FirstName* field is required. You can run this validation code manually outside of the context of the Entity Framework. Listing 3-3 shows a class that can run validation on an entity and report the errors.

**LISTING 3-3** Running manual validation

```
public static class GenericValidator<T>
{
    public static IList<ValidationResult> Validate(T entity)
    {
        var results = new List<ValidationResult>();
        var context = new ValidationContext(entity, null, null);
        Validator.TryValidateObject(entity, context, results);
        return results;
    }
}
```

The Entity Framework also creates foreign keys and primary keys in the database for your entities. They ensure that you don't have entities with the same ID and that the relationships between your entities, such as from *Customer* to *Address*, are correct.

> **MORE INFO**  **ENTITY FRAMEWORK**
>
> For more information about the Entity Framework, see the Microsoft documentation at *http://msdn.microsoft.com/en-us/data/ef.aspx*. You can also read *Programming Entity Framework: DbContext* by Julia Lerman and Rowan Miller (O'Reilly Media, 2012).

Another important topic when managing data integrity with a database is using *transactions*. A transaction helps you group a set of related operations on a database. It ensures that those operations are seen as one distinct action. If one fails, they all fail and can easily be rolled back.

You can also run into problems when your users work *concurrently* with the same set of data. By using transactions, you can configure your database to throw an exception when there is a conflicting update. In your application, you can catch those exceptions and write code that handles the conflict. You could, for example, allow the user to choose which update should win, or you can let the last update win. This helps you maintain your data integrity.

> **MORE INFO**  **TRANSACTIONS**
>
> For more information on using transactions, see Chapter 4, "Implement data access."

# Using *Parse*, *TryParse*, and *Convert*

Most input to your application comes in as a simple string. Maybe you know that it actually represents a number or a valid date, but you have to check this to ensure that the data is valid.

The .NET Framework has some built-in types that help you convert data from one type to another.

The *Parse* and *TryParse* methods can be used when you have a string that you want to convert to a specific data type. For example, if you have a string that you know is a *Boolean* value, you can use the *bool.Parse* method, as Listing 3-4 shows.

**LISTING 3-4** Using *Parse*

```
string value = "true";
bool b = bool.Parse(value);
Console.WriteLine(b); // displays True
```

The *bool.Parse* method uses the *static readonly* fields *TrueString* and *FalseString* to see whether your string is *true* or *false*. If your string contains an invalid value, *Parse* throws a *FormatException*. If you pass a *null* value for the string, you will get an *ArgumentNullException*. *Parse* should be used if you are certain the parsing will succeed. If an exception is thrown, this denotes a real error in your application.

*TryParse* does things differently. You use *TryParse* if you are not sure that the parsing will succeed. You don't want an exception to be thrown and you want to handle invalid conversion gracefully. Look at Listing 3-5 for an example of using the *int.TryParse* method that tries to parse a string to a valid number.

**LISTING 3-5** Using *TryParse*

```
string value = "1";
int result;
bool success = int.TryParse(value, out result);

if (success)
{
    // value is a valid integer, result contains the value
}
else
{
    // value is not a valid integer
}
```

As Listing 3-5 shows, *TryParse* returns a Boolean value that indicates whether the value could be parsed. The *out parameter* contains the resulting value when the operation is successful. If the parsing succeeds, the variable holds the converted value; otherwise, it contains the initial value.

*TryParse* can be used when you are parsing some user input. If the user provides invalid data, you can show a friendly error message and let him try again.

When using the *bool.Parse* or *bool.TryParse* methods, you don't have any extra parsing options. When parsing numbers, you can supply extra options for the style of the number and the specific culture that you want to use. Listing 3-6 shows how you can parse a string that contains a currency symbol and a decimal separator. The *CultureInfo* class can be found in the *System.Globalization* namespace.

LISTING 3-6 Using configuration options when parsing a number

```
CultureInfo english = new CultureInfo("En");
CultureInfo dutch = new CultureInfo("Nl");

string value = "€19,95";
decimal d = decimal.Parse(value, NumberStyles.Currency, dutch);
Console.WriteLine(d.ToString(english)); // Displays 19.95
```

A complex subject is parsing a date and time. You can use the *DateTime.Parse* method for this, which offers several *overloads* (methods with the same name but different arguments):

- *Parse(string)* uses the current thread culture and the *DateTimeStyles.AllowWhiteSpaces*.
- *Parse(string, IFormatProvider)* uses the specified culture and the *DateTimeStyles.Allow-WhiteSpaces*.
- *Parse(string, IFormatProvider, DateTimeStyles)*.

When parsing a *DateTime*, you must take into account things such as time zone differences and cultural differences, especially when working on an application that uses globalization. It's important to parse user input with the correct culture.

> **MORE INFO** **PARSING *DATETIME***
>
> For more information on parsing dates and times, see the MSDN documentation at *http://msdn.microsoft.com/en-us/library/system.datetime.parse.aspx*.

The .NET Framework also offers the *Convert* class to convert between base types. The supported base types are *Boolean, Char, SByte, Byte, Int16, Int32, Int64, UInt16, Uint32, Uint64, Single, Double, Decimal, DateTime*, and *String*. The difference between *Parse/TryParse* and *Convert* is that *Convert* enables *null* values. It doesn't throw an *ArgumentNullException*; instead, it returns the default value for the supplied type, as Listing 3-7 shows.

LISTING 3-7 Using *Convert* with a *null* value

```
int i = Convert.ToInt32(null);
Console.WriteLine(i); // Displays 0
```

A difference between *Convert* and the *Parse* methods is that *Parse* takes a string only as input, while *Convert* can also take other base types as input. Listing 3-8 shows an example of converting a double to an int. The double value is rounded.

LISTING 3-8 Using *Convert* to convert from double to int

```
double d = 23.15;
int i = Convert.ToInt32(d);
Console.WriteLine(i); // Displays 23
```

Methods such as these throw an *OverflowException* when the parsed or converted value is too large for the target type.

**EXAM TIP**

It's important to know that when you are parsing user input, the best choice is the *TryParse* method. Throwing exceptions for "normal" errors is not a best practice. *TryParse* just returns *false* when the value can't be parsed.

# Using regular expressions

A *regular expression* is a specific pattern used to parse and find matches in strings. A regular expression is sometimes called *regex* or *regexp*.

Regular expressions are flexible. For example, the regex *^(\(\d{3}\)|^\d{3}[.-]?)?\d{3}[.-]?\d{4}$* matches North American telephone numbers with or without parentheses around the area code, and with or without hyphens or dots between the numbers.

Regular expressions have a history of being hard to write and use. Luckily, a lot of patterns are already written by someone else. Websites such as *http://regexlib.com/* contain a lot of examples that you can use or adapt to your own needs. Regular expressions can be useful when validating application input, reducing to a few lines of code what can take dozens or more with manual parsing. Maybe you allow a user to use both slashes and dashes to input a valid date. Or you allow white space when entering a ZIP Code. Listing 3-9 shows how cumbersome it is to validate a Dutch ZIP Code manually.

**LISTING 3-9** Manually validating a ZIP Code

```
static bool ValidateZipCode(string zipCode)
{
    // Valid zipcodes: 1234AB | 1234 AB | 1001 AB

    if (zipCode.Length < 6) return false;

    string numberPart = zipCode.Substring(0, 4);
    int number;
    if (!int.TryParse(numberPart, out number)) return false;

    string characterPart = zipCode.Substring(4);

    if (numberPart.StartsWith("0")) return false;
    if (characterPart.Trim().Length < 2) return false;
    if (characterPart.Length == 3 && characterPart.Trim().Length != 2)
        return false;

    return true;
}
```

If you use a regular expression, the code is much shorter. A regular expression that matches Dutch ZIP Codes is *^[1-9][0-9]{3}\s?[a-zA-Z]{2}$*.

You can use this pattern with the *RegEx* class that can be found in the *System.Text.Regular-Expressions* namespace. Listing 3-10 shows how you can use the *RegEx* class to validate a zip code.

LISTING 3-10 Validate a ZIP Code with a regular expression

```
static bool ValidateZipCodeRegEx(string zipCode)
{
    Match match = Regex.Match(zipCode, @"^[1-9][0-9]{3}\s?[a-zA-Z]{2}$",
        RegexOptions.IgnoreCase);
    return match.Success;
}
```

Next to matching application input to a specific pattern, you can also use regular expressions to ensure that input doesn't contain certain restricted characters. You can use regex to replace those characters with another value to remove them from the input.

Especially when working in the context of a web application, it is important to filter the user input. Imagine that a user inputs some HTML inside an input field that is meant for information such as a name or address. The application doesn't validate the input and saves it straight to the database. The next time the user visits the application, the HTML is directly rendered as a part of the page. A user can do a lot of harm by using this technique, so it's important to ensure that input doesn't contain potentially harmful characters.

Listing 3-11 shows an example of using a *RegEx* expression to remove all excessive use of white space. Every single space is allowed but multiple spaces are replaced with a single space.

LISTING 3-11 Collapse multiple spaces with RegEx

```
RegexOptions options = RegexOptions.None;
Regex regex = new Regex(@"[ ]{2,}", options);

string input = "1 2 3 4    5";
string result = regex.Replace(input, " ");

Console.WriteLine(result); // Displays 1 2 3 4 5
```

Although regex looks more difficult than writing the validation code in plain C#, it's definitely worth learning how it works. A regular expression can dramatically simplify your code, and it's worth examining if you are in a situation requiring validation.

## Validating JSON and XML

When exchanging data with other applications, you will often receive *JavaScript Object Notation (JSON)* or *Extensible Markup Language (XML)* data. JSON is a popular format that has its roots in the JavaScript world. It's a compact way to represent some data. XML has a stricter schema and is considered more verbose, but certainly has its uses. It's important to make sure that this data is valid before you start using it.

Valid JSON starts with *{* or *[*, and ends with *}* or *]*. You can easily see whether a string starts with these characters by using the code in Listing 3-12.

**LISTING 3-12** Seeing whether a string contains potential JSON data

```
public static bool IsJson(string input)
{
    input = input.Trim();
    return input.StartsWith("{") && input.EndsWith("}")
            || input.StartsWith("[") && input.EndsWith("]");
}
```

Checking only the start and end characters is, of course, not enough to know whether the whole object can be parsed as JSON. The .NET Framework offers the *JavaScriptSerializer* that you can use to deserialize a JSON string into an object. You can find the *JavaScriptSerializer* in the *System.Web.Extensions* dynamic-link library (DLL) in the *System.Web.Script.Serialization* namespace.

Listing 3-13 shows how you can use the *JavaScriptSerializer*. In this case, you are deserializing the data to a *Dictionary<string,object>*. You can then loop through the dictionary to see the property names and their values.

**LISTING 3-13** Deserializing an object with the *JavaScriptSerializer*

```
var serializer = new JavaScriptSerializer();
var result = serializer.Deserialize<Dictionary<string, object>>(json);
```

If you pass some invalid JSON to this function, an *ArgumentException* is thrown with a message that starts with *"Invalid object passed in"*.

An XML file can be described by using an *XML Schema Definition (XSD)*. This XSD can be used to validate an XML file.

Take, for example, the XML file that is described in Listing 3-14.

**LISTING 3-14** A sample XML with person data

```
<?xml version="1.0" encoding="utf-16" ?>
<Person xmlns:xsi="http://www.w3.org/2001/XMLSchema-
        instance" xmlns:xsd="http://www.w3.org/2001/XMLSchema">
  <FirstName>John</FirstName>
  <LastName>Doe</LastName>
  <Age>42</Age>
</Person>
```

You can create an XSD file for this schema by using the *XML Schema Definition Tool (Xsd. exe)* that is a part of Visual Studio. This tool can generate XML Schema files or C# classes.

The following line will generate an XSD file for the person.xml file:

```
Xsd.exe person.xml
```

The tool creates a file called person.xsd. You can see the content of this XSD file in Listing 3-15.

**LISTING 3-15** A sample XSD file

```
<?xml version="1.0" encoding="utf-8"?>
<xs:schema id="NewDataSet" xmlns="" xmlns:xs="http://www.w3.org/2001/XMLSchema"
  xmlns:msdata="urn:schemas-microsoft-com:xml-msdata">
  <xs:element name="Person">
    <xs:complexType>
      <xs:sequence>
        <xs:element name="FirstName" type="xs:string" minOccurs="0" />
        <xs:element name="LastName" type="xs:string" minOccurs="0" />
        <xs:element name="Age" type="xs:string" minOccurs="0" />
      </xs:sequence>
    </xs:complexType>
  </xs:element>
  <xs:element name="NewDataSet" msdata:IsDataSet="true" msdata:UseCurrentLocale="true">
    <xs:complexType>
      <xs:choice minOccurs="0" maxOccurs="unbounded">
        <xs:element ref="Person" />
      </xs:choice>
    </xs:complexType>
  </xs:element>
</xs:schema>
```

By default, none of the items in the file is required. It does, however, record which elements are possible and what the structure of the file should look like.

You can now use this XSD file to validate an XML file. Listing 3-16 shows a way to do this.

**LISTING 3-16** Validating an XML file with a schema

```
public void ValidateXML()
{
    string xsdPath = "person.xsd";
    string xmlPath = "person.xml";

    XmlReader reader = XmlReader.Create(xmlPath);
    XmlDocument document = new XmlDocument();
    document.Schemas.Add("", xsdPath);
    document.Load(reader);

    ValidationEventHandler eventHandler =
        new ValidationEventHandler(ValidationEventHandler);
    document.Validate(eventHandler);
}

static void ValidationEventHandler(object sender,
    ValidationEventArgs e)
{
    switch (e.Severity)
    {
        case XmlSeverityType.Error:
            Console.WriteLine("Error: {0}", e.Message);
            break;
        case XmlSeverityType.Warning:
            Console.WriteLine("Warning {0}", e.Message);
            break;
    }
}
```

If there is something wrong with the XML file, such as a non-existing element, the *ValidationEventHandler* is called. Depending on the type of validation error, you can decide which action to take.

### Thought experiment

#### Strange errors

In this thought experiment, apply what you've learned about this objective. You can find answers to these questions in the "Answers" section at the end of this chapter.

You have developed a complex web application and deployed it to production. The application is a new hybrid of wiki and a forum. Users can use it to brainstorm on ideas and write a document together.

Suddenly users start contacting your support desk. They are all reporting "that your application looks strange." It suddenly contains extra URLs that link to external websites that are mixed with the original website's layout.

**1.** What could be the problem?

**2.** How will you solve it?

## Objective summary

- Validating application input is important to protect your application against both mistakes and attacks.
- Data integrity should be managed both by your application and your data store.
- The *Parse*, *TryParse*, and *Convert* functions can be used to convert between types.
- Regular expressions, or regex, can be used to match input against a specified pattern or replace specified characters with other values.
- When receiving JSON and XML files, it's important to validate them using the built-in types, such as with *JavaScriptSerializer* and XML Schemas.

## Objective review

Answer the following questions to test your knowledge of the information in this objective. You can find the answers to these questions and explanations of why each answer choice is correct or incorrect in the "Answers" section at the end of this chapter.

1. A user needs to enter a *DateTime* in a text field. You need to parse the value in code. Which method do you use?

   **A.** *DateTime.Parse*

   **B.** *DateTime.TryParse*

   **C.** *Convert.ToDateTime*

   **D.** *Regex.Match.*

2. You are working on a globalized web application. You need to parse a text field where the user enters an amount of money. Which method do you use?

   **A.** *int.TryParse(value, NumberStyles.Currency, UICulture);*

   **B.** *decimal.TryParse(value, NumberStyles.Currency, UICulture);*

   **C.** *decimal.TryParse(value, ServerCulture);*

   **D.** *decimal.TryParse(value)*

3. You need to validate an XML file. What do you use?

   **A.** *JavaScriptSerializer*

   **B.** *RegEx*

   **C.** *StringBuilder*

   **D.** *XSD*

# Objective 3.2 Perform symmetric and asymmetric encryption

Security and cryptography are closely related to each other. Some important steps in building a secure application are the authentication of users, making sure your data stays confidential, and ensuring that no one can tamper with your data. The .NET Framework offers several implementations of popular algorithms that you can use to protect your applications.

> **This objective covers how to:**
> - Use symmetric and asymmetric encryption algorithms.
> - Work with encryption in the .NET Framework.
> - Use hashing.
> - Manage and create certificates.
> - Use the code access permissions from the *System.Security* namespace.
> - Secure string data.

# Using symmetric and asymmetric encryption

Security is about keeping secrets. You can use complex algorithms to encrypt your data, but if you can't keep your passwords and codes secret, everyone will be able to read your private data.

*Cryptography* is about *encrypting* and *decrypting* data. With encryption, you take a piece of *plain text* (regular text that's human readable) and then run an *algorithm* over it. The resulting data looks like a random byte sequence, often called *ciphertext*. Decryption is the opposite process: The byte sequence is transformed into the original plain text data.

In cryptography, you can keep your algorithm secret, or you can use a public algorithm and keep your key secret.

Keeping your algorithm secret is often impractical because you would need to switch algorithms each time someone leaked the algorithm. Instead a *key* is kept secret. A key is used by an algorithm to control the encryption process. An encryption key is the same as a regular password: It shouldn't be easy to guess the key you have chosen.

Another advantage of making the algorithm public is that it's extensively tested. When a successor for the widespread Data Encryption Standard (DES) algorithm became necessary, the American National Institute of Standards and Technology (NIST) invited anyone to submit new algorithms. After the submission period was closed, NIST made the source code for these algorithms public and invited everyone to break them. Some algorithms were broken in a matter of days, and only a small number made it to the final round. Making those algorithms public improved security.

Because the algorithm is public, the key is the thing that should be kept private. The difference in *symmetric* and *asymmetric encryption* strategies lies in the way this key is used. A symmetric algorithm uses one single key to encrypt and decrypt the data. You need to pass your original key to the receiver so he can decrypt your data. And this automatically leads to the problem of securely exchanging keys.

This is where an asymmetric algorithm can be used. An asymmetric algorithm uses two different keys that are mathematically related to each other. Although they are related, it's infeasible to determine one when you know the other. One key is completely *public* and can be read and used by everyone. The other part is *private* and should never be shared with someone else. When you encrypt something with the public key, it can be decrypted by using the private key, and vice versa.

Another difference between symmetric and asymmetric encryption has to do with performance and message size. Symmetric encryption is faster than asymmetric encryption and is well-suited for larger data sets. Asymmetric encryption is not optimized for encrypting long messages, but it can be very useful for decrypting a small key. Combining these two techniques can help you transmit large amounts of data in an encrypted way.

Let's say that Bob and Alice want to send each other a message. They take the following steps:

1. Alice and Bob both generate their own asymmetric key pair.

2. They send each other their public key and keep their private key secret.

3. They both generate a symmetric key and encrypt it only with the other parties' public key (so that it can be encrypted by the private key of the other person).

4. They send their own encrypted symmetric key to one another and decrypt the others symmetric key with their own private key.

5. To send a confidential message, they use the symmetric key of the other person and use it to encrypt their message.

6. The receiving person decrypts the message with their own symmetric key.

As you can see, the asymmetric encryption is used to encrypt a symmetric key. After the key is safely transmitted, Bob and Alice can use it to send larger messages to one another.

Next to using a key, another important concept in cryptography is the *initialization vector (IV)*. An IV is used to add some randomness to encrypting data. If encrypting the same text would always give the same results, this could be used by a potential attacker to break the encryption. The IV makes sure that the same data results in a different encrypted message each time.

---

**EXAM TIP**

Try to remember the differences between symmetric and asymmetric algorithms. A symmetric algorithm uses one key; an asymmetric algorithm uses two: a *key pair* that consists of both a public and a private key.

---

**MORE INFO    SYMMETRIC AND ASYMMETRIC ENCRYPTION**

If you want to know more about encryption a good place to start is *http://msdn.microsoft.com/en-us/library/0ss79b2x.aspx*.

# Working with encryption in the .NET Framework

The .NET Framework offers an extensive set of algorithms for both symmetric and asymmetric encryption.

One symmetric algorithm is the *Advanced Encryption Standard (AES)*. AES is adopted by the U.S. government and is becoming the standard worldwide for both governmental and business use. The .NET Framework has a managed implementation of the AES algorithm in the *AesManaged* class. All cryptography classes can be found in the *System.Security.Cryptography* class.

Listing 3-17 shows an example of using this algorithm to encrypt and decrypt a piece of text. As you can see, AES is a symmetric algorithm that uses a key and IV for encryption. By using the same key and IV, you can decrypt a piece of text. The cryptography classes all work on byte sequences.

**LISTING 3-17** Use a symmetric encryption algorithm

```
public static void EncryptSomeText()
{
    string original = "My secret data!";

    using (SymmetricAlgorithm symmetricAlgorithm =
        new AesManaged())
    {
        byte[] encrypted = Encrypt(symmetricAlgorithm, original);
        string roundtrip = Decrypt(symmetricAlgorithm, encrypted);

        // Displays: My secret data!
        Console.WriteLine("Original:   {0}", original);
        Console.WriteLine("Round Trip: {0}", roundtrip);
    }
}

static byte[] Encrypt(SymmetricAlgorithm aesAlg, string plainText)
{
    ICryptoTransform encryptor = aesAlg.CreateEncryptor(aesAlg.Key, aesAlg.IV);

    using (MemoryStream msEncrypt = new MemoryStream())
    {
        using (CryptoStream csEncrypt =
            new CryptoStream(msEncrypt, encryptor, CryptoStreamMode.Write))
        {
            using (StreamWriter swEncrypt = new StreamWriter(csEncrypt))
            {
                swEncrypt.Write(plainText);
            }
            return msEncrypt.ToArray();
        }
    }
}

static string Decrypt(SymmetricAlgorithm aesAlg, byte[] cipherText)
{
    ICryptoTransform decryptor = aesAlg.CreateDecryptor(aesAlg.Key, aesAlg.IV);

    using (MemoryStream msDecrypt = new MemoryStream(cipherText))
    {
        using (CryptoStream csDecrypt =
            new CryptoStream(msDecrypt, decryptor, CryptoStreamMode.Read))
        {
            using (StreamReader srDecrypt = new StreamReader(csDecrypt))
            {
                return srDecrypt.ReadToEnd();
            }
```

```
      }
    }
}
```

The *SymmetricAlgorithm* class has both a method for creating an *encryptor* and a *decryptor*. By using the *CryptoStream* class, you can encrypt or decrypt a byte sequence.

The .NET Framework also has support for asymmetric encryption. You can use the *RSACryptoServiceProvider* and *DSACryptoServiceProvider* classes. When working with asymmetric encryption, you typically use the public key from another party. You encrypt the data using the public key so only the other party can decrypt the data with their private key.

Listing 3-18 shows how you can create a new instance of the *RSACryptoServiceProvider* and export the public key to XML. By passing *true* to the *ToXmlString* method, you also export the private part of your key.

**LISTING 3-18** Exporting a public key

```
RSACryptoServiceProvider rsa = new RSACryptoServiceProvider();
string publicKeyXML = rsa.ToXmlString(false);
string privateKeyXML = rsa.ToXmlString(true);

Console.WriteLine(publicKeyXML);
Console.WriteLine(privateKeyXML);
 // Displays:
//<RSAKeyValue>
//  <Modulus>
//    tYo35ywTOQOKCNhFPu207bS8rrTk91YaxNcD2ElQ1eoWpdYnoCsdj1KaW/
as9zFLYW5slg5Qq8ltdkxZuU//
fhOj2t+7ZFH8RRAD808GkZTrUi1zv3yqMjQDphHOcNfWh+dQrPmp1ShFxEGuA9Y4Ij9RINU5jcfviPa
//    B1ClLXaGbc=
//  </Modulus>
//  <Exponent>AQAB</Exponent>
//</RSAKeyValue>
//<RSAKeyValue>
//  <Modulus>
//    tYo35ywTOQOKCNhFPu207bS8rrTk91YaxNcD2ElQ1eoWpdYnoCsdj1KaW/as9zFLYW5slg5Qq8ltdkxZuU
//    fhOj2t+7ZFH8RRAD808GkZTrUi1zv3yqMjQDphHOcNfWh+dQrPmp1ShFxEGuA9Y4Ij9RINU5jcfviPa
//    B1ClLXaGbc=
//  </Modulus>
//  <Exponent>AQAB</Exponent>
//  <P>
//    4uhNaN3cPSUzr+KxHmpKyeaD39RT+kWjjDcn/9sTAV/HmDzFzjsiov3KyJ+3XCXucx5TU0lhDOLc/
//    cO+Xrquqw==
//  </P>
//  <Q>
//    zNDVw6oL7YNglrFAeqmgIL3Oj2PkUxrWvoYHCbuFwJKpkWvFBRwZfKXHzzU0zaU5bGdX7M24hW8z5s0
//    eF9CRJQ==
//  </Q>
//  <DP>
//    jkS+/GhWxZPEw5vsF7jnaY3502ZqvPna4HhYwQgX832dRKueDn9vaSidc4sIyWMTDeTOs+LHUfAQRZ/
//    shbKg/w==
//  </DP>
//  <DQ>
```

```
//          HV4QWJboUO0Wi2Ts/umViTxOAudq1LOzeOwU1ENsITmmULCoNlxaFzJaHQ7e/GGlgzKqO80fmRphOc
//          U1fGqudQ==
// </DQ>
// <InverseQ>
//          BW1VUOgXpkRnn2twvb72uxcbK6+o9ns3xa4Ypm+++7vzlg6t/Iyvk94xNJWjjgR+XsSpN6JEtztWol8
//          bv8HEyA==
// </InverseQ>
// <D>
//          IOZUrUNyr+8iA2pWWkowAOhBTZQg7qYfIc8ptjfLO4k544IFGmTV7ZR1vvbcb8vyMkOVxrf/bLKLcOX
//          zWL2rMeWYGuoTbZEeUbrOSlmesHARL7X/feCm9MIyPjhlhJieRVG3h4f+TyAVo7OjmYVcSou+xAaad3
//          7o3Pa8Vny6qIk=
// </D>
//</RSAKeyValue>
```

The public key is the part you want to publish so others can use it to encrypt data. You can send it to someone directly or publish it on a website that belongs to you. Listing 3-19 shows an example of using a public key to encrypt data and decrypt it with the private key.

LISTING 3-19 Using a public and private key to encrypt and decrypt data

```
UnicodeEncoding ByteConverter = new UnicodeEncoding();
byte[] dataToEncrypt = ByteConverter.GetBytes("My Secret Data!");

byte[] encryptedData;
using (RSACryptoServiceProvider RSA = new RSACryptoServiceProvider())
{
    RSA.FromXmlString(publicKeyXML);
    encryptedData = RSA.Encrypt(dataToEncrypt, false);
}

byte[] decryptedData;
using (RSACryptoServiceProvider RSA = new RSACryptoServiceProvider())
{
    RSA.FromXmlString(privateKeyXML);
    decryptedData = RSA.Decrypt(encryptedData, false);
}

string decryptedString = ByteConverter.GetString(decryptedData);
Console.WriteLine(decryptedString); // Displays: My Secret Data!
```

As you can see, you first need to convert the data you want to encrypt to a byte sequence. To encrypt the data, you need only the public key. You then use the private key to decrypt the data.

Because of this, it's important to store the private key in a secure location. If you would store it in plain text on disk or even in a nonsecure memory location, your private key could be extracted and your security would be compromised.

The .NET Framework offers a secure location for storing asymmetric keys in a *key container*. A key container can be specific to a user or to the whole machine. Listing 3-20 shows how to configure an *RSACryptoServiceProvider* to use a key container for saving and loading the asymmetric key.

**LISTING 3-20** Using a key container for storing an asymmetric key

```
string containerName = "SecretContainer";
CspParameters csp = new CspParameters() { KeyContainerName = containerName };
byte[] encryptedData;
using (RSACryptoServiceProvider RSA = new RSACryptoServiceProvider(csp))
{
    encryptedData = RSA.Encrypt(dataToEncrypt, false);
}
```

Loading the key from the key container is the exact same process. You can securely store your asymmetric key without malicious users being able to read it.

## Using hashing

To understand what *hashing* is and see some of the ideas behind a hash code, take a look at Listing 3-21. Listing 3-21 shows an example of how you can implement a set class. A set stores only unique items, so it sees whether an item already exists before adding it.

**LISTING 3-21** A naïve set implementation

```
class Set<T>
{
    private List<T> list = new List<T>();

    public void Insert(T item)
    {
        if (!Contains(item))
            list.Add(item);
    }

    public bool Contains(T item)
    {
        foreach (T member in list)
            if (member.Equals(item))
                return true;
        return false;
    }
}
```

For each item that you add, you have to loop through all existing items. This doesn't scale well and leads to performance problems when you have a large amount of items. It would be nice if you somehow needed to check only a small subgroup instead of all the items.

This is where a *hash code* can be used. Hashing is the process of taking a large set of data and mapping it to a smaller data set of fixed length. For example, mapping all names to a specific integer. Instead of checking the complete name, you would have to use only an integer value.

By using hashing, you can improve the design of the set class. You split the data in a set of buckets. Each bucket contains a subgroup of all the items in the set. Listing 3-22 shows how you can do this.

**LISTING 3-22** A set implementation that uses hashing

```
class Set<T>
{
    private List<T>[] buckets = new List<T>[100];

    public void Insert(T item)
    {
        int bucket = GetBucket(item.GetHashCode());
        if (Contains(item, bucket))
            return;
        if (buckets[bucket] == null)
            buckets[bucket] = new List<T>();
        buckets[bucket].Add(item);
    }
    public bool Contains(T item)
    {
        return Contains(item, GetBucket(item.GetHashCode()));
    }

    private int GetBucket(int hashcode)
    {
        // A Hash code can be negative. To make sure that you end up with a positive
        // value cast the value to an unsigned int. The unchecked block makes sure that
        // you can cast a value larger then int to an int safely.
        unchecked
        {
            return (int)((uint)hashcode % (uint)buckets.Length);
        }
    }

    private bool Contains(T item, int bucket)
    {
        if (buckets[bucket] != null)
            foreach (T member in buckets[bucket])
                if (member.Equals(item))
                    return true;
        return false;
    }
}
```

If you look at the *Contains* method, you can see that it uses the *GetHashCode* method of each item. This method is defined on the base class *Object*. In each type, you can override this method and provide a specific implementation for your type. This method should output an integer code that describes your particular object. As a general guideline, the distribution of hash codes must be as random as possible. This is why the set implementation uses the *GetHashCode* method on each object to calculate in which bucket it should go.

Now your items are distributed over a hundred buckets instead of one single bucket. When you see whether an item exists, you first calculate the hash code, go to the corresponding bucket, and look for the item.

This technique is used by the *Hashtable* and *Dictionary* classes in the .NET Framework. Both use the hash code to store and access items. *Hashtable* is nongeneric collection; *Dictionary* is a generic collection.

A couple of important principles can be deduced from this. First of all, equal items should have equal hash codes. This means that you can check to determine whether two items are equal by checking their hash codes. It also means that your implementation of *GetHashCode* should return the same value during time. It shouldn't depend on changing values such as the current date or time.

---

**MORE INFO** **IMPLEMENTING** ***GETHASHCODE***

For more information on how to implement *GetHashCode* correctly, see *http://msdn.microsoft.com/en-us/library/system.object.gethashcode(v=vs.110).aspx*.

---

These properties are important when looking at hashing in a security context. If you hash a paragraph of text and change only one letter, the hash code will change, so hashing is used to check the integrity of a message.

For example, let's say that Alice and Bob want to send a message to each other. Alice creates a hash of the message and sends both the hash and the message to Bob. Bob creates a hash of the message he has received from Alice and compares the two hash codes with each other. If they match, Bob knows he has received the correct message.

Of course, without any additional encryption, a third party can still tamper with the message by changing both the message and the hash code. Combined with the encryption technologies that the .NET Framework offers, hashing is an important technique to validate the authenticity of a message.

The .NET Framework offers a couple of classes to generate hash values. The algorithms that the .NET Framework offers are optimized hashing algorithms that output a significantly different hash code for a small change in the data.

Listing 3-23 shows an example of using the *SHA256Managed* algorithm to calculate the hash code for a piece of text.

**LISTING 3-23** Using SHA256Managed to calculate a hash code

```
UnicodeEncoding byteConverter = new UnicodeEncoding();
SHA256 sha256 = SHA256.Create();

string data = "A paragraph of text";
byte[] hashA = sha256.ComputeHash(byteConverter.GetBytes(data));
```

```
data = "A paragraph of changed text";
byte[] hashB = sha256.ComputeHash(byteConverter.GetBytes(data));

data = "A paragraph of text";
byte[] hashC = sha256.ComputeHash(byteConverter.GetBytes(data));

Console.WriteLine(hashA.SequenceEqual(hashB)); // Displays: false
Console.WriteLine(hashA.SequenceEqual(hashC)); // Displays: true
```

As you can see, different strings give a different hash code and the same string gives the exact same hash code. This enables you to see whether a string has been altered by comparing the hash codes.

## Managing and creating certificates

*Digital certificates* are the area where both hashing and asymmetric encryption come together. A digital certificate authenticates the identity of any object signed by the certificate. It also helps with protecting the integrity of data.

If Alice sends a message to Bob, she first hashes her message to generate a hash code. Alice then encrypts the hash code with her private key to create a personal signature. Bob receives Alice's message and signature. He decrypts the signature using Alice's public key and now he has both the message and the hash code. He can then hash the message and see whether his hash code and the hash code from Alice match.

A digital certificate is part of a *Public Key Infrastructure* (PKI). A PKI is a system of digital certificates, certificate authorities, and other registration authorities that authenticate and verify the validity of each involved party.

A *Certificate Authority* (CA) is a third-party issuer of certificates that is considered trustworthy by all parties. The CA issues certificates, or *certs*, that contain a public key, a subject to which the certificate is issued, and the details of the CA.

When working on your development or testing environment, you can create certificates by using the *Makecert.exe* tool. This tool generates *X.509 certificates* for testing purposes. The X.509 certificate is a widely used standard for defining digital certificates.

If you open a developer command prompt as administrator, you can run the following command to generate a testing certificate:

```
makecert testCert.cer
```

This command generates a file called *testCert.cer* that you can use as a certificate. You first need to install this certificate on your computer to be able to use it. After installation, it's stored in a *certificate store*. The following line creates a certificate and installs it in a custom certificate store named *testCertStore*:

```
makecert -n "CN=WouterDeKort" -sr currentuser -ss testCertStore
```

Listing 3-24 shows how to use this generated certificate to sign and verify some text. The data is hashed and then signed. When verifying, the same hash algorithm is used to make sure the data has not changed.

**LISTING 3-24** Signing and verifying data with a certificate

```
public static void SignAndVerify()
{
    string textToSign = "Test paragraph";
    byte[] signature = Sign(textToSign, "cn=WouterDeKort");
    // Uncomment this line to make the verification step fail
    // signature[0] = 0;
    Console.WriteLine(Verify(textToSign, signature));
}

static byte[] Sign(string text, string certSubject)
{
    X509Certificate2 cert = GetCertificate();
    var csp = (RSACryptoServiceProvider)cert.PrivateKey;
    byte[] hash = HashData(text);
    return csp.SignHash(hash, CryptoConfig.MapNameToOID("SHA1"));
}

static bool Verify(string text, byte[] signature)
{
    X509Certificate2 cert = GetCertificate();
    var csp = (RSACryptoServiceProvider)cert.PublicKey.Key;
    byte[] hash = HashData(text);
    return csp.VerifyHash(hash,
        CryptoConfig.MapNameToOID("SHA1"),
        signature);
}

private static byte[] HashData(string text)
{
    HashAlgorithm hashAlgorithm = new SHA1Managed();
    UnicodeEncoding encoding = new UnicodeEncoding();
    byte[] data = encoding.GetBytes(text);
    byte[] hash = hashAlgorithm .ComputeHash(data);
    return hash;
}

private static X509Certificate2 GetCertificate()
{
    X509Store my = new X509Store("testCertStore",
        StoreLocation.CurrentUser);
    my.Open(OpenFlags.ReadOnly);

    var certificate = my.Certificates[0];

    return certificate;
}
```

The *SignHash* method uses the private key of the certificate to create a signature for the data. *VerifyHash* uses the public key of the certificate to see whether the data has changed.

> **MORE INFO**   **USING MAKECERT.EXE**
>
> For more information on how to use makecert.exe, see *http://msdn.microsoft.com/en-us/ library/bfsktky3(v=vs.110).aspx*.

One use of digital certificates is to secure Internet communication. The popular HTTPS communication protocol is used to secure communication between a web server and a client. Digital certificates are used to make sure that the client is talking to the correct web server, not to an imposter.

# Using code access permissions

The days when the only way to get a program on your computer was by using a floppy disk to install it to your hard drive are long gone. Today, you can install programs from a variety of sources, which can lead to several security issues. Your computer is probably running a virus scanner, and you're in the habit of making sure that you know the sender of an e-mail message before you open an attachment.

The .NET Framework helps you protect your computers from malicious code via a mechanism called *code access security (CAS)*. Instead of giving every application full trust, applications can be restricted on the types of resources they can access and the operations they can execute.

When using CAS, your code is the untrusted party. You need to ask for permission to execute certain operations or access protected resources. The *common language runtime (CLR)* enforces security restrictions on managed code and makes sure that your code has the correct permissions to access privileged resources.

Applications that are installed on your computer or on your local intranet have full trust. They can access resources and execute all kinds of operations. When running in a sandboxed environment such as Internet Explorer or SQL Server, CAS restricts the operations that an application can execute.

Each code access permission represents one of the following rights:

- The right to access a protected resource, such as a file
- The right to perform a protected operation, such as accessing unmanaged code

It can also be that you are creating a plug-in system and you want to make sure that third-party plug-ins can't compromise your security. CAS can then be used to restrict the things a plug-in is allowed to do.

CAS performs the following functions in the .NET Framework:

- Defines permissions for accessing system resources.
- Enables code to demand that its callers have specific permissions. For example, a library that exposes methods that create files should enforce that its callers have the right for file input/output.

- Enables code to demand that its callers possess a digital signature. This way, code can make sure that it's only called by callers from a particular organization or location.

- Enforces all those restrictions at runtime.

One important concept of CAS is that each and every element on the current call stack is checked. The *call stack* is a data structure that stores information about all the active methods at a specific moment. So if your application starts in the *Main* method and then calls method *A* which calls method *B*, all three methods will be on the call stack. When method *B* returns, only *Main* and *A* are on the call stack.

CAS walks the call stack and sees whether every element on the stack has the required permissions. This way, you can be sure that a less-trusted method cannot call some restricted code through a highly trusted method.

The base class for all things related to CAS is *System.Security.CodeAccessPermission*. Permissions that inherit from CodeAccessPermission are permissions such as *FileIOPermission*, *ReflectionPermission*, or *SecurityPermission*. When applying one of those permissions, you ask the CLR for the permission to execute a protected operation or access a resource.

You can specify CAS in two ways: *declarative* or *imperative*.

Declarative means that you use attributes to apply security information to your code. Listing 3-25 shows an example of asking for the permission to read all local files by using the *FileIOPermissionAttribute*.

**LISTING 3-25** Declarative CAS

```
[FileIOPermission(SecurityAction.Demand,
    AllLocalFiles = FileIOPermissionAccess.Read)]
public void DeclarativeCAS()
{
    // Method body
}
```

You can also do this in an imperative way, which means that you explicitly ask for the permission in the code. Listing 3-26 shows how you can create a new instance of *FileIOPermission* and demand certain rights.

**LISTING 3-26** Imperative CAS

```
FileIOPermission f = new FileIOPermission(PermissionState.None);
f.AllLocalFiles = FileIOPermissionAccess.Read;
try
{
    f.Demand();
}
catch (SecurityException s)
{
    Console.WriteLine(s.Message);
}
```

**MORE INFO** CODE ACCESS SECURITY

For more information about CAS, see *http://msdn.microsoft.com/en-us/library/c5tk9z76. aspx*.

## Securing string data

A lot of data in your application consists of simple strings. For example, passwords and credit card numbers are both strings. But the default *System.String* implementation is not optimized for security. Using a string for storing sensitive data has a couple of problems:

- The string value can be moved around in memory by the garbage collector leaving multiple copies around.

- The string value is not encrypted. If you run low on memory, it could be that your string is written as plain text to a page file on disk. The same could happen when your application crashes and a memory dump is made.

- *System.String* is immutable. Each change will make a copy of the data, leaving multiple copies around in memory.

- It's impossible to force the garbage collector to remove all copies of your string from memory.

The .NET Framework offers a special class that can help you minimize the surface area an attacker has: *System.Security.SecureString*.

A *SecureString* automatically encrypts its value so the possibility of an attacker finding a plain text version of your string is decreased. A *SecureString* is also pinned to a specific memory location. The garbage collector doesn't move the string around, so you avoid the problem of having multiple copies. *SecureString* is a mutable string that can be made read-only when necessary. Finally, *SecureString* implements *IDisposable* so you can make sure that its content is removed from memory whenever you're done with it.

**MORE INFO** *IDISPOSABLE* AND GARBAGE COLLECTION

For more info on what *IDisposable* is and how to use it, see Chapter 2, "Create and use types." Chapter 2 also discusses how the garbage collector works.

A *SecureString* doesn't completely solve all security problems. Because it needs to be initialized at some point, the data that is used to initialize the *SecureString* is still in memory. To minimize this risk and force you to think about it, *SecureString* can deal with only individual characters at a time. It's not possible to pass a string directly to a *SecureString*. Listing 3-27 shows an example of using a *SecureString*. The application reads one character at a time from the user and appends these characters to the *SecureString*.

LISTING 3-27 Initializing a *SecureString*

```
using (SecureString ss = new SecureString())
{
    Console.Write("Please enter password: ");
    while (true)
    {
        ConsoleKeyInfo cki = Console.ReadKey(true);
        if (cki.Key == ConsoleKey.Enter) break;

        ss.AppendChar(cki.KeyChar);
        Console.Write("*");
    }
    ss.MakeReadOnly();
}
```

As you can see, the *SecureString* is used with a *using* statement, so the *Dispose* method is called when you are done with the string so that it doesn't stay in memory any longer then strictly necessary.

At some point, you probably want to convert the *SecureString* back to a normal string so you can use it. The .NET Framework offers some special functionality for this. It's important to make sure that the regular string is cleared from memory as soon as possible. This is why there is a *try/finally* statement around the code. The *finally* statement makes sure that the string is removed from memory even if there is an exception thrown in the code. Listing 3-28 shows an example of how to do this.

LISTING 3-28 Getting the value of a *SecureString*

```
public static void ConvertToUnsecureString(SecureString securePassword)
{
    IntPtr unmanagedString = IntPtr.Zero;
    try
    {
        unmanagedString = Marshal.SecureStringToGlobalAllocUnicode(securePassword);
        Console.WriteLine(Marshal.PtrToStringUni(unmanagedString));
    }
    finally
    {
        Marshal.ZeroFreeGlobalAllocUnicode(unmanagedString);
    }
}
```

The *Marshal* class is located in the *System.Runtime.InteropServices* namespace. It offers five methods that can be used when you are decrypting a *SecureString*. Those methods accept a *SecureString* and return an *IntPtr*. Each method has a corresponding method that you need to call to zero out the internal buffer. Table 3-1 shows these methods.

TABLE 3-1 Methods for working with *SecureString*

| Decrypt method | Clear memory method |
|---|---|
| *SecureStringToBSTR* | *ZeroFreeBSTR* |
| *SecureStringToCoTaskMemAnsi* | *ZeroFreeCoTaskMemAnsi* |
| *SecureStringToCoTaskMemUnicode* | *ZeroFreeCoTaskMemUnicode* |
| *SecureStringToGlobalAllocAnsi* | *ZeroFreeGlobalAllocAnsi* |
| *SecureStringToGlobalAllocUnicode* | *ZeroFreeGlobalAllocUnicode* |

It's important to realize that a *SecureString* is not completely secure. You can create an application, running in full thrust, which will be able to read the *SecureString* content. However, it *does* add to the complexity of hacking your application. All the small steps you can take to make your application more secure will create a bigger hindrance for an attacker.

## *Thought experiment*
### Choosing your technologies

In this thought experiment, apply what you've learned about this objective. You can find answers to these questions in the "Answers" section at the end of this chapter.

You are working on an application that helps users track their time and shows them when they are most productive. The application runs on a server with a web, desktop, and mobile front end being developed with the .NET Framework.

You are assigned the task of determining which security features should be used in the application.

Make a list of the possible technologies that can be used to secure the application.

## Objective summary

- A symmetric algorithm uses the same key to encrypt and decrypt data.
- An asymmetric algorithm uses a public and private key that are mathematically linked.
- Hashing is the process of converting a large amount of data to a smaller hash code.
- Digital certificates can be used to verify the authenticity of an author.
- CAS are used to restrict the resources and operations an application can access and execute.
- *System.Security.SecureString* can be used to keep sensitive string data in memory.

# Objective review

Answer the following questions to test your knowledge of the information in this objective. You can find the answers to these questions and explanations of why each answer choice is correct or incorrect in the "Answers" section at the end of this chapter.

1. Bob and Alice are using an asymmetric algorithm to exchange data. Which key should they send to the other party to make this possible?

   A. Bob sends Alice his private key, and Alice sends Bob her public key.

   B. Bob sends Alice his private key, and Alice sends Bob her private key.

   C. Bob sends Alice his public key, and Alice sends Bob her public key.

   D. Bob sends Alice his public key, and Alice sends Bob her private key.

2. You need to encrypt a large amount of data. Which algorithm do you use?

   A. SHA256

   B. RSACryptoServiceProvider

   C. MD5CryptoServiceProvider

   D. AesManaged

3. You need to send sensitive data to another party and you want to make sure that no one tampers with the data. Which method do you use?

   A. *X509Certificate2.SignHash*

   B. *RSACryptoServiceProvider.Encrypt*

   C. *UnicodeEncoding.GetBytes*

   D. *Marshal.ZeroFreeBSTR*

# Objective 3.3 Manage assemblies

When building your applications, you work with source code files and projects, but this is not the way your application is deployed. The C# compiler takes your source code and produces *assemblies*. Managing those assemblies is important when you are deploying applications to production environments or distributing them to other parties.

> **This objective covers how to:**
> - Explain what an assembly is.
> - Sign assemblies using strong names.
> - Put an assembly in the GAC.
> - Version assemblies and implement side-by-side hosting.
> - Create a WinMD assembly.

# What is an assembly?

Before Microsoft released the .NET Framework, the *Component Object Model (COM)* was dominant, but there were several problems.

One of those problems was known as *"DLL hell."* Microsoft and other software companies distributed *DLLs* that can be used as building blocks by other applications. Problems start to arise when a company distributes a new version of a DLL without fully testing it against all applications that depend on it (which can be numerous applications which makes thorough testing almost impossible). Updating one application can lead to problems in another, seemingly unrelated applications.

Another problem had to do with the way applications were installed. Often an application would have to make changes to several parts of your system. Of course, there would be application directories copied to your system, but also changes were made to the registry and shortcuts were deployed. This made the installation process more difficult because uninstalling an application is hard and sometimes leaves traces of an application behind.

A third issue is security. Because applications made so many changes during installation, it was hard for a user to determine what was actually installed. It could be that one application in turn installs other components that form a security risk.

The .NET Framework addresses these issues and tries to solve them by making some radical changes. One important component of those changes is the concept of an *assembly*. An assembly still has the .dll (or .exe) extension like previous Windows components. Internally, however, they are completely different.

Assemblies are *completely self-contained;* they don't need to write any information to the registry or some other location. Assemblies contain all the information they need to run. This is called the assembly's *manifest*.

Another important aspect is that an assembly is *language-neutral*. You can write some C# code, compile it to an assembly, and then use the assembly directly from other .NET languages such as F# or Visual Basic.

In contrast to an old DLL, an assembly can be *versioned*, which enables you to have different versions of a specific assembly on one system without causing conflicts.

One other important change is the way assemblies are *deployed*. If you want, you can deploy an application by simply copying it to a new machine. All the assemblies that are required are deployed locally in the new application folder. An assembly can even contain resource files, such as images, that are directly embedded in the assembly. You can also choose to deploy an assembly in a shared way so it can be used by multiple applications.

# Signing assemblies using a strong name

The *CLR* supports two different types of assemblies: *strong-named assemblies* and *regular assemblies*.

A regular assembly is what Visual Studio generates for you by default. It's structurally identical to a strong-named assembly. They both contain metadata, header, manifest, and all the types that are in your assembly.

A strong-named assembly is signed with a public/private key pair that uniquely identifies the publisher of the assembly and the content of the assembly. A strong name consists of the simple text name of the assembly, its version number, and culture information. It also contains a public key and a digital signature.

Strongly naming an assembly has several benefits:

- **Strong names guarantee uniqueness.** Your unique private key is used to generate the name for your assembly. No other assembly can have the exact same strong name.

- **Strong names protect your versioning lineage.** Because you control the private key, you are the only one who can distribute updates to your assemblies. Users can be sure that the new version originates from the same publisher.

- **Strong names provide a strong integrity check.** The .NET Framework sees whether a strong-named assembly has changed since the moment it was signed.

Overall, you can see that a strong-named assembly ensures a user that they can trust the origin and content of an assembly.

You generate a strong-named assembly by using your own private key to sign the assembly. Other users can verify the assembly by using the public key that is distributed with the assembly.

> **MORE INFO  PUBLIC AND PRIVATE KEY USAGE**
>
> For more information on using private and public keys to generate a digital signature see the section "Objective 3.2: Perform symmetric and asymmetric encryption" earlier in this chapter.

Signing an assembly can be done both at the command line and by using Visual Studio. The first step you have to take is to generate a *key pair*. A key pair is usually a file with an *.snk* extension that contains your public/private key information.

When using the developer command prompt, you can run the following command to generate a new key pair file:

```
sn -k myKey.snk
```

An easier way is to use Visual Studio to generate the key pair file for you. You can open the property page of the project you want to sign and then navigate to the Signing tab, as shown in Figure 3-1.

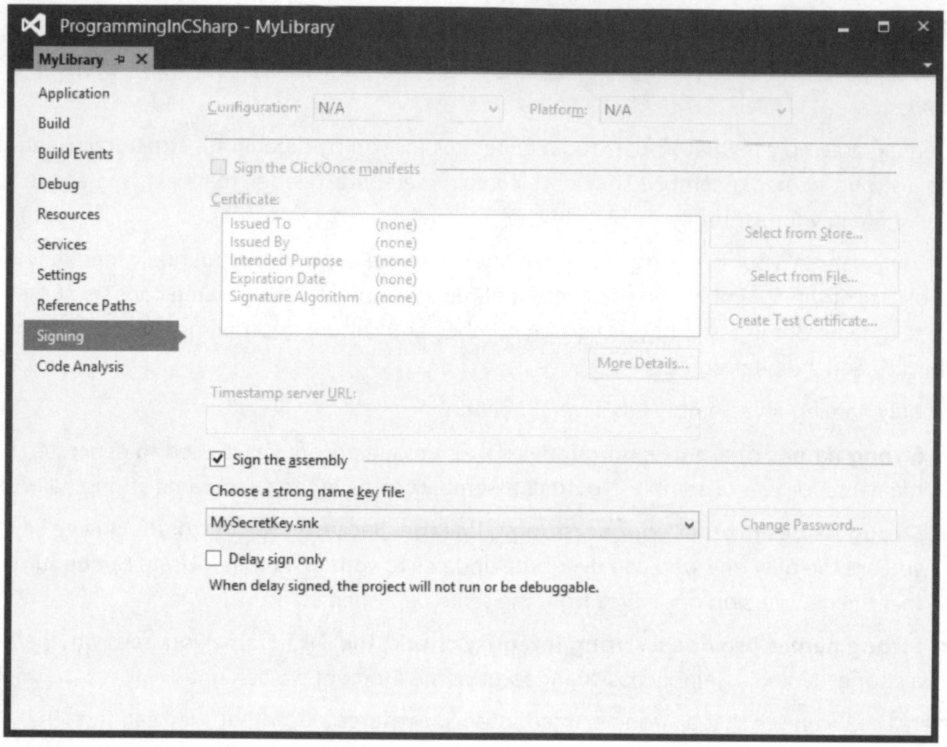

**FIGURE 3-1** The Signing page in Visual Studio

By enabling the signing of the assembly, you can let Visual Studio generate a new key file, which is then added to your project and is used in the compilation step to strongly sign your assembly.

A strong-named assembly can reference only other assemblies that are also strongly named. This is to avoid security flaws where a depending assembly could be changed to influence the behavior of a strong-named assembly. When you add a reference to a regular assembly and try to invoke code from that assembly, the compiler issues an error:

```
Assembly generation failed -- Referenced assembly 'MyLib' does not have a strong name
```

After signing an assembly, you can view the public key by using the *Strong Name tool (Sn. exe)* that's installed with Visual Studio. One of the strongly named assemblies that's installed with the .NET Framework is *System.Data*. Listing 3-29 shows how you can get the public key of this assembly.

**LISTING 3-29** Inspecting the public key of a signed assembly

```
C:\>sn -Tp C:\Windows\Microsoft.NET\Framework\v4.0.30319\System.D
ata.dll

Microsoft (R) .NET Framework Strong Name Utility  Version 4.0.30319.17929
Copyright (c) Microsoft Corporation.  All rights reserved.

Identity public key (hash algorithm: Unknown):
00000000000000000400000000000000

Signature public key (hash algorithm: sha256):
002400000c8000001401000006020000002400005253413100080000010001006133 99aff18ef1
a2c2514a273a42d9042b72321f1757102df9ebada69923e2738406c21e5b801552ab8d200a65a2
35e001ac9adc25f2d811eb09496a4c6a59d4619589c69f5baf0c4179a47311d92555cd006acc8b
5959f2bd6e10e360c34537a1d266da8085856583c85d81da7f3ec01ed9564c58d93d713cd0172c
8e23a10f0239b80c96b07736f5d8b022542a4e74251a5f432824318b3539a5a087f8e53d2f135f
9ca47f3bb2e10aff0af0849504fb7cea3ff192dc8de0edad64c68efde34c56d302ad55fd6e80f3
02d5efcdeae953658d3452561b5f36c542efdbdd9f888538d374cef106acf7d93a4445c3c73cd9
11f0571aaf3d54da12b11ddec375b3

Public key token is b77a5c561934e089
```

The *public key token* is a small string that represents the public key. It is generated by hashing the public key and taking the last eight bytes. If you reference another assembly, you store only the public key token, which preserves space in the assembly manifest. The CLR does not use the public key token when making security decisions because it could happen that several public keys have the same public key token.

Within an organization, it's important to secure the private key. If all employees have access to the private key, someone might leak or steal the key. They are then able to distribute assemblies that look legitimate. But without access to the private key, developers can't sign the assembly and use it while building the application.

To avoid this problem, you can use a feature called *delayed* or *partial signing*. When using delayed signing, you use only the public key to sign an assembly and you delay using the private key until the project is ready for deployment. If you look at Figure 3-1, you can see that there is an option to activate delayed signing in Visual Studio.

> **IMPORTANT  ORIGIN OF A STRONG-NAMED ASSEMBLY**
>
> One thing that's important to understand is that a strongly named assembly does not prove that the assembly comes from the original publisher. It only shows that the person who created the assembly has access to the private key.
>
> If you want to make sure that users can verify you as the publisher, you have to use something called *Authenticode*. Authenticode is a technology that uses digital certificates to identify the publisher of an application. You need to buy a certificate online and then use that certificate to sign your application.
>
> For more information on Authenticode, see *http://technet.microsoft.com/en-us/library/ cc750035.aspx*.

# Putting an assembly in the GAC

Assemblies that are local to an application are called *private assemblies*. You can easily deploy an application that depends on private assemblies by copying it to a new location.

Another way to deploy an assembly is to deploy it to the global assembly cache *(GAC)*. The GAC is a specialized library for storing assemblies. It is machine-wide and it is one of the locations the *CLR* checks when looking for an assembly.

Normally, you want to avoid installing assemblies in the GAC. One reason to deploy to the GAC is when an assembly is shared by multiple applications. Other reasons for installing an assembly into the GAC can be the enhanced security (normally only users with administrator rights can alter the GAC) or the situation where you want to deploy multiple versions of the same assembly.

Deploying an assembly in the GAC can be done in two ways:

- For production scenarios, use a specific installation program that has access to the GAC such as the *Windows Installer 2.0*.

- In development scenarios, use a tool called the *Global Assembly Cache tool (Gacutil.exe)*.

You can view the content of your GAC by running the following command from a developer command prompt:

```
gacutil -l
```

This returns a list of all the assemblies that are installed in the GAC.

Installing an assembly in the GAC can be done with the following command:

```
gacutil –i [assembly name]
```

You can also remove an assembly from the GAC:

```
gacutil –u [assembly name]
```

When referencing a shared assembly from your project, you can add a reference to the file located in the GAC or to a local copy of it. When Visual Studio detects that there is a GAC version of the DLL you are referencing, it will add a reference to the GAC, not to the local version.

# Versioning assemblies

In stark contrast with how DLLs worked before the .NET Framework, an assembly has a *version number*. Inside the assembly manifest, the assembly records its own version number and the version numbers of all the assemblies that it references.

Each assembly has a version number that has the following format:

*{Major Version}.{Minor Version}.{Build Number}.{Revision}*

- The Major Version is manually incremented for each major release. A major release should contain many new features or breaking changes.

- The Minor Version is incremented for minor releases that introduce only some small changes to existing features.

- The Build Number is automatically incremented for each build by the build server. This way, each build has a unique identification number that can be used to track it.

- The Revision is used for patches to the production environment.

When building an assembly, there are two version numbers that you need to take into account: the file version number and the .NET assembly version number.

If you create a new project in Visual Studio, it automatically adds an *AssemblyInfo.cs* file to the properties of your project.

This file contains the following two lines:

```
[assembly: AssemblyVersion("1.0.0.0")]
[assembly: AssemblyFileVersion("1.0.0.0")]
```

*AssemblyFileVersionAttribute* is the one that should be incremented with each build. This is not something you want to do on the client, where it would get incremented with every developer build. Instead, you should integrate this into your build process on your build server.

*AssemblyVersionAttribute* should be incremented manually. This should be done when you plan to deploy a specific version to production.

Because the version of an assembly is important when the runtime tries to locate an assembly, you can deploy multiple versions of the same assembly to the GAC and avoid the DLL problem that happened with regular DLL files. This is called *side-by-side hosting*, in which multiple versions of an assembly are hosted together on one computer.

The process of finding the correct assembly starts with the version number that is mentioned in the manifest file of the original assembly to determine which assembly to load. These bindings can be influenced with specific configuration files, however.

Three configuration files are used:

- Application configuration files
- Publisher policy files
- Machine configuration files

Those configuration files can be used to influence the binding of referenced assemblies. Suppose, for example, that you have deployed an assembly to the GAC and a couple of applications depend on it. Suddenly a bug is discovered and you create a fix for it. The new assembly has a new version number and you want to make sure that all applications use the new assembly.

You can do this by using a *publisher policy file*. In such a configuration file, you specify that if the CLR looks for a specific assembly, it should bind to the new version. Listing 3-30 shows an example of how such a file would look.

**LISTING 3-30** Redirecting assembly bindings to a newer version

```xml
<configuration>
  <runtime>
    <assemblyBinding xmlns="urn:schemas-microsoft-com:asm.v1">
      <dependentAssembly>
        <assemblyIdentity name="myAssembly"
                          publicKeyToken="32ab4ba45e0a69a1"
                          culture="en-us" />
        <!-- Redirecting to version 2.0.0.0 of the assembly. -->
        <bindingRedirect oldVersion="1.0.0.0"
                         newVersion="2.0.0.0"/>
      </dependentAssembly>
    </assemblyBinding>
  </runtime>
</configuration>
```

This file instructs the CLR to bind to version 2 of the assembly instead of version 1. You need to deploy such a publisher policy to the GAC so that the CLR can use it when binding assemblies.

> **MORE INFO**   **PUBLISHER POLICY FILES**
>
> For more information on how to create and deploy a publisher profile file see *http://msdn. microsoft.com/en-us/library/8f6988ab.aspx.*

If you have an assembly deployed privately with your application, the CLR starts looking for it in the current application directory. If it can't find the assembly, it throws a *FileNotFoundException.*

You can specify extra locations where the CLR should look in the configuration file of the application. You use the probing section for this as Listing 3-31 shows.

**LISTING 3-31** Specifying additional locations for assemblies

```xml
<?xml version="1.0" encoding="utf-8" ?>
<configuration>
  <runtime>
    <assemblyBinding xmlns="urn:schemas-microsoft-com:asm.v1">
      <probing privatePath="MyLibraries"/>
    </assemblyBinding>
  </runtime>
</configuration>
```

Another option is using the *codebase* element. A codebase element can specify a location for an assembly that is outside of the application's directory. This way you can locate an assembly that's on another computer on the network or somewhere on the Internet. These assemblies have to be strongly named if they are not in the current application's folder. When the assembly is located on another computer, it's downloaded to a special folder in the GAC. Listing 3-32 shows an example of using the codebase element to specify the location of an assembly somewhere on the web.

**LISTING 3-32** Specifying additional locations for assemblies

```xml
<?xml version="1.0" encoding="utf-8" ?>
<configuration>
  <runtime>
    <assemblyBinding xmlns="urn:schemas-microsoft-com:asm.v1">
      <dependentAssembly>
        <codeBase version="1.0.0.0"
          href= "http://www.mydomain.com/ReferencedAssembly.dll"/>
      </dependentAssembly>
    </assemblyBinding>
  </runtime>
</configuration>
```

**EXAM TIP**

The probing option can be used only to point to locations that are relative to the application path. If you want to locate assemblies somewhere else, you have to use the codebase element.

## Creating a WinMD assembly

With the introduction of Windows 8, Microsoft introduced the new *WinRT runtime*. WinRT is completely written in native C++. There is no managed environment, no CLR, and no Just-In-Time (JIT) compiler.

> **NOTE  WINRT VS. WINDOWS RT**
>
> Although WinRT and Windows RT look similar, they are two completely different things. WinRT is Windows Runtime. Windows RT is a special version of Windows 8 for devices using ARM-based processors. This version of Windows is deployed on tablet devices such as the Microsoft Surface. It can run only Windows Store applications.

Developing apps for Windows 8, however, can be done in languages such as JavaScript and C#. A regular C++ native component does not include metadata. But metadata is necessary to create the correct mapping between the native components and the other languages. To make this work, Microsoft created a new file type named *Windows Metadata (WinMD) files*.

If you are running Windows 8, you can find these files located in *C:\Windows\System32\WinMetadata*. The format of these files is the same as used by the .NET Framework for *the Common Language Infrastructure (CLI)*.

WinMD files can contain both code and metadata. The ones that you find in your *System32* directory contain only metadata, however. This metadata is used by Visual Studio to provide IntelliSense. At runtime, the metadata tells the CLI that the implementation of all the methods found in them is supplied by the runtime. This is why the files don't have to contain actual code; they make sure that the methods are mapped to the correct methods in WinRT.

One thing to note is that WinRT does not offer access to all the functionality of the .NET Framework 4.5. Instead, a lot of duplicate, legacy, or badly designed application programming interfaces (APIs) were removed. This all helps to make sure that WinRT apps can be ported to other platforms and use only the best APIs available.

If you want to create your own WinMD assembly, you do so by creating a *Windows Runtime component* in Visual Studio. You should do this only when you are creating a component that should be used from different programming languages such as JavaScript and C#. If you are working only with C#, you should create a new *"Class Library (Windows Store apps)"* project.

The Windows Runtime component compiles down to a *.winmd file* that you can then use.

There are a couple of restrictions on your Windows Runtime component that you need to be aware of:

- The fields, parameters, and return values of all the public types and members in your component must be Windows Runtime types.

- Public classes and interfaces can contain methods, properties and events. A public class or interface cannot do the following, however:

  - Be generic

  - Implement an interface that is not a Windows Runtime interface

  - Derive from types that are not inside the Windows Runtime

- Public classes must be sealed.

- Public structures can have only public fields as members, which must be value types or strings.

- All public types must have a root namespace that matches the assembly name and does not start with *Windows*.

If you create a valid Windows Runtime Component, you can then use this library when building a Windows 8 app. This way you can, for example, build some complex code in C# and then call it from your JavaScript Windows Store app.

## Thought experiment
### Choosing your technologies

In this thought experiment, apply what you've learned about this objective. You can find answers to these questions in the "Answers" section at the end of this chapter.

You are discussing the reasons why you want to sign an assembly that you have built. The assembly will be distributed with a desktop application you are building. The assembly won't be shared by other applications.

1. Should you sign the assembly?

2. What are the advantages and disadvantages of signing?

# Objective summary

- An assembly is a compiled unit of code that contains metadata.
- An assembly can be strongly signed to make sure that no one can tamper with the content.
- Signed assemblies can be put in the GAC.
- An assembly can be versioned, and applications will use the assembly version they were developed with. It's possible to use configuration files to change these bindings.
- A WinMD assembly is a special type of assembly that is used by WinRT to map non-native languages to the native WinRT components.

# Objective review

Answer the following questions to test your knowledge of the information in this objective. You can find the answers to these questions and explanations of why each answer choice is correct or incorrect in the "Answers" section at the end of this chapter.

1. You are building a strong-named assembly and you want to reference a regular assembly to reuse some code you built. What do you have to do?

   A. You first need to put the assembly in the GAC.

   B. Nothing. Referencing another assembly to use some code is always possible.

   C. You need to sign the other assembly before using it.

   D. You need to use the public key token of the other assembly to reference it.

2. You are building an assembly that will be used by a couple of server applications. You want to make the update process of this assembly as smooth as possible. Which steps should you take? (Choose all that apply.)

   A. Create a WinMD Metadata file.

   B. Deploy the assembly to the GAC.

   C. Add an *assemblyBinding* section to each client application that points to the location of the assembly.

   D. Strongly name the assembly.

3. You want to deploy an assembly to a shared location on the intranet. Which steps should you take? (Choose all that apply.)

   A. Strongly name the assembly.

   B. Use the codebase configuration element in the applications that use the assembly.

   C. Deploy the assembly to the GAC.

   D. Use the *assemblyBinding* configuration element with the probing option.

# Objective 3.4 Debug an application

No matter how good your development process is, from time to time you will have a *bug* in your application. *Debugging* is the process of removing those errors from your application. The C# compiler and Visual Studio help you a lot with finding and fixing the bugs in your application.

> **This objective covers how to:**
> - Choose an appropriate build type.
> - Create and manage compiler directives.
> - Manage program database files and symbols.

## Build configurations

If you create a new project in Visual Studio, it creates two *default build configurations* for you:

- Release mode
- Debug mode

If you compile your project, the settings from these configurations are used to configure what the compiler does. In *release mode*, the compiled code is fully optimized, and no extra information for debugging purposes is created.

In *debug mode*, there is no optimization applied, and additional information is outputted. The difference between these two configurations is clear when you execute the program in Listing 3-33.

**LISTING 3-33** A simple console application

```
using System;
using System.Threading;

public static class Program
{
    public static void Main()
    {
        Timer t = new Timer(TimerCallback, null, 0, 2000);
        Console.ReadLine();
    }

    private static void TimerCallback(Object o)
    {
        Console.WriteLine("In TimerCallback: " + DateTime.Now);
        GC.Collect();
    }
}
```

This console application creates an instance of a *Timer* object and then sets the timer to fire every 2 seconds. When it does, it outputs the current data and time. It also calls *GC.Collect* to force the garbage collector to run. Normally, you would never do this, but in this example it shows some interesting behavior.

When you run this application in debug mode, it does a nice job of outputting the time every 2 seconds and keeps on doing this until you terminate the application.

But when you execute this application in release mode, it outputs the current date and time only once. This demonstrates the difference between a debug and a release build. When executing a release build, the compiler optimizes the code. In this scenario, it sees that the *Timer* object is not used anymore, so it's no longer considered a root object and the garbage collector removes it from memory.

> **MORE INFO** GARBAGE COLLECTOR
>
> For more information on the garbage collector, see Chapter 2.

In debug configuration, the compiler inserts extra *no-operation (NOP) instructions* and *branch instructions*. NOP instructions are instructions that effectively don't do anything (for example, an assignment to a variable that's never used). A branch instruction is a piece of code that is executed conditionally (for example, when some variable is true or false). When the compiler sees that a certain branch is never executed, it can remove it from the compiled output. When optimizing the code, the compiler can also choose to inline short methods, effectively removing a method from the output.

In the real world, you don't suddenly have to start worrying about your objects being garbage collected and your code going wrong in release mode. The *Timer* object is a special case and normally you wouldn't have any problems with this. But it does illustrate the difference between a release and a debug build. The extra information that the compiler outputs in a debug build can be used to debug your application in Visual Studio.

One thing you can do is set a breakpoint. Figure 3-2 shows an example of setting a breakpoint in the application shown in Listing 3-31.

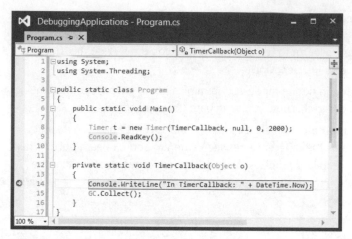

**FIGURE 3-2** Setting a breakpoint in Visual Studio

As you can see, the breakpoint on line 14 is currently active. This means that the debugger has paused the application, and you can now use Visual Studio to inspect and edit values and influence the flow of your program.

> **MORE INFO   DEBUGGING USING VISUAL STUDIO**
>
> For more information on how to use the debugger in Visual Studio, see *http://msdn.micro-soft.com/en-us/library/k0k771bt.aspx.*

While you are working on your application, the debug configuration is the most useful. But when you are ready to deploy your application to a production environment, it's important to make sure that you use the release configuration to get the best performance.

## Creating and managing compiler directives

Some programming languages have the concept of a *preprocessor*, which is a program that goes through your code and applies some changes to your code before handing it off to the compiler.

C# does not have a specialized preprocessor, but it does support *preprocessor compiler directives*, which are special instructions to the compiler to help in the compilation process.

One example of a preprocessor directive is *#if.* Listing 3-34 shows an example.

**LISTING 3-34** Checking for the debug symbol

```
public void DebugDirective()
{
    #if DEBUG
        Console.WriteLine("Debug mode");
    #else
        Console.WriteLine("Not debug");
    #endif
}
```

The output of this method depends on the build configuration you use. If you have set your build configuration to Debug, it outputs "Debug mode"; otherwise, it shows "Not debug".

When using the *#if* directive, you can use the operators you are used to from C#: == (equality), != (inequality), && (and), || (or) and ! (not) to test for *true* or *false*.

The *debug symbol* is defined by Visual Studio when you use the default configuration for debug. It does so by passing the */debug* command to the compiler. You can define your own symbols by using the *#define* directive. Listing 3-35 shows how to define your own symbol and use it later on to see whether it exists. It's important that the definition comes before any other code in the file.

**LISTING 3-35** Defining a custom symbol

```
#define MySymbol

// …

public void UseCustomSymbol()
{
    #if MySymbol
        Console.WriteLine("Custom symbol is defined");
    #endif
}
```

Using directives this way can make your code harder to understand, and you should try to avoid them if possible. A scenario in which using preprocessor directives can be necessary is when you are building a library that targets multiple platforms. When building a .NET library that targets platforms such as Silverlight, WinRT, and different versions of the .NET Framework, you can use the preprocessor directives to smooth out the differences between the platforms.

Listing 3-36 shows an example of the differences between WinRT and .NET 4.5. In .NET 4.5, you can get the assembly of a type directly from the *Assembly* property. In WinRT, however, this API has changed, and you need to call *GetTypeInfo*. By using a preprocessor directive, you can reuse a lot of your code and adjust your code only for the differences.

**LISTING 3-36** Using preprocessor directives to target multiple platforms

```
public Assembly LoadAssembly<T>()
{
    #if !WINRT
        Assembly assembly = typeof(T).Assembly;
    #else
        Assembly assembly = typeof(T).GetTypeInfo().Assembly;
    #endif

    return assembly;
}
```

Another preprocessor directive is *#undef*, which can be used to remove the definition of a symbol. This can be used in a situation where you want to debug a piece of code that's normally included only in a release build. You can then use the *#undef* directive to remove the debug symbol.

Two other directives are *#warning* and *#error*. You can include them in your code to report an error or warning to the compiler. Listing 3-37 shows an example.

**LISTING 3-37** The *warning* and *error* directives

```
#warning This code is obsolete

#if DEBUG
#error Debug build is not allowed
#endif
```

If you paste this code into a Visual Studio project and build the Debug configuration, you will see a warning and an error (see Figure 3-3).

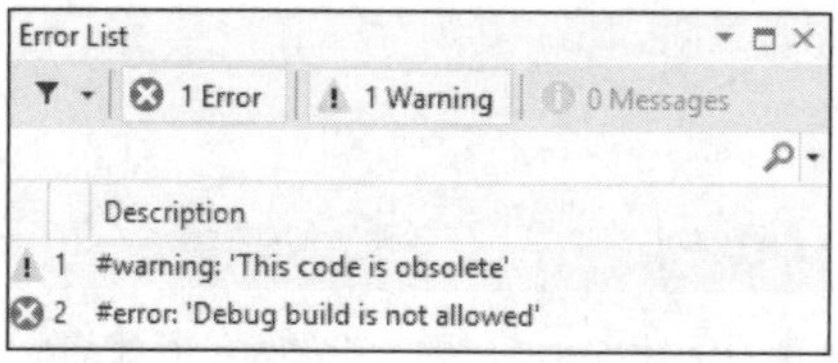

**FIGURE 3-3** A warning and an error

When working with code generation features, you sometimes remove or add lines to a source file before it is compiled. If an error occurs in your code, the compiler will report a line number in your file that is out of sync with how you see the code. The *#line* directive can be used to modify the compiler's line number and even the name of the file. You can also hide a line of code from the debugger. If you debug code using the *#line hide* directive, the debugger skips the hidden parts. Listing 3-38 shows an example of using the *#line* directive.

**LISTING 3-38** The *line* directive

```
#line 200 "OtherFileName"
    int a;    // line 200
#line default
    int b;    // line 4
#line hidden
    int c; // hidden
    int d; // line 7
```

When building an application, you sometimes willingly write some code that triggers a warning. You don't want to change the code, but you do want to hide the warning. You can do this by using the *#pragma* warning directive. Listing 3-39 shows an example of disabling and enabling all warnings.

**LISTING 3-39** The *pragma* warning directive

```
#pragma warning disable
 while (false)
{
    Console.WriteLine("Unreachable code");
}
#pragma warning restore
```

You can also choose to disable or restore specific warnings, as shown in Listing 3-40. The compiler won't report a warning for the *int i* statement, but it will report a warning for the un-reachable code. You can find the specific error codes in your Output Window in Visual Studio.

**LISTING 3-40** Disabling and enabling specific warnings

```
#pragma warning disable 0162, 0168
int i;
#pragma warning restore 0162
while (false)
{
    Console.WriteLine("Unreachable code");
}
#pragma warning restore
```

Often, preprocessor directives are used to include or exclude a certain piece of code depending on the build configuration. The .NET Framework has the *ConditionalAttribute* that you can use as an alternative. Maybe you want a certain function called only when you are building a debug configuration. Listing 3-41 shows how this can be done using preprocessor directives.

**LISTING 3-41** Call a method only in a debug build

```
public void SomeMethod()
{
    #if DEBUG
    Log("Step1");
    #endif
}
private static void Log(string message)
{
    Console.WriteLine("message");
}
```

It's inconvenient to have to wrap each call to the method in preprocessor directives. Instead, you can use the *ConditionalAttribute*, which signals to the compiler that calls to the method should be included only in the compiled program when the condition is *true*. Listing 3-42 shows an example.

LISTING 3-42 Applying the *ConditionalAttribute*

```
[Conditional("DEBUG")]
private static void Log(string message)
{
    Console.WriteLine("message");
}
```

Another attribute that can be useful when debugging is *DebuggerDisplayAttribute*. By default, the debugger in Visual Studio calls *ToString* on each object that you want to inspect for a value. For simple objects, such as ints or strings, this is no problem because they have an overload for *ToString* that displays their value. But for types that don't override *ToString*, the default implementation shows the name of the type, which is not useful when debugging. Of course, you can start overriding all *ToString* methods and give them an implementation that's useful for debugging purposes, but that implementation will also show up in your release build.

As an alternative, you can use the *DebuggerDisplayAttribute* found in the *System.Diagnostics* namespace. This attribute is used by the Visual Studio debugger to display an object. Listing 3-43 shows an example.

LISTING 3-43 Applying the *DebuggerDisplayAttribute*

```
[DebuggerDisplay("Name = {FirstName} {LastName")]
public class Person
{
    public string FirstName { get; set; }
    public string LastName { get; set; }
}
```

# Managing program database files and symbols

When compiling your programs, you have the option of creating an extra file with the extension *.pdb*. This file is called a *program database (PDB) file*, which is an extra data source that annotates your application's code with additional information that can be useful during debugging.

You can construct the compiler to create a PDB file by specifying the */debug:full* or */debug:pdbonly* switches. When you specify the full flag, a PDB file is created, and the specific assembly has debug information. With the *pdbonly* flag, the generated assembly is not modified, and only the PDB file is generated. The latter option is recommended when you are doing a release build.

A .NET PDB file contains two pieces of information:

- Source file names and their lines
- Local variable names

This data is not contained in the .NET assemblies, but you can imagine how it helps with debugging.

When you load a module, the debugger starts looking for the corresponding PDB file. It does this by looking for a PDB file with the same name that sits in the same directory as the application or library. So when you have a *MyApp.dll*, the debugger looks for *MyApp.pdb*. When it finds a file with a matching name, it compares an internal ID that is created by the compiler. The ID, which is a *globally unique identifier (GUID)*, should match exactly. This way, the debugger knows that you are using the correct PDB file and it can show the correct source code for your application while you are debugging.

The important thing is that this GUID is created at compile time, so if you recompile your application, you get a new PDB file that matches your recompiled build exactly. Thus, you can't debug a build from yesterday by using the PDB file that you created today; the GUIDs won't match up, and the debugger won't accept the PDB file.

When you execute a debug session in Visual Studio, there are no problems most of the time. Your code and the running application match exactly, and Visual Studio lets you debug the application. But when you want to debug an application that's currently in production, you need the matching PDB file to debug the application.

You can see the effects of missing PDB files when you run the console application from Listing 3-44 and put a breakpoint somewhere in the *Main* function.

**LISTING 3-44** Examining PDB files

```
using System;

namespace PdbFiles
{
    class Program
    {
        static void Main(string[] args)
        {
            Console.WriteLine("Hello World");
            Console.ReadKey();
        }
    }
}
```

After hitting the breakpoint, you can open two interesting windows. The first one is the *Modules* window that you can find in the *Debug* menu (see Figure 3-4).

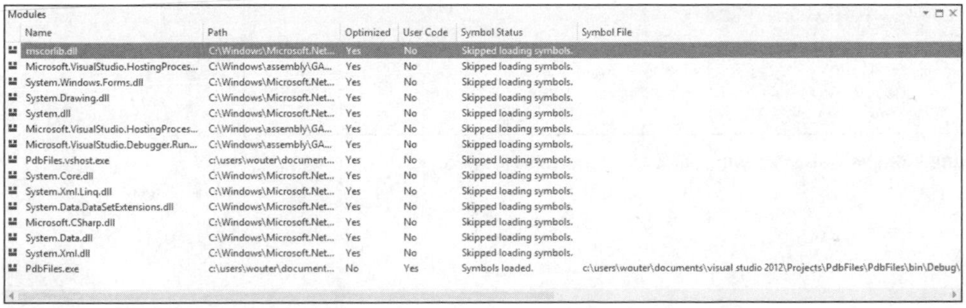
Modules

| Name | Path | Optimized | User Code | Symbol Status | Symbol File |
|---|---|---|---|---|---|
| mscorlib.dll | C:\Windows\Microsoft.Net... | Yes | No | Skipped loading symbols. | |
| Microsoft.VisualStudio.HostingProces... | C:\Windows\assembly\GA... | Yes | No | Skipped loading symbols. | |
| System.Windows.Forms.dll | C:\Windows\Microsoft.Net... | Yes | No | Skipped loading symbols. | |
| System.Drawing.dll | C:\Windows\Microsoft.Net... | Yes | No | Skipped loading symbols. | |
| System.dll | C:\Windows\Microsoft.Net... | Yes | No | Skipped loading symbols. | |
| Microsoft.VisualStudio.HostingProces... | C:\Windows\assembly\GA... | Yes | No | Skipped loading symbols. | |
| Microsoft.VisualStudio.Debugger.Run... | C:\Windows\assembly\GA... | Yes | No | Skipped loading symbols. | |
| PdbFiles.vshost.exe | c:\users\wouter\document... | Yes | No | Skipped loading symbols. | |
| System.Core.dll | C:\Windows\Microsoft.Net... | Yes | No | Skipped loading symbols. | |
| System.Xml.Linq.dll | C:\Windows\Microsoft.Net... | Yes | No | Skipped loading symbols. | |
| System.Data.DataSetExtensions.dll | C:\Windows\Microsoft.Net... | Yes | No | Skipped loading symbols. | |
| Microsoft.CSharp.dll | C:\Windows\Microsoft.Net... | Yes | No | Skipped loading symbols. | |
| System.Data.dll | C:\Windows\Microsoft.Net... | Yes | No | Skipped loading symbols. | |
| System.Xml.dll | C:\Windows\Microsoft.Net... | Yes | No | Skipped loading symbols. | |
| PdbFiles.exe | c:\users\wouter\document... | No | Yes | Symbols loaded. | c:\users\wouter\documents\visual studio 2012\Projects\PdbFiles\PdbFiles\bin\Debug\ |

**FIGURE 3-4** The Modules window

The Modules window shows a couple of interesting things. It shows a list of all the DLLs required to run your program. As you can see, only the last file, *PdbFiles.exe*, has a corresponding symbol file loaded. All the others have *User Code* set to *No* and have the message *Skipped Loading Symbols* because the debugger can't find the corresponding PDB file for those modules.

Another area where you miss the PDB files is when you look in the *Call Stack* window from the Debug menu. Figure 3-5 shows what the Call Stack window looks like.

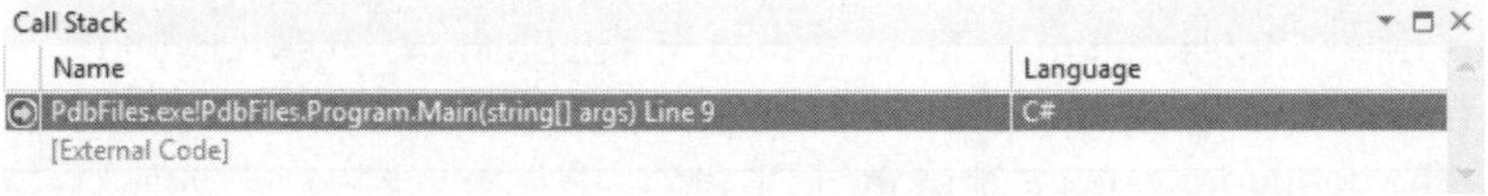

**FIGURE 3-5** The Call Stack window

As you can see, the debugger knows that you are currently in the *Main* method of your application. All other code, however, is seen as *External Code*.

Microsoft has helpfully published its PDB files to its *Symbol Server*, which is a way to expose the PDB files of applications to the debugger so it can easily find the files. The Symbol Server also helps the debugger handle the different versions of PDB files so that it knows how to find the matching version for each build.

If you want to use the Microsoft Symbol Server, you first need to turn off the Enable Just My Code option (you can find this option in Tools → Options → Debugging → General). Tell the debugger where to find the Microsoft symbol files. You can do this in the same Options section by selecting Symbols and then selecting the Microsoft Symbol Servers option.

When you now start debugging, the debugger will download the PDB files from the Microsoft Symbol Server. If you look at the Modules window, you will see that all the modules have their symbols loaded. You will also see that the Call Stack window shows a lot more information than it did previously (see Figure 3-6).

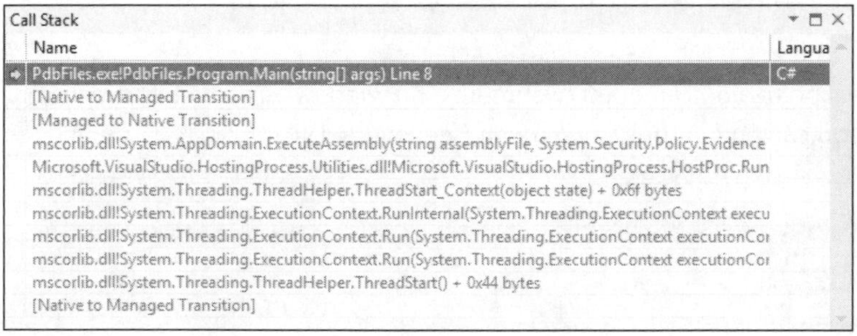

**FIGURE 3-6** The Call Stack window with all modules loaded

When building your own projects, it's important to set up a Symbol Server for your internal use. The easiest way to do this is to use *Team Foundation Server (TFS)* to manage your source code and builds. TFS has an option to publish all the PDB files from your builds to a shared location, which can then act as a Symbol Server for Visual Studio, enabling you to debug all previous versions of an application without having the source code around.

> **MORE INFO**   **SYMBOL SERVER**
>
> For more information on setting up your own Symbol Server, see *http://msdn.microsoft.com/en-us/library/ms680693(VS.85).aspx.*

**EXAM TIP**

Remember how important it is to save your PDB files somewhere. If you throw them away, you immediately lose the opportunity to debug that specific build of your application.

When a full-sized PDB file is built by the compiler, it contains two distinct collections of information: private and public symbol data. A public symbol file contains less data. It exposes only the items that are accessible from one source file to another. Items visible in only one object file, such as local variables, are not in the public symbol part.

When publishing symbol files to the outside world, as Microsoft did, you can choose to remove the private information. When you are dealing with intellectual property that you don't want to be exposed, this is an important step.

You can do this by using the *PDBCopy* tool. PDBCopy is a part of the Debugging Tools for Windows that you install as a part of the Windows Software Development Kit (SDK). The following line shows an example of stripping the private data from a PDB file:

```
pdbcopy mysymbols.pdb publicsymbols.pdb -p
```

This code takes a *mysymbols.pdb* file and creates a file *publicsymbols.pdb* file without the private symbol data.

> **MORE INFO**   **PDBCOPY**
>
> For more information on using PDBCopy, see *http://msdn.microsoft.com/en-us/library/windows/hardware/ff560131(v=vs.85).aspx.*

## Objective summary

- Visual Studio build configurations can be used to configure the compiler.
- A debug build outputs a nonoptimized version of the code that contains extra instructions to help debugging.
- A release build outputs optimized code that can be deployed to a production environment.
- Compiler directives can be used to give extra instructions to the compiler. You can use them, for example, to include code only in certain build configurations or to suppress certain warnings.
- A program database (PDB) file contains extra information that is required when debugging an application.

## Objective review

Answer the following questions to test your knowledge of the information in this objective. You can find the answers to these questions and explanations of why each answer choice is correct or incorrect in the "Answers" section at the end of this chapter.

1. You are ready to deploy your code to a production server. Which configuration do you deploy?

   **A.** Debug configuration

   **B.** Release configuration

   **C.** Custom configuration with PDB files

   **D.** Release configuration built with the */debug:full* compiler flag

2. You are debugging an application for a web shop and are inspecting a lot of *Order* classes. What can you do to make your debugging easier?

   **A.** Use the *DebuggerDisplayAttribute* on the *Order* class.

   **B.** Override *ToString* on the *Order* class.

   **C.** Use the *ConditionalAttribute* on the *Order* class.

   **D.** Use the *#line* compiler directive to make sure you can find the correct location when an exception occurs.

3. You are using custom code generation to insert security checks into your classes. When an exception happens, you're having troubling finding the correct line in your source code. What should you do?

   **A.** Use *#error* to signal the error from your code so that it's easier to find.

   **B.** Use *#line* hidden to hide unnecessary lines from the debugger.

   **C.** Use the *ConditionalAttribute* to remove the security checks from your debug build.

   **D.** Use the *#line* directive with the correct line numbers in your generated code to restore the original line numbers.

# Objective 3.5 Implement diagnostics in an application

When your application is in production, you still want to make sure that everything is working the way it should. Maybe customers are reporting errors in a certain area of the application, and you can't find their cause. It might be that your application is performing worse then you anticipated and you are getting complaints from users. The .NET Framework offers features that can help you to fix these issues.

---

**This objective covers how to:**

- Implement logging and tracing.
- Profile your applications.
- Create and monitor performance counters.

---

## Logging and tracing

When your application is running on a production server, it's sometimes impossible to attach a debugger because of security restrictions or the nature of the application. If the application runs on multiple servers in a distributed environment, such as Windows Azure, a regular debugger won't always help you find the error.

Because of this, it's important that you implement a *logging and tracing strategy* right from the start. *Tracing* is a way for you to monitor the execution of your application while it's running. Tracing information can be detailed; it can show which methods are entered, decisions are made, and errors or warnings happen while the application is running.

Tracing can generate a huge amount of information and it's something that you enable when you need to investigate an issue in a production application.

Logging is always enabled and is used for error reporting. You can configure your logging to collect the data in some centralized way. Maybe you want an e-mail or text message when there is a serious issue. Other errors can be logged to a file or a database.

The .NET Framework offers classes that can help you with logging and tracing in the *System.Diagnostics* namespace. One such class is the *Debug* class, which can, as its name suggests, be used only in a debug build. This is because the *ConditionalAttribute* with a value of *DEBUG* is applied to the *Debug* class. You can use it for basic logging and executing assertions on your code. Listing 3-45 shows an example of using the *Debug* class.

**LISTING 3-45** Using the *Debug* class

```
Debug.WriteLine("Starting application");
Debug.Indent();
int i = 1 + 2;
Debug.Assert(i == 3);
Debug.WriteLineIf(i > 0, "i is greater than 0");
```

By default, the *Debug* class writes its output to the Output window in Visual Studio. If the *Debug.Assert* statement fails, you get a message box showing the current stack trace of the application. This message box asks you to retry, abort, or ignore the assertion failure. You can use *Debug.Assert* to indicate a bug in your code that you want pointed out to you while developing your application.

Another class that you can use is the *TraceSource* class, which was added in .NET 2.0 and should be used instead of the static *Trace* class.

Listing 3-46 shows how to use the *TraceSource* class.

**LISTING 3-46** Using the *TraceSource* class

```
TraceSource traceSource = new TraceSource("myTraceSource",
    SourceLevels.All);

traceSource.TraceInformation("Tracing application..");
traceSource.TraceEvent(TraceEventType.Critical, 0, "Critical trace");
traceSource.TraceData(TraceEventType.Information, 1,
    new object[] { "a", "b", "c" });

traceSource.Flush();
traceSource.Close();

// Outputs:
// myTraceSource Information: 0 : Tracing application..
// myTraceSource Critical: 0 : Critical trace
// myTraceSource Information: 1 : a, b, c
```

As you can see, you can pass a parameter of type *TraceEventType* to the trace methods. You use this to specify the severity of the event that is happening. This information is later used by the *TraceSource* to determine which information should be output.

You can use several different options for the *TraceEventType* enum:

- **Critical**   This is the most severe option. It should be used sparingly and only for very serious and irrecoverable errors.

- **Error**   This enum member has a slightly lower priority than Critical, but it still indicates that something is wrong in the application. It should typically be used to flag a problem that has been handled or recovered from.

- **Warning**   This value indicates something unusual has occurred that may be worth investigating further. For example, you notice that a certain operation suddenly takes longer to process than normal or you flag a warning that the server is getting low on memory.

- **Information**   This value indicates that the process is executing correctly, but there is some interesting information to include in the tracing output file. It may be information that a user has logged onto a system or that something has been added to the database.

- **Verbose**   This is the loosest of all the severity related values in the enum. It should be used for information that is not indicating anything wrong with the application and is likely to appear in vast quantities. For example, when instrumenting all methods in a type to trace their beginning and ending, it is typical to use the verbose event type.

- **Stop**, **Start**, **Suspend**, **Resume**, **Transfer**   These event types are not indications of severity, but mark the trace event as relating to the logical flow of the application. They are known as *activity event types* and mark a logical operation's starting or stopping, or transferring control to another logical operation.

The second argument to the trace methods is the *event ID number*. This number does not have any predefined meaning; it's just another way to group your events together. You could, for example, group your database calls as numbers 10000–10999 and your web service calls as 11000–11999 to more easily tell what area of your application a trace entry is related.

The third parameter is a string that contains the message that should be traced. When you are using the *TraceData* method, you can pass extra arguments that should be output to the trace.

Writing all information to the Output window can be useful during debug sessions, but not in a production environment. To change this behavior, both the *Debug* and *TraceSource* classes have a *Listeners* property. This property holds a collection of *TraceListeners, which* process the information from the *Write, Fail,* and *Trace* methods.

Out of the box, both the *Debug* and the *TraceSource* class use an instance of the *DefaultTraceListener* class. The *DefaultTraceListener* writes to the Output window and shows the message box when assertion fails.

You can use several other *TraceListeners* that are a part of the .NET Framework. Table 3-2 shows a list of the available listeners.

**TABLE 3-2** *TraceListeners* in the .NET Framework

| Name | Output |
|---|---|
| *ConsoleTraceListener* | Standard output or error stream |
| *DelimitedListTraceListener* | *TextWriter* |
| *EventLogTraceListener* | *EventLog* |
| *EventSchemaTraceListener* | XML-encoded, schema-compliant log file |
| *TextWriterTraceListener* | *TextWriter* |
| *XmlWriterTraceListener* | XML-encoded data to a *TextWriter* or stream. |

If you don't want the *DefaultTraceListener* to be active, you need to clear the current listeners collection. You can add as many listeners as you want. In the example in Listing 3-47, the *DefaultTraceListener* is removed, and a *TextWriteTraceListener* is configured. After running this code, an output file is created named *Tracefile.txt* that contains the output of the trace.

**LISTING 3-47** Configuring *TraceListener*.

```
Stream outputFile = File.Create("tracefile.txt");
TextWriterTraceListener textListener =
    new TextWriterTraceListener(outputFile);

TraceSource traceSource = new TraceSource("myTraceSource",
    SourceLevels.All);

traceSource.Listeners.Clear();
traceSource.Listeners.Add(textListener);

traceSource.TraceInformation("Trace output");

traceSource.Flush();
traceSource.Close();
```

You can define your own trace listeners by inheriting from the *TraceListener* base class and specifying your own implementation for the trace methods.

Specifying the listeners through code can be useful, but it's not something you can easily change after the application is deployed. Instead of configuring the listeners through code, you can also use a configuration file.

Listing 3-48 shows an example of configuring your trace source from a configuration file.

**LISTING 3-48** Using a configuration file for tracing

```xml
<?xml version="1.0" encoding="utf-8" ?>
<configuration>
  <system.diagnostics>
    <sources>
      <source name="myTraceSource" switchName="defaultSwitch">
        <listeners>
          <add initializeData="output.txt"
              type="System.Diagnostics.TextWriterTraceListeer"
              name="myLocalListener">
              <filter type="System.Diagnostics.EventTypeFilter"
               initializeData="Warning"/>
          </add>
          <add name="consoleListener" />
          <remove name="Default"/>
        </listeners>
      </source>
    </sources>
    <sharedListeners>
      <add initializeData="output.xml" type="System.Diagnostics.XmlWriterTraceListener"
          name="xmlListener" traceOutputOptions="None" />
      <add type="System.Diagnostics.ConsoleTraceListener" name="consoleListener"
          traceOutputOptions="None" />
    </sharedListeners>
    <switches>
      <add name="defaultSwitch" value="All" />
    </switches>
  </system.diagnostics>
</configuration>
```

Through the configuration file, you have a lot of flexibility. In this case, you configure a trace source named *myTraceSource* to use two listeners: one to a file and the other to the console. The console listener is defined as a shared listener so that you can use it for multiple trace sources.

The configuration file also defines a *switch*, which is used by a trace source to determine whether it should do something with a trace message it receives. This way, you can determine which trace messages you want to see. Lowering the number of messages enhances performance and will result in a smaller output file. After you have found the particular area that you want to focus on, you can set your switch to a more detailed level.

While switches work for a whole trace source, a *filter* is applied to an individual listener. When you have multiple listeners for one single trace source, you can use filters to determine which trace events are actually processed by the listener. You could have a listener that sends text messages only for the critical events in a trace source, for example.

Next to writing trace information to a file or database, you can also write events to the *Windows Event Log*. You do this by using the *EventLog* class in the *System.Diagnostics* namespace. To use the *EventLog* class, you need to run with an account that has the appropriate permissions to create event logs. When running it from Visual Studio, you have to run Visual Studio as an administrator.

Listing 3-49 shows an example of how to create a new log and write some data to it.

**LISTING 3-49** Writing data to the event log

```
using System;
using System.Diagnostics;

class MySample
{
    public static void Main()
    {
        if (!EventLog.SourceExists("MySource"))
        {
            EventLog.CreateEventSource("MySource", "MyNewLog");
            Console.WriteLine("CreatedEventSource");
            Console.WriteLine("Please restart application");
            Console.ReadKey();
            return;
        }

        EventLog myLog = new EventLog();
        myLog.Source = "MySource";
        myLog.WriteEntry("Log event!");
    }
}
```

These messages can then be viewed by the Windows Event Viewer. Figure 3-7 shows the Event Viewer with the newly logged message.

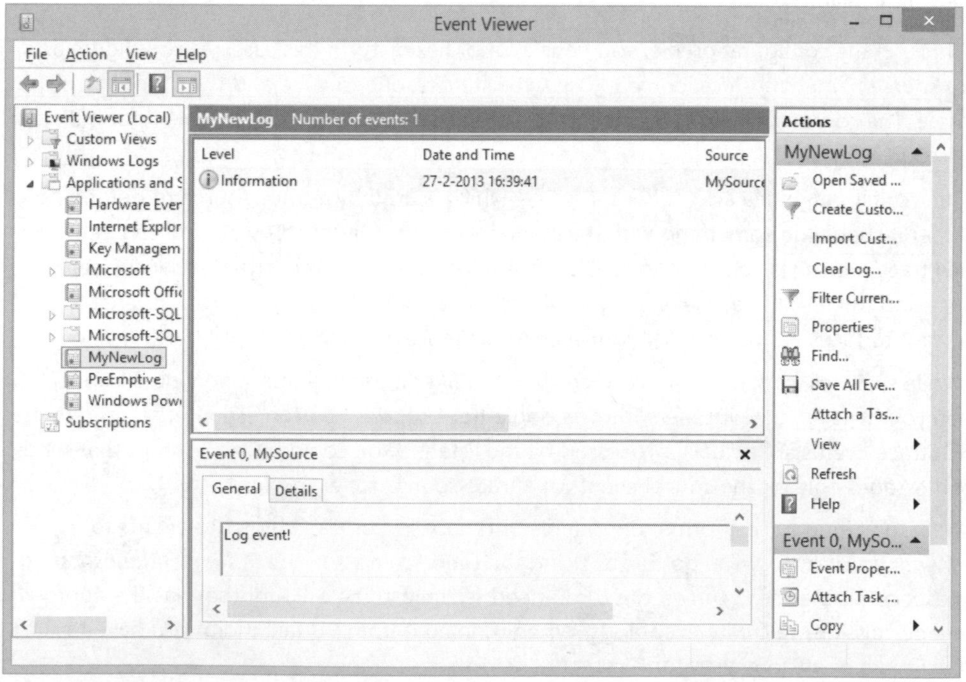

**FIGURE 3-7** The Windows Event Viewer with a new custom event

You can also read programmatically from the event log. You do this by getting an *EventLogEntry* from the *Entries* property of the *EventLog*. Listing 3-50 shows how you can read the latest entry in the event log *"MyNewLog"*.

LISTING 3-50 Reading data from the event log.

```
EventLog log = new EventLog("MyNewLog");

Console.WriteLine("Total entries: " + log.Entries.Count);
EventLogEntry last = log.Entries[log.Entries.Count - 1];
Console.WriteLine("Index:    " + last.Index);
Console.WriteLine("Source:   " + last.Source);
Console.WriteLine("Type:     " + last.EntryType);
Console.WriteLine("Time:     " + last.TimeWritten);
Console.WriteLine("Message: " + last.Message);
```

The *EventLog* also gives you the option to subscribe to changes in the event log. It exposes a special *EntryWritten* event that you can subscribe to for changes. You could use this, for example, to alert your system administrators of critical situations so they don't have to monitor the event log manually. Listing 3-51 shows how to subscribe to changes in the event log.

LISTING 3-51 Writing data to the event log

```
using System;
using System.Diagnostics;

class EventLogSample
{
    public static void Main()
    {
        EventLog applicationLog = new EventLog("Application", ".", "testEventLogEvent");
        applicationLog.EntryWritten += (sender, e) =>
        {

            Console.WriteLine(e.Entry.Message);
        };
        applicationLog.EnableRaisingEvents = true;
        applicationLog.WriteEntry("Test message", EventLogEntryType.Information);

        Console.ReadKey();


    }
}
```

# Profiling your application

When looking for a performance problem, the only real way to find it is measure, not guess. Maybe you have a feeling where the problem is but just making some random changes and then verifying that your applications performance has improved is really hard.

Most of the time, performance is seen as the amount of time something takes. That's not the only performance criterion, however. Maybe you are working on an application that processes lots of data, and constraints are not so much in time as perhaps in memory usage.

*Profiling* is the process of determining how your application uses certain resources. You can check, for example, how much memory your program uses, which methods are being called, and how long each method takes to execute. This information is required when you have a performance bottleneck and you want to find the cause.

With performance, one thing is always true: Don't get into premature optimizations. Worrying whether some algorithm will be faster than another algorithm could be important, but if you haven't profiled your application, you won't even know if that algorithm is the bottleneck of your application. Because of this, a guideline is to write your code as easy and maintainable as possible. When you run into performance problems, you can use a profiler to actually measure which part of your application is causing problems.

A simple way of measuring the execution time of some code is by using the *Stopwatch* class that can be found in the *System.Diagnostics* namespace. Listing 3-52 shows how you can initialize and use a *StopWatch*.

**LISTING 3-52** Using the *StopWatch* class

```
using System;
using System.Diagnostics;
using System.Text;

namespace Profiling
{
    class Program
    {
        const int numberOfIterations = 100000;
        static void Main(string[] args)
        {

            Stopwatch sw = new Stopwatch();
            sw.Start();
            Algorithm1();
            sw.Stop();

            Console.WriteLine(sw.Elapsed);

            sw.Reset();
            sw.Start();
            Algorithm2();
            sw.Stop();
```

```
            Console.WriteLine(sw.Elapsed);
            Console.WriteLine("Ready…");
            Console.ReadLine();            }

        private static void Algorithm2()
        {
            string result = "";

            for (int x = 0; x < numberOfIterations; x++)
            {
                result += 'a';
            }
        }

        private static void Algorithm1()
        {
            StringBuilder sb = new StringBuilder();
            for (int x = 0; x < numberOfIterations; x++)
            {
                sb.Append('a');

            }

            string result = sb.ToString();
        }
    }
}

// Displays
// 00:00:00.0007635
// 00:00:01.4071420
```

As you can see, the *StopWatch* class has a *Start*, *Stop*, and *Reset* method. You can get the elapsed time in milliseconds, in ticks, or formatted as in the example.

Visual Studio 2012 also includes an extensive set of profiling tools. To use them, you need Visual Studio Ultimate, Premium, or Professional edition.

When using the profiler, the easiest way is to use the Performance Wizard. You can find this wizard in the Analyze menu in Visual Studio. Figure 3-8 shows the first page of the wizard.

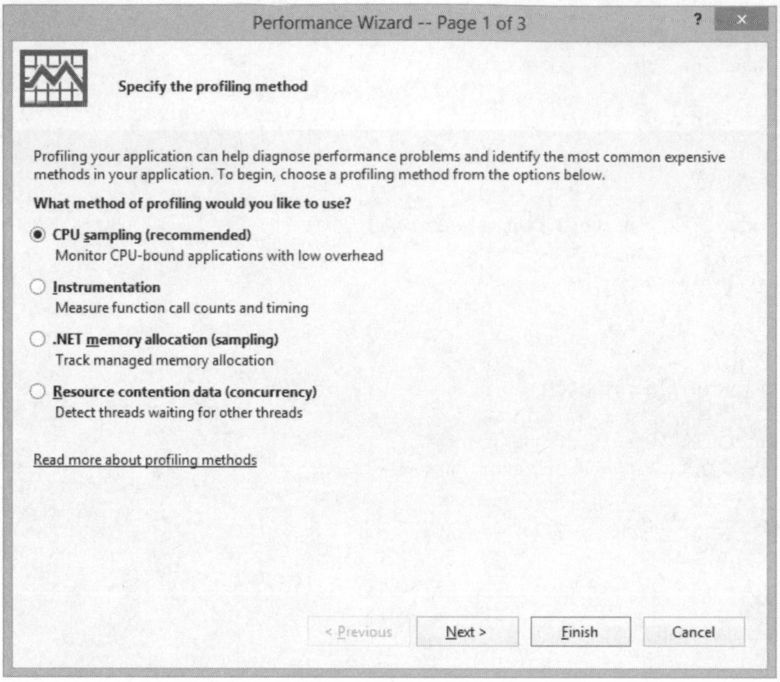

**FIGURE 3-8** Performance Wizard

When profiling your applications, you have four options:

- **CPU sampling**   This is the most lightweight option. It has little effect on the application. You use it for an initial search for your performance problems.

- **Instrumentation**   This method injects code into your compiled file that captures timing information for each function that is called. With instrumentation, you can find problems that have to do with input/output (I/O) or you can closely examine a particular method.

- **.NET memory allocation**   This method interrupts your program each time the application allocates a new object or when the object is collected by the garbage collector to give you a good idea of how memory is being used in your program.

- **Resource contention data**   This method can be used in multithreaded applications to find out why methods have to wait for each other before they can access a shared resource.

If you run the application from Listing 3-49 without the *Stopwatch* code and profile it with the CPU Sampling option, you see a report that looks like the one in Figure 3-9.

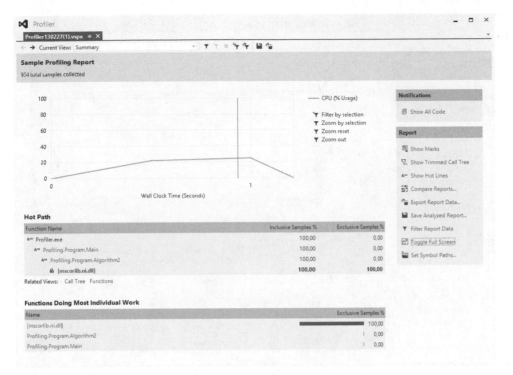

**FIGURE 3-9** Profiler report

In this case, a lot of time is spent inside the *Mscorlib.dll, in which* the implementation of the string and *StringBuilder* classes resides. But you can also see that the function on the second place is *Algorithm2*. You can use this report to drill into individual methods and check which methods should be optimized.

> **MORE INFO** **VISUAL STUDIO PROFILER**
>
> For more information on how to use the Visual Studio profiler, see *http://msdn.microsoft. com/en-us/library/z9z62c29.aspx*.

## Creating and monitoring performance counters

Windows provides a large number of categorized *performance counters* that you can use to monitor your hardware, services, applications, and drivers. Examples of performance counters are those that display your CPU usage and memory usage, but also application-specific counters such as the length of a query in SQL Server.

The performance counters that Windows offers can be viewed with a special program called *Perfmon.exe*. Figure 3-10 shows what the Performance Monitor looks like when examining some data about the CPU.

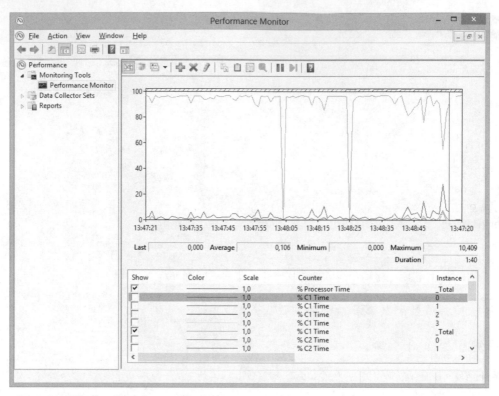

**FIGURE 3-10** Windows Performance Monitor

You can read the values of the performance counters from code by using the *PerformanceCounter* class found in the *System.Diagnostics* namespace. Listing 3-50 shows an example of accessing a performance counter to read the amount of available memory and display it on-screen.

**LISTING 3-53** Reading data from a performance counter

```
using System;
using System.Diagnostics;

namespace PerformanceCounters
{
    class Program
    {
        static void Main(string[] args)
        {
            Console.WriteLine("Press escape key to stop");
            using (PerformanceCounter pc =
                        new PerformanceCounter("Memory", "Available Bytes"))
            {
                string text = "Available memory: ";
                Console.Write(text);
                do
                {
```

```
            while (!Console.KeyAvailable)
            {
                Console.Write(pc.RawValue);
                Console.SetCursorPosition(text.Length, Console.CursorTop);
            }
        } while (Console.ReadKey(true).Key != ConsoleKey.Escape);
    }
  }
 }
}
```

All performance counters are part of a category, and within that category they have a unique name. To access the performance counters, your application has to run under full trust, or the account that it's running under should be an administrator or be a part of the Performance Monitor Users group.

All performance counters implement *IDisposable* because they access unmanaged resources. After you're done with the performance counter, it's best to immediately dispose of it.

---

**MORE INFO    IDISPOSABLE**

For more information on implementing and using *IDisposable*, see Chapter 2.

---

Performance counters come in several different types. The type definition determines how the counter interacts with the monitoring applications. Some types that can be useful are the following:

- *NumberOfItems32/NumberOfItems64*   These types can be used for counting the number of operations or items. *NumberOfItems64* is the same as *NumberOfItems32*, except that it uses a larger field to accommodate for larger values.

- *RateOfCountsPerSecond32/RateOfCountsPerSecond64*   These types can be used to calculate the amount per second of an item or operation. *RateOfCountsPerSecond64* is the same as *RateOfCountsPerSecond32*, except that it uses larger fields to accommodate for larger values.

- *AvergateTimer32*   Calculates the average time to perform a process or process an item.

Listing 3-54 shows an example of creating and using your own performance counters. The first time, the application will create two new performance counters. The second time, it will increment both counters by one. If you run this program (as administrator) and keep an eye on the Windows Performance Monitoring tool, you will see the two counters update.

**LISTING 3-54** Reading data from a performance counter

```csharp
using System;
using System.Diagnostics;

namespace PerformanceCounters
{
    class Program
    {

        static void Main(string[] args)
        {
            if (CreatePerformanceCounters())
            {
                Console.WriteLine("Created performance counters");
                Console.WriteLine("Please restart application");
                Console.ReadKey();
                return;
            }
            var totalOperationsCounter = new PerformanceCounter(
                "MyCategory",
                "# operations executed",
                "",
                false);
            var operationsPerSecondCounter = new PerformanceCounter(
                "MyCategory",
                "# operations / sec",
                "",
                false);

            totalOperationsCounter.Increment();
            operationsPerSecondCounter.Increment();
        }
        private static bool CreatePerformanceCounters()
        {
            if (!PerformanceCounterCategory.Exists("MyCategory"))
            {
                CounterCreationDataCollection counters =
                    new CounterCreationDataCollection
                {
                    new CounterCreationData(
                        "# operations executed",
                        "Total number of operations executed",
                        PerformanceCounterType.NumberOfItems32),
                    new CounterCreationData(
                        "# operations / sec",
                        "Number of operations executed per second",
                        PerformanceCounterType.RateOfCountsPerSecond32)
                };

                PerformanceCounterCategory.Create("MyCategory",
                        "Sample category for Codeproject", counters);

                return true;
            }
```

```
            return false;
        }
    }
}
```

Creating your own performance counters can be a huge help when checking on the health of your application. You can create another application to read them (some kind of dashboard application), or you can use the Performance Counter Monitor tool that Windows provides.

> ### *Thought experiment*
> ### Building a logging and tracing strategy
>
> In this thought experiment, apply what you've learned about this objective. You can find answers to these questions in the "Answers" section at the end of this chapter.
>
> You are building an online web shop that will be hosted in a distributed environment. Your web shop needs to scale well, so performance is an important concept.
>
> 1. Which events would you write to a trace source in a web shop?
>
> 2. How can you use performance counters to keep an eye on your performance?

## Objective summary

- Logging and tracing are important to monitor an application that is in production and should be implemented right from the start.
- You can use the *Debug* and *TraceSource* classes to log and trace messages. By configuring different listeners, you can configure your application to know which data to send where.
- When you are experiencing performance problems, you can profile your application to find the root cause and fix it.
- Performance counters can be used to constantly monitor the health of your applications.

## Objective review

Answer the following questions to test your knowledge of the information in this objective. You can find the answers to these questions and explanations of why each answer choice is correct or incorrect in the "Answers" section at the end of this chapter.

1. You are using the *TraceSource* class to trace data for your application. You want to trace data when an order cannot be submitted to the database and you are going to perform a retry. Which *TraceEventType* should you use?

   A. *Information*

   B. *Verbose*

   C. *Critical*

   D. *Error*

2. Users are reporting errors in your application, and you want to configure your application to output more trace data. Which configuration setting should you change?

   A. *NumberOfItems32*

   B. *Listener*

   C. *Filter*

   D. *Switch*

3. You are working on a global application with lots of users. The operation staff requests information on how many user logons per second are occurring. What should you do?

   A. Add a *TraceSource* and write each logon to a text file.

   B. Implement a performance counter using the *RateOfCountsPerSecond64* type.

   C. Instrument your application with the profiler so you can see exactly how many times the logon method is called.

   D. Use the *EventLog* class to write an event to the event log for each logon.

# Chapter summary

- Validating application input is important to ensure the stability and security of your application. You can use the *Parse*, *TryParse*, and *Convert* functions to parse user input. Regular Expressions can be used for matching patterns.

- Cryptography uses symmetric and asymmetric algorithms together with hashing to secure data.

- Code access permissions can be used to restrict the types of operations a program may execute.

- An assembly is a self-contained unit that contains application code and metadata. An assembly can be signed, versioned, and shared by putting it in the GAC.

- By selecting the correct build configurations, you can output additional information to create program database files that can be used to debug an application.

- By using logging, tracing, and performance counters, you can monitor an application while it's in production.

# Answers

This section contains the solutions to the thought experiments and answers to the lesson review questions in this chapter.

## Objective 3.1: Thought experiment

1. It looks like malicious users are entering HTML in the text fields. This data gets submitted to the server and rendered the next time the page is viewed.

2. You need to use regular expressions to restrict the user input. By making clear which characters you allow, you can strip the input of the HTML characters and make sure they are not showing up in the page layout.

## Objective 3.1: Review

1. **Correct answer:** B

   A. **Incorrect:** *Parse* will throw an exception when the user enters an invalid date,, which is not uncommon.

   B. **Correct:** *TryParse* will see whether the entered value is a valid date. If not, it will return gracefully instead of throwing an exception.

   C. **Incorrect:** Convert.*ToDateTime* uses *Parse* internally. This will throw an exception when entered data is in the wrong format.

   D. **Incorrect:** *RegEx.Match* can be used to see whether the input is a valid date. It can't convert the input string to a *DateTime* object.

2. **Correct answer:** B

   A. **Incorrect:** Money should not be stored in an integer because it can't store decimal numbers.

   B. **Correct:** You need to specify the *NumberStyles.Currency* and the culture that the user is using to parse the *DateTime* correctly.

   C. **Incorrect:** Using the server culture doesn't account for the differences in user culture. You also need the *NumberStyles.Currency* parameter to make sure the user can enter a currency symbol.

   D. **Incorrect:** Leaving off the culture defaults to the culture of the operating system. You also need the *NumberStyles.Currency* parameter to make sure the user can enter a currency symbol.

# Objective 3.2: Thought experiment

You can use numerous security features, including these:

- Digital certificates to make sure the application can be safely installed on desktop machines.

- Asymmetric encryption to send data to the server by using the public key to encrypt the data.

- Asymmetric encryption to send data from the server to the client. The server encrypts with the private key; the client decrypts with the public key.

- Code access permissions to make sure that your application can run in sandboxed environments.

# Objective 3.2: Review

1. **Correct answer:** C

    A. **Incorrect:** The private key should always be kept confidential.

    B. **Incorrect:** The private key should always be kept confidential.

    C. **Correct:** By sending each other their public key, they can then encrypt data with the other party's public key to send them data.

    D. **Incorrect:** The private key should always be kept confidential.

2. **Correct answer:** D

    A. **Incorrect:** *SHA256* is a hashing algorithm. It can't be used to encrypt data.

    B. **Incorrect:** *RSACryptoServiceProvider* is an asymmetric encryption algorithm. Asymmetric algorithms are not suited for encrypting large amounts of data.

    C. **Incorrect:** *MD5CryptoServiceProvider* is a hashing algorithm. It can't be used to encrypt data.

    D. **Correct:** *AesManaged* is a symmetric algorithm that can be used to encrypt large amounts of data.

3. **Correct answers:** A, C

    A. **Correct:** Using the digital certificate X509 can be used to sign hashed data. If the other party uses the *Verify* method, it can check that the hash hasn't changed.

    B. **Incorrect:** This method encrypts the data with an asymmetric algorithm. It doesn't ensure that the data hasn't been tampered with.

    C. **Correct:** *UnicodeEncoding.GetBytes* converts a string to a byte sequence. It doesn't protect the data in any way.

    D. **Incorrect:** The *Marshal* class should be used when working with *System.SecureString*. The *ZeroFreeBSTR* method can be used to zero out an area of memory that contained an insecure string.

# Objective 3.3: Thought experiment

1. Yes, you should sign the assembly.

2. Signing the assembly protects the assembly against tampering. The .NET Framework will check that the assembly hasn't been altered between signing and running.

3. Signing is also a requirement to be able to use a digital certificate so users of your application will know that you are the publisher of the application.

4. A disadvantage could be that you can no longer reference other nonsigned assemblies. If you own these assemblies, you can sign them yourself. If not, you would have to ask their publisher to sign them.

# Objective 3.3: Review

1. **Correct answer:** C

   A. **Incorrect:** An assembly in the GAC needs to be strongly named. Your assembly still won't be able to reference the nonsigned assembly.

   B. **Incorrect:** A strong-named assembly cannot reference a non-strong-named assembly.

   C. **Correct:** You need to strongly name the other assembly before you can reference it.

   D. **Incorrect:** The public key token is a part of the manifest of a strong-named assembly. The non-strong-named assembly doesn't have this key information. It needs to be strongly named first.

2. **Correct answer:** B

   A. **Incorrect:** A WinMD file is used by the WinRT in Windows 8. It shouldn't be used outside of this context.

   B. **Correct:** A shared assembly can be deployed in the GAC. Other applications can reference it there. When you want to update it, you can do so by deploying the new version to the GAC. By using configuration files, you can then let other applications reference your new assembly.

   C. **Incorrect:** You can use the *assemblyBinding* configuration element to add extra search locations for an assembly. This would ask for changes to each client application, however. The GAC is the location where a shared assembly needs to be deployed.

   D. **Incorrect:** Strongly naming an assembly doesn't make it a shared assembly. Each application would still require its own copy.

3. **Correct answers:** A, B

    A. **Correct:** Strongly naming the assembly is required to be able to reference it on the intranet

    B. **Correct:** The codebase configuration element can be used to have local client applications know they can find an assembly on another location such as the intranet.

    C. **Incorrect:** Deploying it to the GAC won't put the assembly on the intranet.

    D. **Incorrect:** The probing option can be used only to give additional locations relative to the application path. It can't be used to point to the intranet.

## Objective 3.4: Thought experiment

1. No, you don't have to do this. Although a debug version will contain more information, you can debug the release version if you have the correct PDB file.

2. You need to make sure that you have the correct PDB file that matches the build that's running on your server. You need this file to launch a debugging session.

3. A Symbol Server stores your PDB files and helps your debugger find the correct version. If you have a Symbol Server in place, you can easily start a debugging session to your server, and your debugger will find the correct PDB files automatically.

## Objective 3.4: Review

1. **Correct answer:** B

    A. **Incorrect:** A debug configuration is not fully optimized and is not suitable for a production environment.

    B. **Correct:** A release configuration is fully optimized and will give the best results in a production environment.

    C. **Incorrect:** PDB files are necessary only when debugging an application.

    D. **Incorrect:** The */debug:full* flag adds extra information to your application for debugging purposes.

2. **Correct answer:** A

    A. **Correct:** The *DebuggerDisplayAttribute* helps you in supplying a more helpful description when inspecting an item through the debugger.

    B. **Incorrect:** Overriding *ToString* does help, but a better solution is to use the *DebuggerDisplayAttribute* because this won't influence your code in production.

    C. **Incorrect:** The *ConditionalAttribute* can be used to remove code from your compiled application. Most of the time, it's used to remove certain calls when doing a release build.

    D. **Incorrect:** The *#line* directive is used to change the line numbers of your code. Normally, this won't be necessary.

3. **Correct answer:** D

    **A.** **Incorrect:** *#error* will signal an error at compile time.

    **B.** **Incorrect:** *#line* hidden will remove the extra generated lines from the debugger, but it won't restore your line numbers.

    **C.** **Incorrect:** This is a dangerous solution because it creates different behavior between debug and release builds. You won't be able to test your security checks while working with a debug build.

    **D.** **Correct:** The *#line* directive can be used to tell the compiler to change the line number of a line of code. This way, you can remove the line numbers for the generated code so that exceptions will match the original code.

# Objective 3.5: Thought experiment

1. Examples could be the following:

    ■ **Critical**   An irrecoverable error occurs, such as the database which is down so users can't place any orders.

    ■ **Error**   While submitting an order, the system notices that the database can't be reached and tries to resubmit the order.

    ■ **Warning**   The time it takes to submit an order is suddenly taking longer than expected.

    ■ **Information**   A new order is submitted successfully.

    ■ **Verbose**   Here you can trace all application events such as the beginning of the order process, how the user navigates through your web shop, and which decisions he makes.

2. You can use performance counters to keep track of how many orders are submitted and how long it takes to save them to the database. In the same way, you can see whether loading the product catalog is taking too long.

# Objective 3.5: Review

1. **Correct answer:** D

    **A.** **Incorrect:** A failing order is not something that should be seen as only an informative event. It should be treated as something critical.

    **B.** **Incorrect:** Verbose should be used only for very detailed tracing messages.

    **C.** **Incorrect:** You can still recover from the error, which makes it a severity of Error, not Critical.

    **D.** **Correct:** You should let the operators know that something is wrong and that you are trying to recover. If recovery fails, you should log a Critical event.

2. **Correct answer:** D

   A. **Incorrect:** *NumberOfItems32* is an option for creating a performance counter.

   B. **Incorrect:** A listener determines what is done with the tracing events. It doesn't influence which events are traced.

   C. **Incorrect:** A filter is used to filter the message that a listener processes. It doesn't influence which events are traced.

   D. **Correct:** The switch value determines which trace events should be handled. By lowering the severity for the switch, you will see more trace events in your output.

3. **Correct answer:** B

   A. **Incorrect:** Writing the events to a text file will still require a tool to parse the text file and give results to the operation staff.

   B. **Correct:** This performance counter will help the operation staff to see exactly what happens every second.

   C. **Incorrect:** Profiler instrumentation will really slow down the performance of your application. It's also something that's not easy readable by your operations staff.

   D. **Incorrect:** Although the event log can be read by the operation staff, they will have to manually count all events to calculate the logons per second.

# CHAPTER 4

# Implement data access

Each application that you create depends on some type of data. Together we already produce so much data that we're speaking about big data. When building your applications, you will often need to work with data from all kinds of storage types. Maybe a file on a hard drive, a relational database, or a service that some other application exposes.

In this chapter, you learn how to work with files, databases, and web services. You look at how *Language Integrated Query* (LINQ) can help you with writing readable, strongly typed queries against all kinds of data sources.

When working with data, you also need to know about *serializing* your data. In this chapter, you learn about different kinds of serialization and how you configure it to suit your needs.

When you talk about data, you also need in-memory constructs to work with it. This is where *collections* come in. In this chapter, you look at the collections .NET Framework offers for various different scenarios and how you can create your own collections.

### Objectives in this chapter:
- Objective 4.1: Perform I/O operations
- Objective 4.2: Consume data
- Objective 4.3: Query and manipulate data and objects by using LINQ
- Objective 4.4. Serialize and deserialize data
- Objective 4.5. Store data in and retrieve data from collections

## Objective 4.1: Perform I/O operations

Working with files is a common task when building an application. Sometimes you have to create a file to store data or to parse a file and extract some content from it. Maybe you are writing plain text or binary data—this is where a Stream object can be used. Maybe you are using streams to send bytes over the network to another application. The .NET Framework also offers support for those scenarios.

Another important topic when it comes to dealing with input/output (I/O) is performance. The new async keyword in C# can be used to easily implement asynchronous operations that can improve usability and scalability of your application.

# Working with files

*Files* are an important aspect of almost every application. That's why the .NET Framework offers an infrastructure that can help you with all your file-related work. All the necessary types can be found in the *System.IO* namespace.

## Drives

When working with the file system, you obviously start with a storage medium, which can be a hard drive, CD player, or another storage type. The .NET Framework offers the *DriveInfo* class to access the drives on your computer. A *DriveInfo* object doesn't have any specific methods for dealing with drives (for example, there is not an eject method for a CD player). It does have several properties to access information such as the name of the drive, size, and available free space. Listing 4-1 shows how to enumerate the current drives and display some information about them.

**LISTING 4-1** Listing drive information

```
DriveInfo[] drivesInfo = DriveInfo.GetDrives();

foreach (DriveInfo driveInfo in drivesInfo)
{
    Console.WriteLine("Drive {0}", driveInfo.Name);
    Console.WriteLine("  File type: {0}", driveInfo.DriveType);

    if (driveInfo.IsReady == true)
    {
        Console.WriteLine("  Volume label: {0}", driveInfo.VolumeLabel);
        Console.WriteLine("  File system: {0}", driveInfo.DriveFormat);
        Console.WriteLine(
            "  Available space to current user:{0, 15} bytes",
            driveInfo.AvailableFreeSpace);

        Console.WriteLine(
            "  Total available space:          {0, 15} bytes",
            driveInfo.TotalFreeSpace);

        Console.WriteLine(
            "  Total size of drive:            {0, 15} bytes ",
            driveInfo.TotalSize);
    }
}
```

# Directories

A drive contains a list of directories and files. To work with those items, you can use the *DirectoryInfo* object or the static *Directory* class. Both classes offer access to your folder structure. When executing only a single operation against your file system, it can be more efficient to use the static *Directory* class. When you want to execute multiple operations against a folder, *DirectoryInfo* is a better choice.

You can use both classes to create a new folder. When you create a new folder, you automatically have both read and write rights to the folder. Listing 4-2 shows how to create a new directory with the static *Directory* class or *DirectoryInfo*.

**LISTING 4-2** Creating a new directory

```
var directory = Directory.CreateDirectory(@"C:\Temp\ProgrammingInCSharp\Directory");

var directoryInfo = new DirectoryInfo(@"C:\Temp\ProgrammingInCSharp\DirectoryInfo");
directoryInfo.Create();
```

As you can see, a *DirectoryInfo* object can be initialized with a non-existing folder. Calling *Create* will create the directory. After creating the folder, you can call other instance members on the *DirectoryInfo* object that now points to the newly created folder.

You might try to create a new directory in a location in which you don't have sufficient permissions. In such a case, a *UnauthorizedAccessException* will be thrown.

You can also remove a folder, but trying to remove a folder that doesn't exist throws *DirectoryNotFoundException*. You can use the *Exists* method on the static *Directory* class or the *Exists* property on the *DirectoryInfo* object to determine whether a folder exists (see Listing 4-3).

**LISTING 4-3** Deleting an existing directory

```
if (Directory.Exists(@"C:\Temp\ProgrammingInCSharp\Directory"))
{
    Directory.Delete(@"C:\Temp\ProgrammingInCSharp\Directory");
}

var directoryInfo = new DirectoryInfo(@"C:\Temp\ProgrammingInCSharp\DirectoryInfo");
if (directoryInfo.Exists)
{
    directoryInfo.Delete();
}
```

One important thing to remember when working with directories and files is that the operating system controls access to all elements on your local computer or on a shared network drive. Access to folders can be arranged by using the *DirectorySecurity* class from the *System.Security.AccessControl* namespace. Listing 4-4 shows how you can use these to allow everyone to access a folder. This, of course, requires that the executing program has the rights to make this modification.

**LISTING 4-4** Setting access control for a directory

```
DirectoryInfo directoryInfo = new DirectoryInfo("TestDirectory");
directoryInfo.Create();
DirectorySecurity directorySecurity = directoryInfo.GetAccessControl();
directorySecurity.AddAccessRule(
        new FileSystemAccessRule("everyone",
                                    FileSystemRights.ReadAndExecute,
                                    AccessControlType.Allow));
directoryInfo.SetAccessControl(directorySecurity);
```

Besides methods for creating and removing directories, you can also query a method for attributes, subdirectories, or files.

The *Directory* and *DirectoryInfo* classes both have a method for retrieving all subdirectories of a given directory. This returns an array of *DirectoryInfo* objects.

You can specify a search pattern and an enumeration of type *SearchOption* that enables you to automatically search only the top folder or all subfolders. When looping through all folders, it can be that you are trying to access a folder without the required access rights. This throws an *UnauthorizedAccessException*. When you use *SearchOption.AllDirectories* and an exception is thrown, you won't get any results. Listing 4-5 shows an example of walking the directory tree manually and handling any exception that can occur. It also shows how to use a search pattern to limit the results to all folders containing the character *a*. It limits the recursive depth of the function to make sure you can control how long the method takes to execute.

**LISTING 4-5** Building a directory tree

```
private static void ListDirectories(DirectoryInfo directoryInfo,
    string searchPattern, int maxLevel, int currentLevel)
{
    if (currentLevel >= maxLevel )
    {
        return;
    }

    string indent = new string('-', currentLevel);

    try
    {
        DirectoryInfo[] subDirectories = directoryInfo.GetDirectories(searchPattern);

        foreach (DirectoryInfo subDirectory in subDirectories)
        {
            Console.WriteLine(indent + subDirectory.Name);
            ListDirectories(subDirectory, searchPattern,maxLevel, currentLevel + 1);
        }
    }
    catch (UnauthorizedAccessException)
    {
        // You don't have access to this folder.
        Console.WriteLine(indent + "Can't access: " + directoryInfo.Name);
        return;
    }
```

```
    catch (DirectoryNotFoundException)
    {
        // The folder is removed while iterating
        Console.WriteLine(indent + "Can't find: " + directoryInfo.Name);
        return;
    }
}

// List the subdirectories for Program Files containing the character 'a' with a maximum
depth of 5

DirectoryInfo directoryInfo = new DirectoryInfo(@"C:\Program Files");
ListDirectories(directoryInfo, "*a*", 5, 0);
```

A search pattern can consist of several wildcard characters that form a search pattern as you can see in Table 4-1.

**TABLE 4-1** Wildcards for a search pattern

| Wildcard character | Description | Example |
|---|---|---|
| * | Zero or more characters | *m* matches Common Files and Media, but not Windows |
| ? | Exactly one character | ?edia matches Media, but not Windows Media Player |

When working with a huge directory tree, it can be more efficient to use *EnumerateDirectories* instead of *GetDirectories*. When using *EnumerateDirectories*, you can start enumerating the collection before it's been completely retrieved. When using *GetDirectories*, you get a list of folder names and you have to wait until the whole list of names is ready.

Another method that can come in handy is the method *MoveTo* on *DirectoryInfo* or *Move* on *Directory* classes when you want to move an existing directory to a new location. Listing 4-6 shows how to use them.

**LISTING 4-6** Moving a directory

```
Directory.Move(@"C:\source", @"c:\destination");

DirectoryInfo directoryInfo = new DirectoryInfo(@"C:\Source");
directoryInfo.MoveTo(@"C:\destination");
```

Besides checking which subdirectories a certain directory contains, you can also work with the files that a directory contains. As you can see in Listing 4-7, the static *Directory.GetFiles(string path)* function returns an array of strings, whereas the *DirectoryInfo.GetFiles()* returns an array of FileInfo objects. This brings us to the next topic.

LISTING 4-7 Listing all the files in a directory

```
foreach (string file in Directory.GetFiles(@"C:\Windows"))
{
    Console.WriteLine(file);
}


DirectoryInfo directoryInfo = new DirectoryInfo(@"C:\Windows");
foreach (FileInfo fileInfo in directoryInfo.GetFiles())
{
    Console.WriteLine(fileInfo.FullName);
}
```

## Working with files

Directories are necessary only to give some structure to the files they need to store. Just as with directories, you can use both a static *File* class and a *FileInfo* object to access files.

You can determine whether a file exists and when it does, you can take action, such as deleting it. Listing 4-8 shows how to see whether a file exists and delete it if it does.

**LISTING 4-8** Deleting a file

```
string path = @"c:\temp\test.txt";

if (File.Exists(path))
{
    File.Delete(path);
}

FileInfo fileInfo = new FileInfo(path);

if (fileInfo.Exists)
{
    fileInfo.Delete();
}
```

You can also move files around by using the *File.Move(string source, string destination)* or *FileInfo.MoveTo(string destination)*. Moving a file deletes the original if the move is successful. If that's not what you want, you can also use *Copy* and *CopyTo*. Listing 4-9 shows how to move a file; Listing 4-10 shows how to copy a file.

**LISTING 4-9** Moving a file

```
string path = @"c:\temp\test.txt";
string destPath = @"c:\temp\destTest.txt";

File.CreateText(path).Close();
File.Move(path, destPath);

FileInfo fileInfo = new FileInfo(path);
fileInfo.MoveTo(destPath);
```

**LISTING 4-10** Copying a file

```
string path = @"c:\temp\test.txt";
string destPath = @"c:\temp\destTest.txt";

File.CreateText(path).Close();
File.Copy(path, destPath);

FileInfo fileInfo = new FileInfo(path);
fileInfo.CopyTo(destPath);
```

## Working with paths

When accessing files, you often have a need for combining a directory and a file name. Manually concatenating them by using simple string addition can work, but it is error-prone. For example, adding the strings shown in Listing 4-11 results in an invalid path.

**LISTING 4-11** Don't manually concatenate strings to form a file path

```
string folder = @"C:\temp";
string fileName = "test.dat";

string fullPath = folder + fileName; // Results in C:\temptest.dat
```

The static class *Path* that can be found in *System.IO* has some helper methods for dealing with these kinds of situations. One of these methods is the static *Combine* method that has a number of overloads that accept multiple string parameters. Listing 4-12 shows how the *Combine* method results in a correct path.

**LISTING 4-12** Using *Path.Combine*

```
string folder = @"C:\temp";
string fileName = "test.dat";

string fullPath = Path.Combine(folder, fileName); // Results in C:\\temp\\test.dat
```

The Path class offers some other helpful methods: *GetDirectoryName*, *GetExtensions*, *GetFileName*, and *GetPathRoot*. Listing 4-13 shows how you can use these methods on a string that contains a full path.

**LISTING 4-13** Using other Path methods to parse a path

```
string path = @"C:\temp\subdir\file.txt";

Console.WriteLine(Path.GetDirectoryName(path)); // Displays C:\temp\subdir
Console.WriteLine(Path.GetExtension(path)); // Displays .txt
Console.WriteLine(Path.GetFileName(path)); // Displays file.txt
Console.WriteLine(Path.GetPathRoot(path)); // Displays C:\
```

The Path class can also help you when you need to temporarily store some data. You can use *GetRandomFileName* to create a random file or directory name. *GetTempPath* returns the location of the current user's temporary folder, and *GetTempFileName* creates a temporary file that you can then use to store some data in.

**EXAM TIP**

Never try to manually add strings together to form a path. Always use the Path class when combining multiple strings together to form a legal path.

# Working with streams

Of course, the most interesting thing you do with files is to create and read them. When working with files in the .NET Framework, it's important to know about the *Stream* class, which is a base class that is used in the .NET Framework for I/O operations. It's an abstraction of a sequence of bytes. For example, a file is, in essence, a sequence of bytes stored on your hard drive or a DVD, but a network socket also works with sequences of bytes just as an inter-process communication pipe. The Stream class provides a generic interface for all these types of input/output.

## The base *Stream* class

A stream has three fundamental operations:

- Reading
- Writing
- Seeking

*Reading* from a stream means that you get a series of bytes. You can then translate those into some meaningful data such as text or deserialize them to an object.

*Writing* is the reverse operation: You translate an object into a series of bytes and then send it off to the stream. It can then be sent across the network or persisted to a file on some other storage medium, such as a hard disk.

*Seeking* refers to the fact that some streams have the concept of a current position. You can query for the current position of a cursor and move it around. *Seeking* isn't supported by all streams. Files mostly support *seeking* (depending on the file type). But a *network socket* doesn't have the concept of a current position. You can't move forward or backward in a stream of bytes that is being sent to you over a network cable.

When working with the *File* and *FileInfo* classes, you will often deal with a *FileStream*, which supports the methods for reading and writing bytes in files, and for setting the current position by executing a seek operation. Listing 4-14 shows how to create a file by using a *FileStream*.

**LISTING 4-14** Create and use a *FileStream*

```
string path = @»c:\temp\test.dat»;

using (FileStream fileStream = File.Create(path))
{
    string myValue = "MyValue";
    byte[] data = Encoding.UTF8.GetBytes(myValue);
    fileStream.Write(data, 0, data.Length);
}
```

When writing to a FileStream, you can use the synchronous method *Write*, which expects a *byte array*. A simple *File* object does not store text directly. As already mentioned, a *Stream* works with bytes, so you need to convert your text into bytes.

> **MORE INFO**   **USING SYNCHRONOUS AND ASYNCHRONOUS I/O OPERATIONS**
>
> For more information about the difference between asynchronous and synchronous I/O operations, see the section "Implementing asynchronous I/O operations" later in this chapter.

## Encoding and decoding

The process of converting characters into bytes (and the other way around) is called *encoding* and *decoding*. The Unicode Consortium is responsible for maintaining a standard that describes how this should happen.

A *char*, which is the most basic character type, is equivalent to a single Unicode character taking 2 bytes in memory. A *string* is simply a sequence of chars. *System.Text.Encoding* is the class that helps you convert between bytes and strings.

The .NET Framework offers several encoding standards that you can use. *UTF-8* is one that suffices for general purpose use. It can represent all Unicode characters and it is used as the default encoding in a lot of the .NET Framework classes. Other encodings are *ASCII*, *BigEndianUnicode*, *Unicode*, *UTF32*, and *UTF7*.

To make this a little easier when working with text, the File class also supports a *CreateText* method that creates a file with an UTF-8 encoding for you. *CreateText* returns a *StreamWriter*, a class that inherits from *TextWriter* and enables you to directly write characters to a *Stream* with a particular encoding, as shown in Listing 4-15.

**LISTING 4-15** Using *File.CreateText* with a *StreamWriter*

```
string path = @»c:\temp\test.dat»;

using (StreamWriter streamWriter = File.CreateText(path))
{
    string myValue = «MyValue»;
    streamWriter.Write(myValue);
}
```

Of course, you will also want to read data from a file. You can do this by directly using a *FileStream* object, reading the bytes, and converting them back to a string with the correct encoding. Listing 4-16 shows how to read the bytes from a file and convert them to a string with UTF-8 encoding.

**LISTING 4-16** Opening a *FileStream* and decode the bytes to a string

```
using (FileStream fileStream = File.OpenRead(path))
{
    byte[] data = new byte[fileStream.Length];

    for (int index = 0; index < fileStream.Length; index++)
    {
        data[index] = (byte)fileStream.ReadByte();
    }
    Console.WriteLine(Encoding.UTF8.GetString(data)); // Displays: MyValue
}
```

If you know that you are parsing a text file, you can also use a *StreamReader* (as the opposite of the *StreamWriter*) to read a text file. The *StreamReader* uses a default encoding and returns the bytes to you as a string (see Listing 4-17).

**LISTING 4-17** Opening a TextFile and reading the content

```
using (StreamReader streamWriter = File.OpenText(path))
{
    Console.WriteLine(streamWriter.ReadLine()); // Displays: MyValue
}
```

## Using different types of streams together

Because of the way *Streams* are designed, you can couple multiple *Stream* objects together to perform a more complex operation. This principle is called the *decorator pattern*. For example, when you want to compress some data you can use a *GZipStream.*, which takes another *Stream* object in its constructor. The second *Stream* is used as the input or output for the compression algorithm. By giving it a *FileStream* object, you can easily compress some data (such as another file) and store it to disk. You can also use a *MemoryStream* as the input or output for a *GZipStream*. You can find the *GZipStream* in the *System.IO.Compression* namespace. Listing 4-18 creates some data, writes it to a file, and then compresses the file. As you can see, the compressed file is a lot smaller than the original file.

> **MORE INFO**   **DECORATOR PATTERN**
>
> For more information about the decorator pattern, see *http://en.wikipedia.org/wiki/Decorator_pattern*.

**LISTING 4-18** Compressing data with a *GZipStream*

```
string folder = @»c:\temp»;
string uncompressedFilePath = Path.Combine(folder, "uncompressed.dat");
string compressedFilePath = Path.Combine(folder, "compressed.gz");
byte[] dataToCompress = Enumerable.Repeat((byte)'a', 1024 * 1024).ToArray();

using (FileStream uncompressedFileStream = File.Create(uncompressedFilePath))
{
```

```
        uncompressedFileStream.Write(dataToCompress, 0, dataToCompress.Length);
}
using (FileStream compressedFileStream = File.Create(compressedFilePath))
{
    using (GZipStream compressionStream = new GZipStream(
                compressedFileStream, CompressionMode.Compress))
    {
        compressionStream.Write(dataToCompress, 0, dataToCompress.Length);
    }
}

FileInfo uncompressedFile = new FileInfo(uncompressedFilePath);
FileInfo compressedFile = new FileInfo(compressedFilePath);

Console.WriteLine(uncompressedFile.Length); // Displays 1048576
Console.WriteLine(compressedFile.Length); // Displays 1052
```

As Listing 4-18 shows, you can pass another *Stream* to the constructor of a *GZipStream*. When writing data to the *GZipStream*, it compresses the data and then immediately forwards it to the *FileStream*.

Another example where this can be used is with a *BufferedStream*. Hard drives are optimized for reading larger blocks of data. Reading a file byte by byte can be slower than reading big chunks of data and processing them byte by byte. Just as with the *GZipStream*, the *BufferedStream* takes another *Stream* in its constructor. The *BufferedStream* helps you with checking to determine whether it's possible to read or write larger chunks of data at once. Listing 4-19 shows how to write some data to a *BufferedStream* that wraps a *FileStream*.

**LISTING 4-19** Using a *BufferedStream*

```
string path = @»c:\temp\bufferedStream.txt»;

using (FileStream fileStream = File.Create(path))
{
    using (BufferedStream bufferedStream = new BufferedStream(fileStream))
    {
        using (StreamWriter streamWriter = new StreamWriter(bufferedStream))
        {
            streamWriter.WriteLine(«A line of text.»);
        }
    }
}
```

# The file system is not just for you

In this chapter, you have already seen on multiple occasions that a check is performed to determine whether a file exists on disk. You also created files, opened them, and moved some data in and out. But is it true that if *File.Exists* returns *false*, you can safely assume the file is not there when you want to create it?

No, because you are not the only user accessing the file system. While you are working with the file system, some other users are doing the exact same thing. Maybe they remove the folder you wanted to use to create a new file. Or they suddenly change the permissions on a file so you can't access it any more.

Normally, when dealing with a situation in which multiple users access shared resources, we start using a locking mechanism to synchronize resource usage. C# has a locking mechanism that you can use to synchronize access to code when multiple threads are involved. This ensures that a certain piece of code cannot be executed simultaneously at the same moment in time.

> **MORE INFO** LOCKING
>
> For more infomation on how to synchronize access to resources by using a locking mecha-nism, see Chapter 1, "Manage program flow."

However, the file system does not have these locking mechanisms. It is a multithreaded system, but without any of the safety regulations that you want to see.

Take the code in Listing 4-20, which determines whether a file exists and then reads all text in it.

**LISTING 4-20** Depending on *File.Exists* when reading file content

```
private static string ReadAllText()
{
    string path = @"C:\temp\test.txt";

    if (File.Exists(path))
    {
        return File.ReadAllText(path);
    }
    return string.Empty;
}
```

Another user might remove the file between the call to *Exists* and *ReadAllText*, which would cause an exception to be thrown. You can, however, anticipate the exceptions that can be thrown and make sure that your application knows how to deal with them. See Listing 4-21.

**LISTING 4-21** Using exception handling when opening a file

```
string path = @"C:\temp\test.txt";

try
{
    return File.ReadAllText(path);
}
catch (DirectoryNotFoundException) { }
catch (FileNotFoundException) { }

return string.Empty;
```

When working with the file system, you need to remind yourself that exceptions can and will occur. Good exception handling is important for a robust application that works with files.

> **MORE INFO** **EXCEPTION HANDLING**
>
> For more information on how to handle exceptions and create a robust application, see Chapter 1.

# Communicating over the network

The .NET Framework has support for enabling your applications to communicate across a network. The *System.Net* namespace defines a large number of classes that hide the complexity of executing network operations while providing an easy-to-use interface.

Of all those members, the ones that you will probably use the most are *WebRequest* and *WebResponse*. These classes are abstract base classes that offer support for communicating over a network. Specific implementations define the protocol to use for communication. For example, you can use *HttpWebRequest* and *HttpWebResponse* when using the HTTP protocol.

## *WebRequest* and *WebResponse*

*WebRequest* and *WebResponse* form a pair of classes that you can use together to send a request for information and then receive the response with the data you requested.

A *WebRequest* is created by using a static *Create* method on the *WebRequest* class. The *Create* method inspects the address that you pass to it and then selects the correct protocol implementation. If you would pass the address *http://www.microsoft.com* to it, it would see that you are working with the HTTP protocol and it would return an *HttpWebRequest*. After creating the correct *WebRequest*, you can set other properties such as authentication or caching instructions.

When you are finished composing your request, you call the *GetResponse* method to execute the request and retrieve the response (see Listing 4-22).

**LISTING 4-22** Executing a web request

```
WebRequest request = WebRequest.Create("http://www.microsoft.com");
WebResponse response = request.GetResponse();

StreamReader responseStream = new StreamReader(response.GetResponseStream());
string responseText = responseStream.ReadToEnd();

Console.WriteLine(responseText); // Displays the HTML of the website

response.Close();
```

# Implementing asynchronous I/O operations

When working with I/O, you often have to wait for an operation to finish. Maybe you have to wait before a file is read from your hard drive or before a network request returns from somewhere in the world.

All the code that you've seen until now in this chapter is called *synchronous* code. The code is executed line by line and waits till each method is finished. An innocent-looking line of code can suddenly take a whole lot of time while you are waiting for it to finish. This can have a severe impact on the user experience and the scalability of your application.

When you create a desktop application such as a Windows Presentation Foundation (WPF), WinForm, or Windows Store application, your application has one main thread that is responsible for updating the user interface. This thread is responsible for processing all user activity. If this thread is busy with something else, the application appears to be unresponsive. Most users will then try to close such an application because they think something is wrong. It's important to execute long-running operations on another thread, which ensures that your application stays responsive while it's executing the long-running operation in the background.

With a server application, things are a little different. When the user hits your ASP.NET web server, he has to wait before the request is finished. If the page takes a long time to load, the user perceives this as poor performance. What's happening on the server is that a thread is picking up the request and starts creating the response for the user. The server starts collecting data, producing HTML, and performing all kinds of other actions. A server has a limited number of threads for handling incoming requests. When a thread is waiting for I/O to happen, it can't work on any other requests. When all threads are busy, and a new request comes in, the new request is queued. This issue is called "thread pool starvation." All threads are waiting for some I/O to happen with a CPU load of 0%, and the response times for new requests will go through the roof.

This is where async operations can be useful. When your application waits for some external response that's not CPU-bound, you can make your code work asynchronously to remain responsive and to free the main thread for other requests.

Async code was already possible before C#5. You could use the *Event-based Asynchronous Programming* pattern to wire up your code to continue processing when an external request finishes. However, writing asynchronous code completely by hand and getting all the small details right is difficult, especially when you need exception handling. It's no trivial task to make sure that your code handles all situations well.

## Async/await

C#5 introduced the new *async/await* keywords. Async/await signal to the compiler that you want to execute some asynchronous code. The compiler then is responsible for turning your "synchronous-looking" code into a state machine that handles all possible situations.

I/O is one area of the .NET Framework that benefits greatly from the new support for *async/await*. When you look through the I/O methods in this chapter, you will see many methods have an async equivalent that returns *Task* or *Task<T>*.

It's important to know that the static *File* class does not support real asynchronous I/O. If you call asynchronous methods, it fakes this by using another thread from the thread pool to work with the file. For real async I/O, you need to use the *FileStream* object and pass a true value for the *useAsync* parameter.

Listing 4-23 shows an example of how to write asynchronously to a file. The *Write* method is replaced by *WriteAsync*, the method is marked with the *async* modifier to signal to the compiler that you want some help on transforming your code, and finally you use the *await* keyword on the returned task.

LISTING 4-23 Writing asynchronously to a file

```
public  async Task CreateAndWriteAsyncToFile()
{
    using (FileStream stream = new FileStream("test.dat", FileMode.Create,
        FileAccess.Write, FileShare.None, 4096, true))
    {
        byte[] data = new byte[100000];
        new Random().NextBytes(data);

        await stream.WriteAsync(data, 0, data.Length);
    }
}
```

The returned *Task* object represents some ongoing work by encapsulating the state of the asynchronous operation. Eventually, the *Task* object returns the result of the operation or exceptions that were asynchronously raised.

In the case of Listing 4-23, the method doesn't have any value that's returned to the caller. That's why *WriteAsync* returns a regular *Task* object. When a method does have a return value, it returns *Task<T>*, where *T* is the type of the value that is returned.

In Listing 4-24, the *GetStringAsync* method is used. This method returns *Task<string>*, which means that eventually when the process is finished, a string value is available (or an exception).

LISTING 4-24 Executing an asynchronous HTTP request

```
public async Task ReadAsyncHttpRequest()
{
    HttpClient client = new HttpClient();
    string result = await client.GetStringAsync("http://www.microsoft.com");
}
```

Whenever the .NET Framework offers an async equivalent of a synchronous method, it is best to use it. It creates a better user experience and a more scalable application. However, when you are working on a performance-critical application, it pays to know what the compiler does for you. If you are uncertain, use a profiler to actually measure the difference so you can make an informed decision.

## Running I/O operations in parallel

Real asynchronous I/O makes sure that your thread can do other work until the operating system notifies your application that the I/O is ready. Multiple async I/O operations can still be executed one after the other.

When you look at Listing 4-25, you can see that multiple awaits are used in one method. With the current code, each web request starts when the previous one is finished. The thread won't be blocked while running these requests, but the amount of time the method takes is the sum of the three web requests.

**LISTING 4-25** Executing multiple awaits

```
public async Task ExecuteMultipleRequests()
{
    HttpClient client = new HttpClient();

    string microsoft= await client.GetStringAsync("http://www.microsoft.com");
    string msdn = await client.GetStringAsync("http://msdn.microsoft.com");
    string blogs = await client.GetStringAsync("http://blogs.msdn.com/");
}
```

You can also write code that will execute those operations in *parallel*. If you would execute those requests in parallel, you would only have to wait as long as the longest request takes (the other two will already be finished). You can do this by using the static method *Task.WhenAll* (see Listing 4-26). As soon as you call *GetStringAsync*, the async operation gets started. However, you don't immediately wait for the result. Instead, you let all three requests start and then you wait for them to finish. Now, all three operations run parallel, which can save you a lot of time.

**LISTING 4-26** Executing multiple requests in parallel

```
public async Task ExecuteMultipleRequestsInParallel()
{
    HttpClient client = new HttpClient();

    Task microsoft = client.GetStringAsync("http://www.microsoft.com");
    Task msdn =  client.GetStringAsync("http://msdn.microsoft.com");
    Task blogs = client.GetStringAsync("http://blogs.msdn.com/");

    await Task.WhenAll(microsoft, msdn, blogs);
}
```

Using *Tasks* and *async/await* makes using asynchronous code a lot easier. Whenever possible, determine whether an operation is taking a long time and is not CPU-bound. If true or likely to be true, running it asynchronously is a good idea.

## Objective summary

- You can work with drives by using *Drive* and *DriveInfo*.

- For folders, you can use *Directory* and *DirectoryInfo*.

- *File* and *FileInfo* offer methods to work with files.

- The static *Path* class can help you in creating and parsing file paths.

- *Streams* are an abstract way of working with a series of bytes.

- There are many *Stream* implementations for dealing with files, network operations, and any other types of I/O.

- Remember that the file system can be accessed and changed by multiple users at the same time. You need to keep this in mind when creating reliable applications.

- When performing network requests, you can use the *WebRequest* and *WebResponse* classes from the *System.Net* namespace.

- Asynchronous I/O can help you create a better user experience and a more scalable application.

## Objective review

Answer the following questions to test your knowledge of the information in this objective. You can find the answers to these questions and explanations of why each answer choice is correct or incorrect in the "Answers" section at the end of this chapter.

1. You are creating a new file to store some log data. Each time a new log entry is necessary, you write a string to the file. Which method do you use?

   A. File.CreateText

   B. FileInfo.Create

   C. File.Create

   D. File.AppendText

2. You have built a complex calculation algorithm. It takes quite some time to complete and you want to make sure that your application remains responsive. What do you do?

   A. Use async/await.

   B. Run the code synchronously.

   C. Use Task.Run.

   D. Use a BackgroundWorker.

3. You are writing an application that will be deployed to Western countries. It outputs user activity to a text file. Which encoding should you use?

   A. UTF-8

   B. UTF-7

   C. ASCII

   D. UTF-32

# Objective 4.2: Consume data

Data management is one of the most important aspects of an application. Imagine that you can create only applications that store their data in memory. As soon as the user quits, all data is lost, and subsequent launches require reentering of all necessary data. Of course, this would be an impossible situation to work with, which is why the .NET Framework helps you store your data in a persistent way. This can be done in a database by directly using *ADO.NET* or the *Entity Framework*. You can also store and request data from an external web service and retrieve the response in *JavaScript Object Notation* (JSON) or *Extensible Markup Language* (XML). The .NET Framework helps you execute these requests and parse the returned data.

> **This objective covers how to:**
> - Retrieve and update data in a database.
> - Consume JSON and XML.
> - Access web services.

# Working with a database

In the .NET Framework, you can find various types of data-related classes in the *System.Data.dll*. The data access code in the .NET Framework is under the umbrella of *ADO.NET, which* consists of two conceptual parts: connected and disconnected data.

When using the connected parts of *ADO.NET*, you explicitly connect to a database and use that as the underlying data store. You execute queries by using *Structured Query Language* (SQL) to create, read, update, and delete data (commonly known as *CRUD* operations). Those queries are used by the *ADO.NET* infrastructure and forwarded to your database of choice. When working in the connected fashion, you use, among others, *Connection* objects, *Command* objects, and *DataReader* objects.

In the disconnected world, you work with *DataSets* and *DataTables* that mimic the structure of a relational database in memory. You can use them to work with offline data and later sync them to a database when you are online. A *DataSet* that is created after executing a query against a connected database can then be manipulated in memory, and the changes can be sent back to the data store by using a *DataAdapter*.

> **MORE INFO**  **DISCONNECTED DATA**
>
> For more information on working with data in a disconnected fashion, see *http://msdn. microsoft.com/en-us/library/zb0sdh0b.aspx.*

## Providers

In the world around you, there are many different types of databases. You can use Microsoft SQL Server, Oracle, and MySQL, among others. The .NET Framework offers features for working with data in all these types of databases in a standard way.

A .NET Framework *data provider* is used for connecting to a database, executing commands, and working the resulting data. The .NET Framework data providers provide a thin layer that integrates with a specific database, so you can create programs that can work with different types of databases without having to change any code.

## Connecting to a database

When you are working with data in a database, the first step you have to take is create a *connection* to the specific database. A connection is established by using a *connection string*, which contains all the information that the .NET Framework needs to know: the type of database, the location of the database, and how to authenticate against the database.

Connections in the .NET Framework all inherit from the *DbConnection* base class. The *SqlConnection* can be used to establish a connection to a Microsoft SQL Server database. Because the *DbConnection* class uses a real, unmanaged database connection, it's important to make sure that you properly close the connection when you're finished with it. Because of this, the *DbConnection* class implements *IDisposable*, so you can deterministically close the connection and free any associated unmanaged objects. As discussed in Chapter 2, a using clause will call the *DbConnections* Dispose method, which automatically closes the connection. Listing 4-27 shows how to do this.

**LISTING 4-27** A *SqlConnection* with a using statement to automatically close it

```
using (SqlConnection connection = new SqlConnection(connectionString))
{
    connection.Open();
    // Execute operations against the database
} // Connection is automatically closed.
```

A typical connection string might look like the following example:

```
"Persist Security Info=False;Integrated Security=true;Initial Catalog=Northwind;server=(
local)"
```

This connection string describes where the database is located, how it's named, and some details about how to authenticate against the database. The basic format of a connection string is a series of key/value pairs connected by an equal sign (=), all separated by semicolons (;).

> **MORE INFO  CONNECTION STRINGS**
>
> If you are looking for specific information for creating your own connection string, you can look at *http://www.connectionstrings.com/*. Here you can find examples of connection strings for different providers with different settings.

When you need to build a connection string dynamically, you can use one of the several *DbConnectionStringBuilder* classes. For example, you can use *OracleConnectionStringBuilder* to build a connection string for an Oracle database and *SqlConnectionStringBuilder* for a Microsoft SQL Server database. Listing 4-28 shows how to use the *SqlConnectionStringBuilder* to create a new connection string programmatically.

**LISTING 4-28** Creating a connection string with *SqlConnectionStringBuilder*

```
var sqlConnectionStringBuilder = new SqlConnectionStringBuilder();

sqlConnectionStringBuilder.DataSource = @"(localdb)\v11.0";
sqlConnectionStringBuilder.InitialCatalog = "ProgrammingInCSharp";

string connectionString = sqlConnectionStringBuilder.ToString();
```

Hard-coding a connection string is usually not the best way to configure an application. When you deploy an application to a testing, staging, or production environment, the connection string often has to change, and most of the time this is done by an IT professional who doesn't have (and doesn't want to have!) any programming experience.

Because of this, you can easily store connection strings in an outside configuration file. Depending on the type of application, you use the *app.config* or *web.config* file. These files can be used to store all kinds of configuration settings for an application. You can also use other configuration files, which you reference from these files.

An example of a connection string in the app.config file of an application is shown in Listing 4-29.

**LISTING 4-29** Putting a connection string in the *app.config* file

```xml
<?xml version="1.0" encoding="utf-8" ?>
<configuration>
    <connectionStrings>
        <add name="ProgrammingInCSharpConnection"
     providerName="System.Data.SqlClient"
     connectionString="Data Source=(localdb)\v11.0;Initial Catalog=ProgrammingInCSharp;"
/>
    </connectionStrings>
</configuration>
```

If you want to use the connection string in your application, you can use the *ConfigurationManager.ConnectionStrings* property from the *System.Configuration.dll*. You can access connection strings both by index and by name. Listing 4-30 shows how to access a connection string by name and use it to open a database connection.

**LISTING 4-30** Using a connection string from an external configuration file

```csharp
string connectionString = ConfigurationManager.
            ConnectionStrings["ProgrammingInCSharpConnection"].ConnectionString;

using (SqlConnection connection = new SqlConnection(connectionString))
{
    connection.Open();
}
```

> **MORE INFO**  **CONNECTION STRINGS FOR DIFFERENT CONFIGURATIONS**
>
> When you want to have different connection strings for different configurations (such as staging, testing, and production) you can use a special transformation syntax that changes your configuration file depending on the configuration you want to build. For more information see *http://msdn.microsoft.com/en-us/library/dd465326.aspx*.

Connecting to a database is a time-consuming operation. Having a connection open for too long is also a problem because it can lead to other users not being able to connect. To minimize the costs of repeatedly opening and closing connections, ADO.NET applies an optimization that's called *connection pooling*.

When using SQL Server, a pool of connections is maintained by your application. When a new connection is requested, the .NET Framework checks to see whether there is an open connection in the pool. If there is one, it doesn't have to open a new connection and do all the initial setup steps. By default, connection pooling is enabled, which can give you a huge performance improvement.

## Reading data

After the connection is established, you can start sending queries to the database. Queries are constructed using SQL, which is a special syntax optimized for working with databases.

> **MORE INFO** SQL
>
> For more information on SQL, see *http://msdn.microsoft.com/en-us/library/bb510741.aspx.*

Let's say you are working with a database table similar to the one in Table 4-2.

**TABLE 4-2** Example table structure

| Column name | Data type | Nullable |
| --- | --- | --- |
| id | int, Primary Key | False |
| FirstName | varchar(30) | False |
| MiddleName | varchar(30) | True |
| LastName | varchar(30) | False |

You can create this table with the SQL from Listing 4-31.

**LISTING 4-31** Using SQL script to create a table

```
CREATE TABLE dbo.People
(
    [id]        INT         NOT NULL IDENTITY,
    [FirstName] VARCHAR(30) NOT NULL,
    [MiddleName] VARCHAR(30) NULL,
    [LastName]  VARCHAR(30) NOT NULL
);
```

If you want to select a couple of rows from this table, you first need to define a SQL statement. A SQL query can then be executed by using a *SqlCommand* object. A *SqlCommand* can return a *SqlDataReader* that keeps track of where you are in the result set. It gives you access to each row and the columns it contains.

Listing 4-32 shows how you can use this to loop through the rows in the *People* table and display the results. ADO.NET also supports the new *async/await* keywords so you can execute queries asynchronously.

**LISTING 4-32** Executing a SQL select command

```
public async Task SelectDataFromTable()
{
    string connectionString = ConfigurationManager.
                ConnectionStrings["ProgrammingInCSharpConnection"].ConnectionString;
```

```
using (SqlConnection connection = new SqlConnection(connectionString))
{
    SqlCommand command = new SqlCommand("SELECT * FROM People", connection);
    await connection.OpenAsync();

    SqlDataReader dataReader = await command.ExecuteReaderAsync();

    while (await dataReader.ReadAsync())
    {
        string formatStringWithMiddleName = "Person ({0}) is named {1} {2} {3}";
        string formatStringWithoutMiddleName = "Person ({0}) is named {1} {3}";

        if ((dataReader["middlename"] == null))
        {
            Console.WriteLine(formatStringWithoutMiddleName,
                dataReader["id"],
                dataReader["firstname"],
                dataReader["lastname"]);
        }
        else
        {
            Console.WriteLine(formatStringWithMiddleName,
                dataReader["id"],
                dataReader["firstname"],
                dataReader["middlename"],
                dataReader["lastname"]);
        }
    }
    dataReader.Close();
}
}
```

A *SqlDataReader* is a forward-only stream of rows. You can't go back while you're reading; only forward. You can access the columns of a resulting row both by index and by name. The *SqlDataReader* offers a couple of methods that can map the value of a column to the corresponding *CLR* type. For example, you can call methods like *GetInt32(int index)*, *GetGuid(int index)*, *GetString(int index)*, and so on.

When executing a query, you can also batch multiple SQL statements together. The *SqlDataReader* returned contains multiple result sets. You can advance to the next result set by calling *NextResult* or *NextResultAsync* on your *SqlDataReader* object. Listing 4-33 shows how to execute a query that runs two result sets.

LISTING 4-33 Executing a SQL query with multiple result sets

```
public async Task SelectMultipleResultSets()
{
    string connectionString = ConfigurationManager.
        ConnectionStrings["ProgrammingInCSharpConnection"].ConnectionString;

    using (SqlConnection connection = new SqlConnection(connectionString))
    {
        SqlCommand command = new SqlCommand("SELECT * FROM People;
            SELECT TOP 1 * FROM People ORDER BY LastName", connection);
```

```
            await connection.OpenAsync();
            SqlDataReader dataReader = await command.ExecuteReaderAsync();
            await ReadQueryResults(dataReader);
            await dataReader.NextResultAsync(); // Move to the next result set
            await ReadQueryResults(dataReader);
        dataReader.Close();
    }
}
private static async Task ReadQueryResults(SqlDataReader dataReader)
{
    while (await dataReader.ReadAsync())
    {
        string formatStringWithMiddleName = "Person ({0}) is named {1} {2} {3}";
        string formatStringWithoutMiddleName = "Person ({0}) is named {1} {3}";
        if ((dataReader["middlename"] == null))
        {
            Console.WriteLine(formatStringWithoutMiddleName,
                dataReader["id"],
                dataReader["firstname"],
                dataReader["lastname"]);
        }
        else
        {
            Console.WriteLine(formatStringWithMiddleName,
                dataReader["id"],
                dataReader["firstname"],
                dataReader["middlename"],
                dataReader["lastname"]);
        }
    }
}
```

## Updating data

Besides selecting data and getting it to the client, you can also update data in the database. You can create new records, update existing ones, or completely remove a record.

You can do it all by using a connection and a command object. But instead of getting back a reader with the resulting rows, you get an integer value back that shows how many rows are affected by your last query. This means that if you execute a stored procedure or chain multiple SQL statements together you will only get the number of records affected by the last query, not across all queries in your procedure. By checking the result you can determine if the correct amount of rows was affected. You use the *ExecuteNonQuery* or *ExecuteNonQuery-Async* method to do this, as shown in Listing 4-34.

**LISTING 4-34** Updating rows with *ExecuteNonQuery*

```
public async Task UpdateRows()
{
    string connectionString = ConfigurationManager.
        ConnectionStrings["ProgrammingInCSharpConnection"].ConnectionString;
```

```
    using (SqlConnection connection = new SqlConnection(connectionString))
    {
        SqlCommand command = new SqlCommand(
            "UPDATE People SET FirstName='John'",
            connection);

        await connection.OpenAsync();
        int numberOfUpdatedRows = await command.ExecuteNonQueryAsync();
        Console.WriteLine("Updated {0} rows", numberOfUpdatedRows);
    }
}
```

## Using parameters

Until now, you have seen only queries that were already completely constructed at compile time. In the real world, however, you often need to use dynamic values when executing a query.

Because a SQL query is nothing more than a simple string, you might be tempted to concatenate multiple strings together to create your query. However, be aware that this is a huge security risk. For example, let's say that you have a form in which people can fill in their names that you will insert into the People table. Your query will look something like this:

```
INSERT INTO People VALUES('John', 'Doe', null)
```

Now, you could read the values that a user enters and then manually construct this string. But what would happen if a user enters the following for a middle name?

```
'); DELETE FROM People; --
```

After executing this query, all data in your People table would be deleted. This security hole is known as SQL injection.

> **MORE INFO  SQL INJECTION**
>
> For more information on SQL injection, see *http://msdn.microsoft.com/en-us/library/ ms161953(v=sql.105).aspx.*

To guard against SQL injection, you should never directly use user input in your SQL strings. Instead of manually building the correct SQL query, you can use parameterized SQL statements (see Listing 4-35).

**LISTING 4-35** Inserting values with a parameterized query

```
public async Task InsertRowWithParameterizedQuery()
{
    string connectionString = ConfigurationManager.
        ConnectionStrings["ProgrammingInCSharpConnection"].ConnectionString;

    using (SqlConnection connection = new SqlConnection(connectionString))
    {
        SqlCommand command = new SqlCommand(
```

```
            "INSERT INTO People([FirstName], [LastName], [MiddleName]) VALUES(@
firstName, @lastName, @middleName)",
            connection);
        await connection.OpenAsync();

        command.Parameters.AddWithValue("@firstName", "John");
        command.Parameters.AddWithValue("@lastName", "Doe");
        command.Parameters.AddWithValue("@middleName", "Little");

        int numberOfInsertedRows = await command.ExecuteNonQueryAsync();
        Console.WriteLine("Inserted {0} rows", numberOfInsertedRows);
    }
}
```

These parameterized queries can be used when running select, update, insert, and delete queries. Besides being much more secure, they also offer better performance. Because the database gets a more generic query, it can more easily find a precompiled execution plan to execute your query.

> **MORE INFO   EXECUTION PLANS**
>
> For more information about execution plans, see *http://msdn.microsoft.com/en-us/library/ms175580.aspx.*

## Using transactions

When working with a database, things can go wrong. Maybe you are executing multiple queries that should be grouped together. If the last one fails, the previous ones are already executed, and suddenly your data can go corrupt.

Because of this, .NET Framework helps you with *transactions*. A transaction has four key properties that are referred to as ACID:

- **Atomicity**   All operations are grouped together. If one fails, they all fail.
- **Consistency**   Transactions bring the database from one valid state to another.
- **Isolation**   Transactions can operate independently of each other. Multiple concurrent transactions won't influence each other. It will be as if they were executed serially.
- **Durability**   The result of a committed transaction is always stored permanently, even if the database crashes immediately thereafter.

When working with transactions, it's easiest to use the *TransactionScope* class. *Transaction-Scope* offers an easy way to work with transactions without requiring you to interact with the transaction itself (see Listing 4-36).

**LISTING 4-36** Using a *TransactionScope*

```
string connectionString = ConfigurationManager.
    ConnectionStrings["ProgrammingInCSharpConnection"].ConnectionString;
```

```
using (TransactionScope transactionScope = new TransactionScope())
{
    using (SqlConnection connection = new SqlConnection(connectionString))
    {
        connection.Open();

        SqlCommand command1 = new SqlCommand(
            "INSERT INTO People ([FirstName], [LastName], [MiddleInitial])
VALUES('John', 'Doe', null)",
            connection);
        SqlCommand command2 = new SqlCommand(
            "INSERT INTO People ([FirstName], [LastName], [MiddleInitial])
VALUES('Jane', 'Doe', null)",
            connection);

        command1.ExecuteNonQuery();
        command2.ExecuteNonQuery();
    }
    transactionScope.Complete();
}
```

If an exception occurs inside the TransactionScope, the whole transaction is rolled back. If nothing goes wrong, you use *TransactionScope.Complete* to complete the transaction. It's important to use the *TransactionScope* inside a using statement so that it is automatically disposed of when it's no longer necessary.

A *TransactionScope* can also be constructed by passing a *TransactionScopeOption* enum to it. By using this enum, you can define the behavior of the *TransactionScope*.

A *TransactionScope* can be constructed with three options:

- **Required** Join the ambient transaction or create a new one if it doesn't exist. If there is an ambient transaction, that transaction controls when the transaction is completed. This is the default scope.
- **RequiresNew** Start a new transaction.
- **Suppress** Don't take part in any transaction.

When using *TransactionScope*, the .NET Framework automatically manages the transaction for you. If your transaction uses nested connections, multiple databases, or multiple resource types, your transaction is promoted to a *distributed transaction*. The promotion to a distributed transaction can have a huge performance hit if it's not necessary. If possible, try to avoid distributed transactions. If you need them, .NET Framework manages it for you.

## Using an Object Relational Mapper (ORM)

One of the problems with a relational database is that it's inherently different from the object-oriented structure that you want to use in your applications. You use objects that have relationship to other objects or that inherit from them. The database uses tables with columns and foreign keys to other tables. This is what's called the *object-relational impedance mismatch*.

You can create complex applications by manually writing your SQL queries and executing them against the database. But when your application grows, and you want to use an object-oriented design, you start running into problems. Of course, you can map the results of your query to objects and create queries from the changes to your objects, but this is a difficult task. Even if you like the challenge, this is not something that will add value for your customers.

This is where Object Relational Mapping (ORM) software comes into play. One such ORM is Microsoft's open source Entity Framework, which lessens the burden of the tedious work of mapping your objects, constructing queries, and keeping track of all the changes.

The Entity Framework can be used with a few different approaches:

- **Database First** You want to map an existing database to your object structure.
- **Model First** You want to design your object model with a graphical designer and then create a database that supports it.
- **Code First** You create your object model in code and then generate a database that can store your data.

Using an ORM is a compromise between performance and development speed. You can imagine how the Entity Framework uses reflection to map from SQL query results to objects, which is always slower than doing it by hand. However, using the Entity Framework will increase your development speed immensely. It enables you to create your application quickly by prioritizing the parts of it that need better performance. The Entity Framework is typically good enough for most situations. If not, you can add a simple stored procedure for the queries that are problematic.

Imagine you have a *Person* class, such as the one shown in Listing 4-37.

LISTING 4-37 A simple *Person* class

```
public class Person
{
    public int Id { get; set; }
    public string Name { get; set; }
}
```

If you want to use Code First to map this entity to a database, you just need to inherit from *DbContext* (a base class that offers access to the Entity Framework) with your own custom context and define the sets of entities you want to use. If necessary, you can then modify the custom mapping to support complex types, inheritance, or other mapping scenarios. Listing 4-38 shows how this can work in a simple application.

LISTING 4-38 Using Code First to map a class to the database

```
public class PeopleContext : DbContext
{
    public IDbSet<Person> People { get; set; }
}

using (PeopleContext ctx = new PeopleContext())
{
```

```
    ctx.People.Add(new Person() { Id = 1, Name = "John Doe" });
    ctx.SaveChanges();
}

using (PeopleContext ctx = new PeopleContext())
{
    Person person = ctx.People.SingleOrDefault(p => p.Id == 1);
    Console.WriteLine(person.Name);
}
```

The default conventions for the Entity Framework immediately notice that there should be one table for storing people. The *id* property is used as primary key, and the *Name* property is mapped to another column. *DbContext* keeps track of all changes you make to your entities and generates update queries for you. The Entity Framework is growing fast and becomes better with each release. If you use a database in your application, using the Entity Framework properly can really improve your development efforts.

> **MORE INFO**  **ENTITY FRAMEWORK**
>
> For more information on the Entity Framework, see *http://msdn.microsoft.com/en-us/data/ef.aspx*.

# Using web services

Another option beyond storing data in a relational database or a file is to use an external service to store data. It can be a web service that you created or it can come from a third party.

With such services, you can exchange data between applications in a loosely coupled way. You only need to know the service address and how to make a request to that service. How the service gets its data is completely hidden from you, and you generally don't have to worry about it.

The .NET Framework has solid support for creating web services. You can build highly flexible web services by using another Microsoft technology called the Windows Communication Foundation (WCF).

## Creating a WCF service

In the past, you had many options when building a service. You could use .NET Remoting, XML Web Services (including SOAP-based services), or Microsoft Message Queues, all with their own options and features. WCF replaces all these technologies with a single, unified, extendable programming model that encompasses the technologies of the past.

A WCF service looks like a regular class. It can have methods with return types, constructors, and other members. The only difference with a regular class are the attributes on the class itself and on its methods that inform the .NET Framework you want to expose your class as a service.

Listing 4-39 shows an example of a simple WCF service. As you can see, the class is decorated with the *ServiceContract* attribute and the method with an *OperationContract* attribute.

**LISTING 4-39** A simple WCF web service

```
[ServiceContract]
public class MyService
{
    [OperationContract]
    public string DoWork(string left, string right)
    {
        return left + right;
    }
}
```

You can create this service by creating a new ASP.NET project and adding a WCF service to it. A WCF service consists of both an *.svc* file and a code-behind file that contains the actual service code. The .svc file contains instructions for how to host your service in Internet Information Services (IIS), so you can put your .svc file with the associated code file in a website hosted by IIS to make it available to your users.

The code file doesn't contain any information about how the service can be called—it doesn't specify an address or a protocol. This is where WCF is superior to previous technologies because it uses the so called ABC model:

- Address
- Binding
- Contract

When building a WCF service, you usually start with the *contract*, which defines which operations your service exposes. The contract is what the outside world expects of your service. After specifying your *contract*, you specify the *bindings*. A binding configures the protocols and transports that can be used to call your service. Maybe your service can be used over HTTP, HTTPS, and a named-pipe connection. You next need to specify the *address*, which is the endpoint that your service exposes. Doing this ensures that there is a physical network address that can be used to call your service with a specific binding.

When working with a previously created WCF service, you can use Visual Studio to create a *service reference* for you. It creates a proxy class in your client project that enables you to access the external service. You can see an example of a proxy class for the *MyService* service in Listing 4-40.

**LISTING 4-40** A generated WCF proxy client

```
namespace Service.Client.ExternalService
{
    [System.CodeDom.Compiler.GeneratedCodeAttribute(«System.ServiceModel», «4.0.0.0»)]
    [System.ServiceModel.ServiceContractAttribute(
        ConfigurationName = «ExternalService.MyService»)]

    public interface MyService
    {
        [System.ServiceModel.OperationContractAttribute(
            Action = "http://tempuri.org/MyService/DoWork",
```

```
            ReplyAction = «http://tempuri.org/MyService/DoWorkResponse»)]
        string DoWork(string left, string right);

        [System.ServiceModel.OperationContractAttribute(
            Action = "http://tempuri.org/MyService/DoWork",
            ReplyAction = «http://tempuri.org/MyService/DoWorkResponse»)]
        System.Threading.Tasks.Task<string> DoWorkAsync(string left, string right);
}

[System.CodeDom.Compiler.GeneratedCodeAttribute(«System.ServiceModel», «4.0.0.0»)]
public interface MyServiceChannel : Service.Client.ExternalService.MyService,
                                    System.ServiceModel.IClientChannel
{ }

[System.Diagnostics.DebuggerStepThroughAttribute()]
[System.CodeDom.Compiler.GeneratedCodeAttribute(«System.ServiceModel», «4.0.0.0»)]
public partial class MyServiceClient :
        System.ServiceModel.ClientBase<Service.Client.ExternalService.MyService>,
        Service.Client.ExternalService.MyService
{
    public MyServiceClient()
    { }

     public MyServiceClient(string endpointConfigurationName) :
        base(endpointConfigurationName)
    { }

    public MyServiceClient(string endpointConfigurationName, string remoteAddress) :
        base(endpointConfigurationName, remoteAddress)
    { }

     public MyServiceClient(string endpointConfigurationName,
        System.ServiceModel.EndpointAddress remoteAddress) :
            base(endpointConfigurationName, remoteAddress)
    { }

    public MyServiceClient(System.ServiceModel.Channels.Binding binding,
        System.ServiceModel.EndpointAddress remoteAddress) :
        base(binding, remoteAddress)
    { }

    public string DoWork(string left, string right)
    {
        return base.Channel.DoWork(left, right);
    }

    public System.Threading.Tasks.Task<string> DoWorkAsync(
                        string left,
                        string right)
    {
        return base.Channel.DoWorkAsync(left, right);
    }
}
}
```

You can use this client just like every regular class. The only difference is that behind the scenes, the proxy client uses the configuration settings from the *app.config* file to look for the *ABC* settings. Listing 4-41 shows how to construct the client and call a method on it.

**LISTING 4-41** Using a WCF proxy client

```
ExternalService.MyServiceClient client = new ExternalService.MyServiceClient();
string result = client.DoWork("John", "Doe");
Console.WriteLine(result); // Displays JohnDoe
```

By using a WCF service with a client proxy, the result from the *DoWork* method is automatically converted to a string. However, when working with other services, the result you get back might be in an entirely different format.

> **MORE INFO   WCF**
>
> If you want to know more about WCF and how you can use it in a variety of scenarios, see
> *http://msdn.microsoft.com/en-us/library/ms731082.aspx.*

# Consuming XML

Extensible Markup Language (XML) is a markup language that consists of a set of rules that define how a document should be formatted. The advantage of XML is that it can be read by both humans and computer programs. It was originally created to be the one and only solution for communication over the Internet between different applications.

Listing 4-42 shows an example XML document.

**LISTING 4-42** XML file

```
<?xml version="1.0" encoding="utf-8" ?>
<people>
  <person firstName="John" lastName="Doe">
    <contactdetails>
      <emailaddress>john@unknown.com</emailaddress>
    </contactdetails>
  </person>
  <person firstName="Jane" lastName="Doe">
    <contactdetails>
      <emailaddress>jane@unknown.com</emailaddress>
      <phonenumber>001122334455</phonenumber>
    </contactdetails>
  </person>
</people>
```

As you can see, an XML document consists of several elements. First, there is an optional line that specifies you are looking at XML. This line is called the *prolog*. It tells something about the encoding that is used and can contain other metadata.

After the prolog comes the content. There should be a single root element that contains the rest of the information. This way, you create a hierarchical tree that defines the relationship between all elements.

Underneath the root element are other child elements. A child element can be a single element that describes some characteristic or several elements that group other elements. Elements can contain attributes, which are name-value pairs associated with an element. An XML document can also contain comments and special processing instructions. The special processing instructions are often contained in a Document Type Definition (DTD) file that is stored externally to the XML and referenced in the prolog.

> **MORE INFO** XML
>
> For more information on XML and its many capabilities, see *http://msdn.microsoft.com/en-us/library/ms256177.aspx*.

## XML in the .NET Framework

Parsing an XML file as if it were a regular text file is a lot of work. The .NET Framework helps you out by providing classes that can be used to parse, create, and edit XML files—both in memory and on disk.

These classes are found in the *System.Xml* namespace. The important classes are listed in Table 4-3.

**TABLE 4-3** Classes for working with XML

| Name | Description |
|------|-------------|
| *XmlReader* | A fast way of reading an XML file. You can move forward only through the file, and nothing is cached. |
| *XmlWriter* | A fast way to create an XML file. Just as with the *XmlReader*, it's forward only and noncached. |
| *XmlDocument* | Represents an in-memory XML document. It supports navigating and editing a document. |
| *XPathNavigator* | Helps with navigating through an XML document to find specific information. |

> **MORE INFO** LINQ TO XML
>
> Another way to work with XML is using LINQ to XML. More info can be found in Objective 4.3, "Query and manipulate data and objects by using LINQ," later in this chapter.

## XmlReader

The *XmlReader* class offers the fastest option of working with XML data. It is an abstract base class that is inherited from by classes such as *XmlTextReader*, *XmlNodeReader*, and *XmlValidatingReader*.

You create a new instance of *XmlReader* by using the static Create method. You can pass this method an instance of *XmlReaderSettings* to configure how the XML should be parsed. This way, you can choose to skip data from your XML file such as white space and comments, or start at a particular position. Listing 4-43 shows an example of how to use an *XmlReader* to parse a string that contains the XML data of Listing 4-42.

**LISTING 4-43** Parsing an XML file with an *XmlReader*

```
string xml = @"<?xml version=""1.0"" encoding=""utf-8"" ?>
                <people>
                  <person firstname=""john"" lastname=""doe"">
                    <contactdetails>
                      <emailaddress>john@unknown.com</emailaddress>
                    </contactdetails>
                  </person>
                  <person firstname=""jane"" lastname=""doe"">
                    <contactdetails>
                      <emailaddress>jane@unknown.com</emailaddress>
                      <phonenumber>001122334455</phonenumber>
                    </contactdetails>
                  </person>
                </people>";

using (StringReader stringReader = new StringReader(xml))
{
    using (XmlReader xmlReader = XmlReader.Create(stringReader,
        new XmlReaderSettings() { IgnoreWhitespace = true }))
    {
        xmlReader.MoveToContent();
        xmlReader.ReadStartElement("People");

        string firstName = xmlReader.GetAttribute("firstName");
        string lastName = xmlReader.GetAttribute("lastName");

        Console.WriteLine("Person: {0} {1}", firstName, lastName);
        xmlReader.ReadStartElement("Person");

        Console.WriteLine("ContactDetails");

        xmlReader.ReadStartElement("ContactDetails");
        string emailAddress = xmlReader.ReadString();

        Console.WriteLine("Email address: {0}", emailAddress);
    }
}
```

As you can see, the *XmlReader* treats the XML like a hierarchy of nodes. This is easier than working with XML as if it were a flat file. By moving to nodes, child nodes, and attributes, you can parse the document for the content you need.

## XmlWriter

When you want to create an XML file you can use the *XmlWriter* class. This class is created by using the static *Create* method and it can be configured by using an instance of the *XmlWriterSettings* class. Listing 4-44 shows how to create a new XML file. As you can see, you have methods for writing the individual elements and attributes.

**LISTING 4-44** Creating an XML file with *XmlWriter*

```
StringWriter stream = new StringWriter();

using (XmlWriter writer = XmlWriter.Create(
    stream,
    new XmlWriterSettings() { Indent = true }))
{
    writer.WriteStartDocument();
    writer.WriteStartElement("People");
    writer.WriteStartElement("Person");
    writer.WriteAttributeString("firstName", "John");
    writer.WriteAttributeString("lastName", "Doe");
    writer.WriteStartElement("ContactDetails");
    writer.WriteElementString("EmailAddress", "john@unknown.com");
    writer.WriteEndElement();
    writer.WriteEndElement();
    writer.Flush();
}

Console.WriteLine(stream.ToString());
```

Just as with the *XmlReader* class, the *XmlWriter* class is aware of the hierarchical structure of XML. However, you need to make sure that you write both the start and the end tag of each element. You can choose to add attributes or to add elements that have a string value as their content.

## XmlDocument

Although *XmlReader* and *XmlWriter* are the fastest options, they are definitely not the easiest to use. When you work with relatively small documents, and performance is not as important, you can use the *XmlDocument* class. Its primary function enables you to edit XML files, and it represents the XML in a hierarchical way in memory, and enables you to easily navigate the document and edit elements in place. After you finish editing the document, you can save it back to a file or stream.

An *XmlDocument* uses a set of *XmlNode* objects to represent the various elements comprising the document. *XmlDocument* inherits from *XmlNode* and adds specific capabilities for loading and saving documents. *XmlNode* helps you with reading content and attributes, and gives you methods for adding child nodes so that you can easily structure your document. Listing 4-45 shows an example in which both the reading and editing capabilities of *XmlDocument* are used on the XML found in Listing 4-43.

**LISTING 4-45** Using *XmlDocument*

```
XmlDocument doc = new XmlDocument();

doc.LoadXml(xml);
XmlNodeList nodes = doc.GetElementsByTagName("Person");

// Output the names of the people in the document
foreach (XmlNode node in nodes)
{
    string firstName = node.Attributes["firstName"].Value;
    string lastName = node.Attributes["lastName"].Value;
    Console.WriteLine("Name: {0} {1}", firstName, lastName);
}

// Start creating a new node
XmlNode newNode = doc.CreateNode(XmlNodeType.Element, "Person", "");

XmlAttribute firstNameAttribute = doc.CreateAttribute("firstName");
firstNameAttribute.Value = "Foo";

XmlAttribute lastNameAttribute = doc.CreateAttribute("lastName");
lastNameAttribute.Value = "Bar";

newNode.Attributes.Append(firstNameAttribute);
newNode.Attributes.Append(lastNameAttribute);

doc.DocumentElement.AppendChild(newNode);
Console.WriteLine("Modified xml...");
doc.Save(Console.Out);

//Displays:
//Name: john doe
//Name: jane doe
//Modified xml...
//<?xml version="1.0" encoding="ibm850"?>
//<people>
//   <person firstname="john" lastname="doe">
//    <contactdetails>
//       <emailaddress>john@unknown.com</emailaddress>
//    </contactdetails>
//   </person>
//   <person firstname="jane" lastname="doe">
//    <contactdetails>
//       <emailaddress>jane@unknown.com</emailaddress>
//       <phonenumber>001122334455</phonenumber>
//    </contactdetails>
//   </person>
//   <person firstname="Foo" lastname="Bar" />
//</people>
```

One nifty feature for navigating through a document is *XPath*, a kind of query language for XML documents. XmlDocument implements *IXPathNavigable* so you can retrieve an *XPathNavigator* object from it. The *XPathNavigator* offers an easy way to navigate through an XML document. You can use methods similar to those in an *XmlDocument* to move from one node to another, or you can use an XPath query. This enables you to select elements or attributes with certain values, similar to the way SQL selects data in a database. Listing 4-46 shows an example of how to use an XPath query to select a *Person* by name.

**LISTING 4-46** Using an XPath query

```
XmlDocument doc = new XmlDocument();
doc.LoadXml(xml); // Can be found in Listing 4-43

XPathNavigator nav = doc.CreateNavigator();
string query = "//People/Person[@firstName='Jane']";
XPathNodeIterator iterator = nav.Select(query);

Console.WriteLine(iterator.Count); // Displays 1

while(iterator.MoveNext())
{
    string firstName = iterator.Current.GetAttribute("firstName","");
    string lastName = iterator.Current.GetAttribute("lastName","");
    Console.WriteLine("Name: {0} {1}", firstName, lastName);
}
```

## Consuming JSON

Another popular format used by many web services is JavaScript Object Notation (JSON). Although XML is useful, it is verbose and has many rules regarding a document's structure. JSON is what's called the "fat-free" alternative to XML. It has an easier grammar and often carries significantly less weight. The example in Listing 4-47 shows how the *People* XML from the previous examples could be represented using JSON.

**LISTING 4-47** A sample JSON file

```
{
  "People": {
    "Person": [
      {
        "firstName": "John",
        "lastName": "Doe",
        "ContactDetails": { "EmailAddress": "john@unknown.com" }
      },
      {
        "firstName": "Jane",
        "lastName": "Doe",
        "ContactDetails": {
          "EmailAddress": "jane@unknown.com",
          "PhoneNumber": "001122334455"
        }
      }
    ]
  }
}
```

When working with XML, you use classes such as *XmlWriter*, *XmlReader*, and *XmlDocument*; JSON does not have classes like them. Normally, when working with JSON, you use a serialization library that helps you convert objects to JSON, and vice versa. One such popular library is Newtonsoft.Json, which is available at *http://json.codeplex.com/*.

JSON is most often used in asynchronous JavaScript and XML (AJAX) scenarios. In reality, AJAX should be called AJAJ because the XML is swapped for JSON now. AJAX is a technology that allows a website to execute background calls to a web server. This is the technique that enables a website to update itself without doing a full page refresh. JSON is particularly useful for this because all JavaScript engines can parse a JSON string into an object by a relatively simple command.

> **MORE INFO**  **SERIALIZING JSON**
>
> For more info on serializing JSON, see Objective 4.4, "Serialize and deserialize data," later in this chapter.

## Thought experiment
### Exchanging data

You are designing a new application that stores data about weather conditions throughout the world. Your business model relies on selling this data to customers so they can use it in their own applications. You use a relational database to store your data, and you access your data through web services that can be accessed by authorized users. You also create regular XML dumps for users that want a local copy of the data.

1. What are the advantages and disadvantages of using the Entity Framework?

2. Which techniques do you plan to use for your web services?

3. How will you expose your data as XML?

## Objective summary

- ADO.NET uses a provider model that enables you to connect to different types of databases.
- You use a *DbConnection* object to create a connection to a database.
- You can execute queries that create, update, read, and delete (CRUD) data from a database.
- When creating queries it's important to use parameterized queries so you avoid SQL injection.

- You can consume a web service from your application by creating a proxy for it.
- You can work with XML by using the *XmlReader*, *XmlWriter*, *XPathNavigator*, and *Xml-Document* classes.

## Objective review

Answer the following questions to test your knowledge of the information in this objective. You can find the answers to these questions and explanations of why each answer choice is correct or incorrect in the "Answers" section at the end of this chapter.

1.  You want to update a specific row in the database. Which objects should you use? (Choose all that apply.)

    A. *SqlCommand*

    B. *SqlDataReader*

    C. *SqlConnection*

    D. *TransactionScope*

2.  You are planning to build an application that will use an object-oriented design. It will be used by multiple users at the same time. Which technology should you use?

    A. XML files

    B. Entity Framework

    C. ADO.NET

    D. Web service

3.  You need to process a large number of XML files in a scheduled service to extract some data. Which class should you use?

    A. *XmlReader*

    B. *XmlDocument*

    C. *XmlWriter*

    D. *FileStream*

# Objective 4.3: Query and manipulate data and objects by using LINQ

In .NET 3.5, a new feature was added to C#: LINQ. LINQ enables you to work with data in an extremely powerful way. It consists of a set of standard, easily learned patterns that enable you to query data. The beautiful thing is that LINQ can be extended to work against different types of data. This enables you to write powerful queries that can be easily understood and maintained.

# Language features that make LINQ possible

To support LINQ, a few language features have been added to C#. These features are useful on their own, but combined together to form LINQ, they shine. Some of these language features help you to construct queries in a nice and elegant way, but other features are sometimes mandatory to even be able to create a query.

Those language constructs are as follows:

- Implicitly typed variables
- Object initialization syntax
- Lambda expressions
- Extension methods
- Anonymous types

## Implicitly typed variables

When working with C#, most of the time you use the static typing system of C#. This means that the compiler knows the type of a certain variable and that it sees whether you use it in the correct way.

For example, the following code will lead to a compile error:

```
int i = 42;
Stream m = new MemoryStream();
string s = i + m; // This line gives a compile error
```

What you are seeing here is called *explicit typing*. You tell the compiler explicitly what the type of each variable is. In C# 3, a new feature was added: *implicit typing*. When using implicit typing, the compiler infers the type of variable for you and then strongly types your variable to that type. Implicitly typed variables can be used only for local variables. You can use implicit typing by using the *var* keyword:

```
var i = 42;
var m = new MemoryStream();
//string s = i + m; // This line still gives a compile error
```

In this code, the compiler infers for you that the type of *i* is int, and *m* is *MemoryStream*. The types are still strongly typed, but you don't specify the type yourself.

Why is this necessary in LINQ? Sometimes when using a LINQ query, the return type is determined at compile time, so you can't specify the return explicitly because you don't know it. You will see an example of this shortly when you get to your first LINQ query.

Besides being mandatory in these situations, implicit typing can also improve the readability of your code. If a user of your code can easily see the type of your variable, implicit typing can be used to avoid repetition. In the following case, *var* can improve readability:

```
Dictionary<string, IEnumerable<Tuple<Type, int>>> data =
    new Dictionary<string, IEnumerable<Tuple<Type, int>>>();
var implicitData = new Dictionary<string, IEnumerable<Tuple<Type, int>>>();
```

In this case, you avoid the repetition of the large type declaration. A reader of your code will immediately see that the type of *implicitData* is a Dictionary. When the type of your variable is unclear, it's better to avoid implicit typing:

```
var whatsMyType = GetData();
```

In this case, a reader of your code would have to inspect the *GetData* method or use IntelliSense in Visual Studio to see what the type of *whatsMyType* is.

## Object initialization syntax

Before C# added object initializers, you had to split creating a new object and setting its properties, as shown in Listing 4-48.

**LISTING 4-48** Creating and initializing an object

```
public class Person
{
    public string FirstName { get; set; }
    public string LastName { get; set; }
}

// Create and initialize a new object
Person p = new Person();
p.FirstName = "John";
p.LastName = "Doe";
```

The new object initialization syntax enables you to combine creating a new object and setting its properties in one statement. Listing 4-49 shows this new syntax.

**LISTING 4-49** Using an object initializer

```
// Create and initialize a new object in one step
Person p = new Person
{
    FirstName ="John",
    LastName = "Doe"
};
```

Although not strictly necessary, it can improve the readability of your code when you use object initializers (see Listing 4-50). The same syntax can be used when creating collections.

LISTING 4-50 Using a collection initializer

```
var people = new List<Person>
{
    new Person
    {
        FirstName = "John",
        LastName = "Doe"
    },
    new Person
    {
        FirstName = "Jane",
        LastName = "Doe"
    }
};
```

Most of the time, objection initialization syntax is some nice syntactic sugar, but when working with anonymous types it is actually required. By using the object initialization syntax, you define the properties that an anonymous type has.

## Lambda expressions

To understand what a lambda expression is, it's important that you first know what an anonymous method is. Anonymous methods were introduced in C# 2.0 to enable you to create a method inline in some code, assign it to a variable, and pass it around. Listing 4-51 shows how to create an anonymous method.

LISTING 4-51 Using an anonymous method

```
Func<int, int> myDelegate =
    delegate(int x)
    {
        return x * 2;
    };
Console.WriteLine(myDelegate(21)); // Displays 42
```

The *Func<T,T>* is one of the built in types of the .NET Framework. It's a shorthand notation for a delegate that takes an int and returns an *int*. You can also use *Action<...>* for specifying a delegate that doesn't have a return value.

*Lambdas* introduce a shorthand notation for creating anonymous functions. The same code can be written by using a lambda:

```
Func<int, int> myDelegate = x => x * 2;
Console.WriteLine(myDelegate(21)); // Displays 42
```

As you can see, the result is the same, but the notation is a lot shorter. Lambdas use the special => notation, which you can read as "becomes" or "for which." When working with

LINQ, you often have to pass a *Fun<>* delegate to a method. By using lambdas, you can streamline your code and save yourself a lot of typing. The syntax gets a little more verbose when you work with multiple arguments or when your lambda contains multiple statements, but it's still a lot more compact than when using an anonymous method.

## Extension methods

*Extension methods* can be used to extend an existing type with new behavior without using inheritance. An extension method is defined in a static class and it uses the special *this* keyword to mark itself as an extension method. Listing 4-52 shows how to create an extension method for *int*.

**LISTING 4-52** Using an extension method

```
public static class IntExtensions
{
    public static int Multiply(this int x, int y)
    {
        return x * y;
    }
}

int x = 2;
Console.WriteLine(x.Multiply(3)); // Displays 6
```

LINQ is entirely based on extension methods. They are defined in the *System.Linq.Enumerables* class and they enable you to call LINQ functions on all enumerable types.

> **MORE INFO**  **EXTENSION METHODS**
>
> For more information on extension methods, see Chapter 2 "Create and use types."

## Anonymous types

When you create *anonymous types*, you use both object initializers and implicit typing. An anonymous type is a type that is shaped at compile time without having a formal class definition. The compiler helps you by creating a type for you and gives a default implementation by overriding the virtual members of *System.Object*.

You create an anonymous type by using the *var* keyword as the type and by using the new operator without specifying a type, as shown in Listing 4-53.

**LISTING 4-53** Creating an anonymous type

```
var person = new
{
    FirstName = "John",
    LastName = "Doe"
};

Console.WriteLine(person.GetType().Name); // Displays "<>f__AnonymousType0`2"
```

Here you see how object initializers can be used to define the properties of an anonymous type. Anonymous types are used in LINQ when you create a so-called *projection*. This means that you select certain properties from a query and form a specific type for it.

## Using LINQ queries

When working with data, be it in memory, from a database, an XML file, or another store, your queries always have the following three steps:

1. Obtain the data.

2. Create a query.

3. Execute the query.

Listing 4-54 shows an example of a simple LINQ query that selects some numbers from an array.

**LISTING 4-54** A LINQ select query

```
int[] data = { 1, 2, 5, 8, 11 };

var result = from d in data
             where d % 2 == 0
             select d;

foreach (int i in result)
{
    Console.WriteLine(i);
}
// Displays 2 8
```

As you can see, the query uses a special syntax: *query syntax*. The CLR that underpins the .NET Framework has no notion of what to do with a query in query syntax. The compiler translates the query syntax into a set of method calls. The previous query can also be written in method syntax:

```
var result = data.Where(d => d % 2 == 0);
```

Of course, there is no *Where* method on an array of integers. This is where the extension methods are used. The LINQ operators are extension methods on *IEnumerable<T>*. You also see how a lambda is used as an argument to the *Where* method. In this case, Where expects an argument of type *Func<int,bool>*, meaning that it expects a *bool* for each given *int*.

You can choose whether you want to use method or query syntax. Often, for smaller queries, the query syntax is easier to read. However, not all LINQ operators are supported in query syntax, so sometimes you are forced to use the method-based syntax. You can also mix the two approaches. The compiler always transforms your query syntax into method syntax.

## Standard LINQ query operators

LINQ has a couple of standard query operators that you can use when working with your data. A LINQ provider maps your query to a specific data store, such as LINQ to XML, LINQ to Entities, or LINQ to Objects. Every LINQ provider is encouraged to implement the standard query operators so you can always use them. This means that you can use these standard operators on almost all data sources, providing a consistent experience.

> **MORE INFO  LINQ SAMPLES**
>
> For examples of how to use all the LINQ operators, see *http://code.msdn.microsoft. com/101-LINQ-Samples-3fb9811b*.

The standard query operators are: *All, Any, Average, Cast, Count, Distinct, GroupBy, Join, Max, Min, OrderBy, OrderByDescending, Select, SelectMany, Skip, SkipWhile, Sum, Take, TakeWhile, ThenBy, ThenByDescending,* and *Where.*

The most basic query that you can create is shown in Listing 4-55.

**LISTING 4-55** LINQ *Select* operator

```
int[] data = { 1, 2, 5, 8, 11 };
var result = from d in data
             select d;
Console.WriteLine(string.Join(", ", result)); // Displays 1, 2, 5, 8, 11
```

In this case, the query is not doing anything special. You could have used the data array directly and it would have produced the same results. However, this query shows how LINQ works. First, you start with a *from statement* and then a data source. This helps the compiler because now it immediately knows what you're working with. Because of this, it can give IntelliSense on the next line. This is different from what you are used to in regular SQL, in which you start with a SELECT clause and then a FROM clause.

You can now make the query somewhat more interesting by adding a filter. This is done by adding a *where* statement. This statement should return a Boolean value that represents if the value should be included in the final result. Listing 4-56 shows how to filter your list for items that are greater than 5.

**LISTING 4-56** LINQ *where* operator

```
int[] data = { 1, 2, 5, 8, 11 };
var result = from d in data
             where d > 5
             select d;
Console.WriteLine(string.Join(", ", result)); // Displays 8, 11
```

Another useful operator is *orderby*, which can be used to sort your collection on a specific value. You can use *orderby* to sort your data in ascending or descending order. Listing 4-57 shows how to sort the data in descending order.

**LISTING 4-57** LINQ *orderby* operator

```
int[] data = { 1, 2, 5, 8, 11 };
var result = from d in data
             where d > 5
             orderby d descending
             select d;
Console.WriteLine(string.Join(", ", result)); // Displays 11, 8
```

You can also combine data from multiple sources. Let's say you have two arrays both containing numbers and you want to multiply them with each other. In your LINQ query, you use multiple *from* statements to combine the data, as shown in Listing 4-58.

**LISTING 4-58** LINQ multiple *from* statements

```
int[] data1 = { 1, 2, 5 };
int[] data2 = { 2, 4, 6};

var result = from d1 in data1
             from d2 in data2
             select d1 * d2;

Console.WriteLine(string.Join(", ", result)); // Displays 2, 4, 6, 4, 8, 12, 10, 20, 30
```

When you are working with some more interesting types LINQ shows its power. Let's say you are working with an *Order* class that has some *OrderLine* objects that point to a *Product* (see Listing 4-59).

**LISTING 4-59** A sample *Order* class for LINQ queries

```
public class Product
{
    public string Description { get; set; }
    public decimal Price { get; set; }
}

public class OrderLine
{
    public int Amount { get; set; }
    public Product Product { get; set; }
}

public class Order
{
    public List<OrderLine> OrderLines { get; set; }
}
```

Now, let's say you want to know the average number of *OrderLines* for a set of *Orders*. You can use a LINQ query to easily calculate this value:

```
var averageNumberOfOrderLines = orders.Average(o => o.OrderLines.Count);
```

As you can see, there is no query syntax for the *Average* method, which is why you need to use the method syntax. Try writing this query without LINQ. It's not hard, but it definitely has a lot more code.

Other useful LINQ operations are *projection* and *grouping*. When using *projection*, you select another type or an anonymous type as the result of your query. You project your results into it to focus only on the properties you really need. When using *grouping*, you group your data by a certain property and then work with that result. An example where this is useful is when you want to know how many items of each *product* you have sold. You can use the query from Listing 4-60 to calculate this.

**LISTING 4-60** Using *group by* and *projection*

```
var result = from o in orders
             from l in o.OrderLines
             group l by l.Product into p
             select new
                 {
                     Product = p.Key,
                     Amount = p.Sum(x => x.Amount)
                 };
```

Another standard operator is the *join* operator. *Join* can be used to combine data from two or more sources. When using the *join* operator, you have to specify the property that needs to be equal, as you can see in Listing 4-61.

**LISTING 4-61** Using *join*

```
string[] popularProductNames = { "A", "B" };
var popularProducts = from p in products
                      join n in popularProductNames on p.Description equals n
                      select p;
```

When you are working with a large data set, you probably want to implement *paging*. When using paging, you don't show all data at once to the user. Instead, you load it one page at a time. When data comes from an external resource such as a database, this can yield a significant performance gain. To implement paging, you can use the *Skip* and *Take* operators. There is no query syntax for them, so you need to use the methods as you can see in Listing 4-62.

**LISTING 4-62** Using *Skip* and *Take* to implement paging

```
var pagedOrders = orders
                  .Skip((pageIndex - 1) * pageSize)
                  .Take(pageSize);
```

**MORE INFO**   **LINQPAD**

LINQPad is an interactive way of testing your queries. You can use it to quickly test a query, convert from SQL to LINQ or just to learn how LINQ works. You can find LINQPad at *http://www.linqpad.net/*.

## How does LINQ work?

Now that you have experimented somewhat with a few queries, you are probably wondering how it all works. Let's say that you wanted to implement the *Where* query operator yourself.

If you look at the source code, you will see that the method definition of *Where* is the following:

```
public static IEnumerable<TSource> Where(
    this IEnumerable<TSource> source,
    Func<TSource, bool> predicate)
```

If you want to create your own implementation, you need to create an extension method with this signature. By removing the using statement for *System.Linq* you can then use your own method.

A basic implementation for this method is shown in Listing 4-63. This omits error checking and handling.

**LISTING 4-63** Implementing *Where*

```
public static class LinqExtensions
{
    public static IEnumerable<TSource> Where<TSource>(
        this IEnumerable<TSource> source,
        Func<TSource, bool> predicate)
    {
        foreach (TSource item in source)
        {
            if (predicate(item))
            {
                yield return item;
            }
        }
    }
}
```

The magical keyword in this code listing is the *yield* return statement. Because the *yield* statement is an implementation of the iterator pattern, the code is not executed until the first call to *MoveNext* is made. This is called *deferred execution*. A LINQ query is not executed until it is iterated, until that moment the query does nothing. A lot of errors when working with LINQ queries happen because people forget when their query is executed.

This is particularly important when you are working with one of the other LINQ providers that work against a database, such as LINQ to Entities or LINQ to SQL (LINQ providers like LINQ to Entities parse the query and transform it to SQL). The query won't be sent to the database until the result is iterated over. That also means that executing a query multiple times hits the database multiple times. Because of this, it is better to save the results of a query in a local variable and use that variable when working with the data.

Iterating can happen when you call a method like *ToList* or when you iterate over the results in a for each statement (which calls the *MoveNext* method on the iterator). Of course, other methods are more complex, but they all follow the same idea.

> **MORE INFO**  **YIELD**
>
> For more information on yield and the iterator pattern, see Chapter 2.

## Using LINQ to XML

One other provider that is part of the .NET Framework is *LINQ to XML*. Normally, you work with XML files by using the *XmlWriter*, *XmlReader*, and *XmlDocument* classes. The advantage of LINQ to XML is that you can use the same query experience that you use in LINQ to Objects or with other LINQ providers.

LINQ to XML helps you create, edit, and parse XML files. If you just have to get some information from an XML file, LINQ to XML offers you an easy query experience. If you need more capabilities, LINQ helps you write powerful queries that are more compact than other XML classes.

## Querying XML

If you want to query an XML file with LINQ to XML, you can use the *XDocument* class to load a file or a string containing XML into memory. The *XDocument* class works with objects of type *XNode*. *XNode* is an abstract class that represents the idea of some segment of content that a document holds. You can use *XDocument.Nodes* to access the nodes that form an XML file, or you can use *XDocument.Descendants* or *XDocument.Elements* to search for a specific set of nodes. One of the nice features of the *XDocument* class is that it represents the XML file in a hierarchical way. Because of this, you can move from a node to child nodes and back to the parent node. Attributes are not considered nodes; instead, they are key/value pairs that belong to a node.

Listing 4-64 shows some sample XML containing a set of people who all have some attributes and contact information.

**LISTING 4-64** Sample XML

```
String xml = @"<?xml version=""1.0"" encoding=""utf-8"" ?>
                    <people>
                      <person firstname=""john"" lastname=""doe"">
                        <contactdetails>
                          <emailaddress>john@unknown.com</emailaddress>
                        </contactdetails>
                      </person>
                      <person firstname=""jane"" lastname=""doe"">
                        <contactdetails>
                          <emailaddress>jane@unknown.com</emailaddress>
                          <phonenumber>001122334455</phonenumber>
                        </contactdetails>
                      </person>
                    </people>";
```

You can use LINQ to XML to execute a query that loads the names of the people from the string of XML. To use LINQ to XML, you have to add a reference to the *System.Xml.Linq* namespace. Listing 4-65 shows how you can use the *Descendants* method and the *Attribute* method to load this data.

**LISTING 4-65** Querying some XML by using LINQ to XML

```
XDocument doc = XDocument.Parse(xml);
IEnumerable<string> personNames = from p in doc.Descendants("Person")
                                  select (string)p.Attribute("firstName")
                                      + " " + (string)p.Attribute("lastName");
foreach (string s in personNames)
{
    Console.WriteLine(s);
}

// Displays:
// John Doe
// Jane Doe
```

One thing to note is that the *Attribute* method returns instances of *XAttribute*. The *XAttribute* has a *Value* property of type string, but it also implements explicit operators, so you can cast it to most of the basic types in C#.

> **MORE INFO    EXPLICIT CAST OPERATORS**
>
> For more information on explicit cast operators, see Chapter 2.

Because LINQ to XML supports the standard LINQ operators, you can easily use operators such as *Where* and *OrderBy* in your XML queries. Listing 4-66 shows how you can filter all people to only those with a phone number and then select their full names in alphabetical order. You also see how easily you can mix both method and query-based syntax.

**LISTING 4-66** Using *Where* and *OrderBy* in a LINQ to XML query

```
XDocument doc = XDocument.Parse(xml);
IEnumerable<string> personNames = from p in doc.Descendants("Person")
                                  where p.Descendants("PhoneNumber").Any()
                                  let name = (string)p.Attribute("firstName")
                                             + " " + (string)p.Attribute("lastName")
                                  orderby name
                                  select name;
```

## Creating XML

Besides querying XML, LINQ to XML can also help you with creating XML in a nice and fluent syntax. You use the class *XElement* for creating your own XML. You can use the *Add* method to construct an XML hierarchy or you can use the *XElement* constructor that takes an array of objects that form the content. This syntax is nice and trim. Listing 4-67 shows an example of how to create some XML.

**LISTING 4-67** Creating XML with the *XElement* class

```
XElement root = new XElement("Root",
        new List<XElement>
        {
            new XElement("Child1"),
            new XElement("Child2"),
            new XElement("Child3")
        },
        new XAttribute("MyAttribute", 42));
root.Save("test.xml");

//Outputs:
//<Root MyAttribute="42">
//    <Child1 />
//    <Child2 />
//    <Child3 />
//</Root>
```

By using object initializers and collection initializers, you can create your XML documents in an easy way.

## Updating XML

When you want to modify a piece of XML, you typically load it into memory, modify the XML by removing and inserting nodes, or changing the content of existing nodes. After you're finished, you save the XML back to the file.

LINQ to XML uses another approach called *functional construction*. Functional construction treats modifying data as a problem of transformation rather than as a detailed manipulation of data. Transformation can take more processor power, but it's easier to write and maintain, and in most situations, these benefits outweigh the costs.

Let's say you are working with the XML from Listing 4-64 and you need to add a phone number for *Joe* and an *IsMale* attribute to all people.

You can use procedural code to do this, as shown in Listing 4-68.

**LISTING 4-68** Updating XML in a procedural way

```
XElement root = XElement.Parse(xml);

foreach (XElement p in root.Descendants("Person"))
{
    string name = (string)p.Attribute("firstName") + (string)p.Attribute("lastName");
    p.Add(new XAttribute("IsMale", name.Contains("John")));
    XElement contactDetails = p.Element("ContactDetails");
    if (!contactDetails.Descendants("PhoneNumber").Any())
    {
        contactDetails.Add(new XElement("PhoneNumber", "001122334455"));
    }
}
```

You can use functional construction to transform this tree into a new one that adds the new attribute and elements by using a LINQ to XML query. Listing 4-69 shows how you can do it.

**LISTING 4-69** Transforming XML with functional creation

```
XElement root = XElement.Parse(xml);

XElement newTree = new XElement("People",
    from p in root.Descendants("Person")
    let name = (string)p.Attribute("firstName") + (string)p.Attribute("lastName")
    let contactDetails = p.Element("ContactDetails")
    select new XElement("Person",
        new XAttribute("IsMale", name.Contains("John")),
        p.Attributes(),
        new XElement("ContactDetails",
            contactDetails.Element("EmailAddress"),
            contactDetails.Element("PhoneNumber")
                ?? new XElement("PhoneNumber", "112233455")
    )));
```

It depends on the difficulty of your modification whether you use the regular procedural or functional way. Especially when the structure of the XML document changes, the functional way can have a lot of benefits.

You are starting a new project in which you can use LINQ for the first time. You have never worked with LINQ before, but you have studied it on your own time and you see its advantages.

You see possibilities for using LINQ to Entities, LINQ to Objects, and LINQ to XML in your projects and you try to introduce them in your company.

However, some of your coworkers are having some doubts. Will LINQ be fast enough? Is it easy to maintain? Do we need to use the method or query syntax?

Try to help your colleagues by answering these questions for them:

1. Does LINQ have any performance problems? If so, should it be avoided?

2. Is LINQ easy to maintain?

3. What are the differences between method and query syntax? Which should be used?

## Objective summary

- LINQ, which stands for Language Integrated Query, is a uniform way of writing queries against multiple data sources.
- Important language features when working with LINQ queries are implicit typing, object initialization syntax, lambdas, extension methods, and anonymous types.
- You can use LINQ with a method-based syntax and the query syntax.
- LINQ queries are deferred-execution, which means that the query executes when it is first iterated.
- You can use LINQ to XML to query, create, and update XML.

## Objective review

Answer the following questions to test your knowledge of the information in this objective. You can find the answers to these questions and explanations of why each answer choice is correct or incorrect in the "Answers" section at the end of this chapter.

1. You have a list of dates. You want to filter the dates to the current year and then select the highest date. Which query do you use?

   **A.** *DateTime result = dates.Where(d => d == DateTime.Now).OrderBy(d => d).First();*

   **B.** *DateTime result = dates.Where(d => d.Year == DateTime.Now.Year). OrderByDescending(d => d).FirstOrDefault();*

   **C.** *DateTime result = dates.Where(d => d.Year == DateTime.Now.Year). OrderByDescending(d => d).First();*

   **D.** *DateTime result = dates.Where(d => d.Year == DateTime.Now.Year). OrderByDescending(d => d).Single();*

2. You are trying to use a LINQ query, but you are getting a compile error that the *Where* method cannot be found. What should you do? (Choose all that apply.)

   **A.** Add a *using System.Linq* statement.

   **B.** Check that you are using a type that implements *IEnumerable*.

   **C.** Change your query from query to method syntax.

   **D.** Change the type of your query to var.

3. You are using the following LINQ to Entities query:

   ```
   var query = from p in myContext.Products
               where p.Price < 50
               select p;
   int numberOfItems = query.Count();
   var products = query.ToList();
   ```

   You are suffering performance problems. How can you improve your query? (Choose all that apply.)

   **A.** Avoid hitting the database multiple times.

   **B.** Don't execute *ToList()* on the query.

   **C.** Use paging.

   **D.** Change the query to method syntax.

# Objective 4.4: Serialize and deserialize data

When building your applications, you will often exchange data with other applications. When sending data to a web service or over a network stream, you first have to transform your data to a flat or binary form. When you receive data, you have to transform the flat or binary data to the objects you want to work with. This process is called serialization and deserialization.

> **This objective covers how to:**
> - Use serialization and deserialization.
> - Use different types of serializers.
> - Configure your objects for serialization.

## Using serialization and deserialization

*Serialization* is the process of transforming an object or object graph that you have in-memory into a stream of bytes or text. Deserialization is the opposite. You take some bytes or text and transform them into an object.

You use serialization when you need to exchange data with another application. This exchange can be done over a network or when you store data into a database or file.

Serialization can become a complex process, especially when you are dealing with a graph of objects that can have cyclic references (a series of references in which the last object references the first). It's not a trivial task to serialize an object.

Another thing to keep in mind is that serialization serializes only the data that an object stores. Methods are not serialized. When you deserialize an object, you need access to the original class definition or you will end up with an object that only stores data. When you want to optimize the amount of data that you have to serialize, you can create a custom *data transfer object (DTO)* that contains only the specific data you need.

The .NET Framework offers classes to help with serializing your object that can be found in the *System.Runtime.Serialization* and *System.Xml.Serialization* namespaces. These classes can help you with serializing and deserializing an object, but also with configuring your own objects so they can be serialized.

The .NET Framework offers three serialization mechanisms that you can use by default:

- *XmlSerializer*
- *DataContractSerializer*
- *BinaryFormatter*

# Using *XmlSerializer*

The *XmlSerializer* was created with the idea of Simple Object Access Protocol (SOAP) messaging in mind. SOAP is a protocol for exchanging information with web services. It uses XML as the format for messages. XML is readable by both humans and machines, and it is independent of the environment it is used in.

The *XmlSerializer* is loosely coupled to your objects. If you add new properties or methods to your objects, the *XmlSerializer* won't notice it. With some simple configuration changes, you can map XML nodes to properties in your objects so both can be modified independently. But the *XmlSerializer* doesn't have the highest performance; it also doesn't maintain the object references you have and it can't work with private fields.

When working with the *XmlSerializer*, it's important that you mark your types with the *[Serializable]* attribute, part of the *SerializableAttribute* class. This informs the .NET Framework that your type should be serializable. It will check your object and all the objects it references to make sure that it can serialize the whole graph. If that's not possible, you will get an exception at runtime.

Listing 4-70 shows an example of how you can serialize an object and then restore it from XML. As you can see, the *Person* class is marked with *Serializable*. All members of the type are automatically serialized if they don't opt out.

**LISTING 4-70** Serializing an object with the *XmlSerializer*

```
[Serializable]
public class Person
{
    public string FirstName { get; set; }
    public string LastName { get; set; }
    public int Age { get; set; }
}

XmlSerializer serializer = new XmlSerializer(typeof(Person));
string xml;
using (StringWriter stringWriter = new StringWriter())
{
    Person p = new Person
    {
        FirstName = "John",
        LastName = "Doe",
        Age = 42
    };
    serializer.Serialize(stringWriter, p);
    xml = stringWriter.ToString();
}

Console.WriteLine(xml);

using (StringReader stringReader = new StringReader(xml))
{
    Person p = (Person)serializer.Deserialize(stringReader);
    Console.WriteLine("{0} {1} is {2} years old", p.FirstName, p.LastName, p.Age);
}
```

```
// Displays
//<?xml version="1.0" encoding="utf-16"?>
//<Person xmlns:xsi="http://www.w3.org/2001/XMLSchema-instance"
// xmlns:xsd="http://www.w3.org/2001/XMLSchema">
//  <FirstName>John</FirstName>
//  <LastName>Doe</LastName>
//  <Age>42</Age>
//</Person>
//John Doe is 42 years old
```

You can configure how the XmlSerializer serializes your type by using attributes. These attributes are defined in the *System.Xml.Serialization* namespace. The following are the important attributes that you will use most of the time:

- *XmlIgnore*
- *XmlAttribute*
- *XmlElement*
- *XmlArray*
- *XmlArrayItem*

By default, each member is serialized as an *XmlElement*. This means that they end up as node in your XML. By using *XmlAttribute*, you can map a member to an attribute on its parent node. *XmlIgnore* can be used to make sure that an element is not serialized. *XmlArray* and *XmlArrayItem* are used when serializing collections. Listing 4-71 shows an example in which all these attributes are used.

**LISTING 4-71** Using the XML attributes to configure serialization

```
[Serializable]
public class Person
{
    public string FirstName { get; set; }
    public string LastName { get; set; }
    public int Age { get; set; }
}

[Serializable]
public class Order
{
    [XmlAttribute]
    public int ID { get; set; }

    [XmlIgnore]
    public bool IsDirty { get; set; }

    [XmlArray("Lines")]
    [XmlArrayItem("OrderLine")]
    public List<OrderLine> OrderLines { get; set; }
}

[Serializable]
public class VIPOrder : Order
```

```
{
    public string Description { get; set; }
}

[Serializable]
public class OrderLine
{
    [XmlAttribute]
    public int ID { get; set; }

    [XmlAttribute]
    public int Amount { get; set; }

    [XmlElement("OrderedProduct")]
    public Product Product { get; set; }
}

[Serializable]
public class Product
{
    [XmlAttribute]
    public int ID { get; set; }
    public decimal Price { get; set; }
    public string Description { get; set; }
}
```

When you serialize this code, you have to make sure the .NET Framework knows that you are using an inheritance hierarchy. Listing 4-72 shows a sample *VIPOrder* and how you can serialize and deserialize it.

**LISTING 4-72** Serializing a derived, complex class to XML

```
private static Order CreateOrder()
{
    Product p1 = new Product { ID = 1, Description = "p2", Price = 9 };
    Product p2 = new Product { ID = 2, Description = "p3", Price = 6 };

    Order order = new VIPOrder
    {
        ID = 4,
        Description = "Order for John Doe. Use the nice giftwrap",
        OrderLines = new List<OrderLine>
        {
            new OrderLine { ID = 5, Amount = 1, Product = p1},
            new OrderLine { ID = 6 ,Amount = 10, Product = p2},
        }
    };

    return order;
}

XmlSerializer serializer = new XmlSerializer(typeof(Order),
    new Type[] { typeof(VIPOrder) });
string xml;
using (StringWriter stringWriter = new StringWriter())
```

```
{
    Order order = CreateOrder();
    serializer.Serialize(stringWriter, order);
    xml = stringWriter.ToString();
}


using (StringReader stringReader = new StringReader(xml))
{
    Order o = (Order)serializer.Deserialize(stringReader);
    // Use the order
}
```

## Using binary serialization

The *XmlSerializer* outputs human-readable text. You can open it in Notepad, for example, to inspect and edit it. But the human readability of the file also adds to its size. By using a *binary format*, you get a smaller result. You can also serialize data that is not suitable for an XML format such as an image.

In essence, using binary serialization looks like using the *XmlSerializer*. You need to mark an item with the *SerializableAttribute* and then you use instance of the binary serializer to serialize an object or an object graph to a *Stream*. The important namespaces are *System. Runtime.Serialization* and *System.Runtime.Serialization.Formatters.Binary*. Listing 4-73 shows how you can take an object, serialize it to a file, and then deserialize it to an object.

**LISTING 4-73** Using binary serialization

```
[Serializable]
public class Person
{
    public int Id { get; set; }
    public string Name { get; set; }
    private bool isDirty = false;
}


Person p = new Person
{
    Id = 1,
    Name = "John Doe"
};

IFormatter formatter = new BinaryFormatter();
using (Stream stream = new FileStream("data.bin", FileMode.Create))
{
    formatter.Serialize(stream, p);
}

using (Stream stream = new FileStream("data.bin", FileMode.Open))
{
    Person dp = (Person)formatter.Deserialize(stream);
}
```

Binary serialization creates a compact stream of bytes. One thing that's different compared with XML serialization is that private fields are serialized by default. Another thing is that during deserialization, no constructors are executed. You have to take this into account when working with binary serialization.

Just as with the *XmlSerializer*, you can prevent fields from being serialized. You do this by using the *[NonSerialized]* attribute. Suppose that you don't want to serialize the *IsDirty* field from the Person class. You can do this by using the code in Listing 4-74.

**LISTING 4-74** Using attributes to control serialization

```
[Serializable]
public class Person
{
    public int Id { get; set; }
    public string Name { get; set; }

    [NonSerialized]
    private bool isDirty = false;
}
```

Binary serialization is more strict than XML serialization. When the XML serializer can't find a specific field, it won't throw an exception; it will just set the property to its default value. The binary serializer is not that forgiving. So it's important to be able to influence the serialization process. You can use the *OptionalFieldAttribute* to make sure that the binary serializer knows that a field is added in a later version and that earlier serialized objects won't contain this field, for example.

You can influence the serialization and deserialization process in four specific phases, namely when starting and finishing an action. You can do this by using the following four attributes:

- *OnDeserializedAttribute*
- *OnDeserializingAttribute*
- *OnSerializedAttribute*
- *OnSerializingAttribute*

You add these attributes to methods inside your class that take a *StreamingContext* as a parameter. Listing 4-75 shows how you can add these methods to the *Person* class.

**LISTING 4-75** Influencing serialization and deserialization

```
[Serializable]
public class Person
{
    public int Id { get; set; }
    public string Name { get; set; }

    [NonSerialized]
    private bool isDirty = false;
```

```
[OnSerializing()]
internal void OnSerializingMethod(StreamingContext context)
{
    Console.WriteLine("OnSerializing.");
}

[OnSerialized()]
internal void OnSerializedMethod(StreamingContext context)
{
    Console.WriteLine("OnSerialized.");
}

[OnDeserializing()]
internal void OnDeserializingMethod(StreamingContext context)
{
    Console.WriteLine("OnDeserializing.");
}

[OnDeserialized()]
internal void OnDeserializedMethod(StreamingContext context)
{
    Console.WriteLine("OnSerialized.");
}
}
```

When serializing and deserializing a Person object, you will get the following output:

```
OnSerializing..
OnSerialized..
OnDeserializing..
OnSerialized..
```

One thing that's important to keep in mind is that a serialized object could expose private data that is security sensitive. Everyone who has permissions to deserialize the file can access your sensitive data. If you have a sensitive class, you should implement the *ISerializable* interface. When implementing this interface, you have control over which values are serialized. You could choose to not serialize sensitive data or possibly encrypt prior to serialization. Listing 4-76 shows how to implement this interface.

**LISTING 4-76** Implementing *ISerializable*

```
[Serializable]
public class PersonComplex : ISerializable
{
    public int Id { get; set; }
    public string Name { get; set; }
    private bool isDirty = false;

    public PersonComplex() { }
    protected PersonComplex(SerializationInfo info, StreamingContext context)
    {
        Id = info.GetInt32("Value1");
        Name = info.GetString("Value2");
        isDirty = info.GetBoolean("Value3");
    }
```

```
[System.Security.Permissions.SecurityPermission(SecurityAction.Demand,
                                        SerializationFormatter = true)]
public void GetObjectData(SerializationInfo info, StreamingContext context)
{
    info.AddValue("Value1", Id);
    info.AddValue("Value2", Name);
    info.AddValue("Value3", isDirty);
}
}
```

As you can see, implementing ISerializable consists of two important parts. The first is the *GetObjectData* method. This method is called when your object is serialized. It should add the values that you want to serialize as key/value pairs to the *SerializationInfo* object that's passed to the method. One thing that's important is that you should mark this method with a *SecurityPermission* attribute (you can find this attribute in the *System.Security.Permissions* namespace) so that it is allowed to execute serialization and deserialization code.

The other important step is adding a special protected constructor that takes a *SerializationInfo* and *StreamingContext*. This constructor is called during deserialization, and you use it to retrieve the values and initialize your object. As you can see, you are free in choosing the names for the values that you add to the *SerializationInfo*.

It's important to implement security checks in your constructor. This way, you can make sure that no one has tampered with the serialized data.

## Using *DataContract*

You have now seen XML and binary serialization. Another type of serialization is used when you use WCF. When your types are used in WCF, they are serialized so they can be sent to other applications. The *Data Contract Serializer* is used by WCF to serialize your objects to XML or JSON.

The most noticeable difference is that you use *DataContractAttribute* instead of *SerializableAttribute*. Another important difference is that members are not serialized by default. You have to explicitly mark them with the *DataMember* attribute.

As with binary serialization, you can use *OnDeserializedAttribute*, *OnDeserializingAttribute*, *OnSerializedAttribute*, and *OnSerializingAttribute* to configure the four phases of the serialization and deserialization process.

Listing 4-77 shows how you can create a *DataContract* for the *Person* class. The *isDirty* field is ignored, and both the *Id* and *Name* property will be serialized.

**LISTING 4-77** Using a *DataContract*

```
[DataContract]
public class PersonDataContract
{
    [DataMember]
    public int Id { get; set; }
```

```
    [DataMember]
    public string Name { get; set; }

    private bool isDirty = false;
}
```

You can use the *DataContractSerializer* from the *System.Runtime.Serialization* namespace in the same way you used the *XmlSerializer* and *BinarySerializer*. You need to specify a *Stream* object that has the input or output when serializing or deserializing an object. Listing 4-78 shows an example.

**LISTING 4-78** Using the *DataContractSerializer*

```
PersonDataContract p = new PersonDataContract
{
    Id = 1,
    Name = "John Doe"
};

using (Stream stream = new FileStream("data.xml", FileMode.Create))
{
    DataContractSerializer ser = new DataContractSerializer(typeof(PersonDataContract));
    ser.WriteObject(stream, p);
}

using (Stream stream = new FileStream("data.xml", FileMode.Open))
{
    DataContractSerializer ser = new DataContractSerializer(typeof(PersonDataContract));
    PersonDataContract result = (PersonDataContract)ser.ReadObject(stream);
}
```

# Using JSON serializer

JSON is a special format that is specifically useful when sending small amounts of data between a web server and a client by using Asynchronous JavaScript and XML (AJAX). Normally, your data is automatically serialized for you when you use a WCF AJAX endpoint or ASP.NET WebApi. When you want to execute this serialization manually, you can use the *DataContractJsonSerializer*. Listing 4-79 shows how to serialize an object manually to JSON.

**LISTING 4-79** Using the *DataContractJsonSerializer*

```
[DataContract]
public class Person
{
    [DataMember]
    public int Id { get; set; }
    [DataMember]
    public string Name { get; set; }
}

Person p - new Person
{
```

```
        Id = 1,
        Name = "John Doe"
    };

    using (MemoryStream stream = new MemoryStream())
    {
        DataContractJsonSerializer ser = new DataContractJsonSerializer(typeof(Person));
        ser.WriteObject(stream, p);

        stream.Position = 0;
        StreamReader streamReader = new StreamReader(stream);
        Console.WriteLine(streamReader.ReadToEnd()); // Displays {"Id":1,"Name":"John Doe"}

        stream.Position = 0;
        Person result = (Person)ser.ReadObject(stream);
    }
```

## *Thought experiment*

### Choosing the correct serialization

You need to serialize some data to a file. The file can then be processed by another .NET application. Your data consists of personal records that store important information such as names, addresses, logon credentials, and contact details.

You are wondering which serialization would be best. You think about XML binary, JSON or using a Data Contract.

**1.** To which format should you serialize the data?

**2.** Which serializer should you use?

**3.** Do you need to implement any specific serialization methods on your type?

## Objective summary

- Serialization is the process of transforming an object to a flat file or a series of bytes.
- Deserialization takes a series of bytes or a flat file and transforms it into an object.
- XML serialization can be done by using the *XmlSerializer*.
- You can use special attributes to configure the *XmlSerializer*.
- Binary serialization can be done by using the *BinaryFormatter* class.
- WCF uses another type of serialization that is performed by the *DataContractSerializer*.
- JSON is a compact text format that can be created by using the *DataContractJsonSerializer*.

# Objective review

Answer the following questions to test your knowledge of the information in this objective. You can find the answers to these questions and explanations of why each answer choice is correct or incorrect in the "Answers" section at the end of this chapter.

1. You need to store a large amount of data, and you want to do this in the most optimal way. Which serializer should you use?

   **A.** *XmlSerializer*

   **B.** *BinaryFormatter*

   **C.** *DataContractSerializer*

   **D.** *DataContractJsonSerializer*

2. You are serializing some sensitive data to a binary format. What should you use? (Choose all that apply.)

   **A.** *XmlSerializer*

   **B.** *ISerializable*

   **C.** *DataContractSerializer*

   **D.** *BinaryFormatter*

3. You want to serialize some data to XML, and you need to make sure that a certain property is not serialized. Which attribute should you use?

   **A.** *XmlElement*

   **B.** *XmlAttribute*

   **C.** *XmlIgnore*

   **D.** *NonSerialized*

# Objective 4.5: Store data in and retrieve data from collections

When you are working with *some* groups of data, you often use a collection. Collection objects are useful when you want to work with data in a flexible way. You might need to add and remove elements from a collection, you might have special performance needs, or you might need to access items. This is why the .NET Framework offers you an extensive set of collections that you can use.

## Using arrays

The most basic type that you can use to store a group of entities is an *array*. Arrays are useful when you are working with a fixed number of objects that all have the same type.

You declare an array by using a special syntax: *type[] arrayName*. The square brackets denote the type as being an array. When creating an array, you are required to specify the number of items it will contain.

Listing 4-80 shows how you can declare an array, fill it, and iterate over it.

**LISTING 4-80** Using an array

```
int[] arrayOfInt = new int[10];

for (int x = 0; x < arrayOfInt.Length; x++)
{
    arrayOfInt[x] = x;
}

foreach (int i in arrayOfInt)
{
    Console.Write(i); // Displays 0123456789
}
```

As you can see, the array is created with a fixed size. Arrays are zero-based, which means that the first element can be found at index 0 and the last element at the length of the array–1. You can loop through an array by using the *Length* property and a *for* loop. Arrays are reference types that inherit from the *Array* class. An array implements *IEnumerable*, so you can use it in a *foreach* loop.

An array can also be initialized directly. The compiler then will check the length for you and create an appropriate array.

```
int[] arrayOfInt = { 0, 1, 2, 3, 4, 5, 6, 7, 8, 9 };
```

Besides declaring single-dimensional arrays, you can also create *multidimensional* and *jagged arrays*.

A two-dimensional array, for example, means that the array has a certain number of rows and columns. You declare it by using a comma (,) in your array declaration. The number of rows and columns can be different. Listing 4-81 shows how to declare a two-dimensional array.

**LISTING 4-81** Using a two-dimensional array

```
string[,] array2D = new string[3, 2] { { "one", "two" }, { "three", "four" },
                      { "five", "six" } };

Console.WriteLine(array2D[0, 0]); // one
Console.WriteLine(array2D[0, 1]); // two
Console.WriteLine(array2D[1, 0]); // three
Console.WriteLine(array2D[1, 1]); // four
Console.WriteLine(array2D[2, 0]); // five
Console.WriteLine(array2D[2, 1]); // six
```

A *jagged array* is an array whose elements are arrays. Because arrays are reference types, the values of a jagged array have a default value of *null*. Listing 4-82 shows how you can create a jagged array by using the initialization syntax.

**LISTING 4-82** Creating a jagged array

```
int[][] jaggedArray =
    {
        new int[] {1,3,5,7,9},
        new int[] {0,2,4,6},
        new int[] {42,21}
    };
```

The biggest problem with arrays is that they are of fixed size. When working with groups of objects, you often want to add or remove items from the collection. This is why the .NET Framework has some other collection types.

## Understanding generic versus nongeneric

Most of the collection types have both a generic and a nongeneric version. When you work with objects of one specific type (or base type), use the generic collection. It will improve type safety and performance because there is no casting required.

The nongeneric collections can be found in *System.Collections*, and generic collections can be found in *System.Collections.Generic*.

If you use a value type as the type parameter for a generic collection, you need to make sure that you eliminate all scenarios in which boxing could occur. For example, if your value type does not implement *IEquatable<T>*, your object needs boxing to call *Object.Equals(Object)* for checking equality. The same is true for the *IComparable<T>* interface.

When using reference types, you won't have these issues.

## Using *List*

One collection type you will probably use most often is the generic *List<T>* collection. The *List* type offers methods for adding and removing items, accessing items by index, and searching and sorting the list.

The *List* type makes sure that there is always enough room to store additional items. If necessary, the internal implementation of the *List* class will increase the size of the array it uses to store its items. *List<T>* can store reference types and it can have a value of null for an item. It can also store duplicate items.

The class definition for *List<T>* has the following form:

```
public class List<T> : IList<T>, ICollection<T>, IList, ICollection,
      IReadOnlyList<T>, IReadOnlyCollection<T>, IEnumerable<T>, IEnumerable
```

*List<T>* implements quite some interfaces. Of course, it implements *IEnumerable<T>* and *IEnumerable*, so you can use it in a *foreach* pattern without worrying about the implementation. *IList* and *ICollection* are the interfaces that define the real usefulness of this collection. *IList<T>* and *ICollection<T>* can be found in Listing 4-83.

**LISTING 4-83** Using *IList<T>* and *ICollection<T>*

```
public interface IList<T> : ICollection<T>, IEnumerable<T>, IEnumerable
{
      T this[int index] { get; set; }
      int IndexOf(T item);
      void Insert(int index, T item);
      void RemoveAt(int index);
}

public interface ICollection<T> : IEnumerable<T>, IEnumerable
{
      int Count { get; }
      bool IsReadOnly { get; }
      void Add(T item);
      void Clear();
      bool Contains(T item);
      void CopyTo(T[] array, int arrayIndex);
      bool Remove(T item);
}
```

Listing 4-84 shows an example of how you can use a *List* by adding, removing, searching, and iterating over items.

**LISTING 4-84** Using *List<T>*

```
List<string> listOfStrings =
    new List<string> { "A", "B", "C", "D", "E" };

for (int x = 0; x < listOfStrings.Count; x++)
    Console.Write(listOfStrings[x]); // Displays: ABCDE

listOfStrings.Remove("A");

Console.WriteLine(listOfStrings[0]); // Displays: B

listOfStrings.Add("F");
```

```
Console.WriteLine(listOfStrings.Count); // Displays: 5

bool hasC = listOfStrings.Contains("C");

Console.WriteLine(hasC); // Displays: true
```

# Using *Dictionary*

A *List<T>* just stores a group of items. It enables duplicates and it quickly finds items.

A *Dictionary<TKey,TValue>* can be used in scenarios in which you want to store items and retrieve them by key, so it doesn't allow duplicate keys. It takes two type parameters: one for the type of the key, and the other for the type of the value.

The *Dictionary* class is implemented as a hash table, which makes retrieving a value very fast, close to O(1). The hash value of a key shouldn't change during time and it can't be null. The value can be null (if it's a reference type).

The class signature of the *Dictionary<TKey,TValue>* class is as follows:

```
public class Dictionary<TKey, TValue> : IDictionary<TKey, TValue>,
    ICollection<KeyValuePair<TKey, TValue>>, IDictionary, ICollection,
    IReadOnlyDictionary<TKey, TValue>, IReadOnlyCollection<KeyValuePair<TKey, TValue>>,
    IEnumerable<KeyValuePair<TKey, TValue>>, IEnumerable, ISerializable,
    IDeserializationCallback
```

The *Dictionary* class works with *KeyValuePair<TKey,TValue>* structures. Listing 4-85 shows how you can work with a *Dictionary*.

**LISTING 4-85** Using *Dictionary<TKey, TValue>*

```
Person p1 = new Person { Id = 1, Name = "Name1" };
Person p2 = new Person { Id = 2, Name = "Name2" };
Person p3 = new Person { Id = 3, Name = "Name3" };

var dict = new Dictionary<int, Person>();
dict.Add(p1.Id, p1);
dict.Add(p2.Id, p2);
dict.Add(p3.Id, p3);

foreach (KeyValuePair<int, Person> v in dict)
{
    Console.WriteLine("{0}: {1}", v.Key, v.Value.Name);
}

dict[0] = new Person { Id = 4, Name = "Name4" };

Person result;
if (!dict.TryGetValue(5, out result))
{
    Console.WriteLine("No person with a key of 5 can be found");
}
```

# Using sets

In some languages, such as Java, there is a special *set* type. In C#, a set is a reserved keyword, but you can use the *HashSet<T>* if you need one. A set is a collection that contains no duplicate elements and has no particular order.

In mathematics, you often perform operations on a set, such as seeing whether a set is a subset of another set, selecting the elements that two sets have in common or that they don't have in common, and combining two sets. HashSet implements the *ISet<T>* interface that has the members you can find in Listing 4-86.

**LISTING 4-86** Using the *ISet<T>* interface

```
public interface ISet<T> : ICollection<T>, IEnumerable<T>, IEnumerable
{
        bool Add(T item);
        void ExceptWith(IEnumerable<T> other);
        void IntersectWith(IEnumerable<T> other);
        bool IsProperSubsetOf(IEnumerable<T> other);
        bool IsProperSupersetOf(IEnumerable<T> other);
        bool IsSubsetOf(IEnumerable<T> other);
        bool IsSupersetOf(IEnumerable<T> other);
        bool Overlaps(IEnumerable<T> other);
        bool SetEquals(IEnumerable<T> other);
        void SymmetricExceptWith(IEnumerable<T> other);
        void UnionWith(IEnumerable<T> other);
}
```

Just as with the other collections, you can easily add new objects to it and iterate over them. Listing 4-87 shows an example of how you can use a *HashSet<T>*.

**LISTING 4-87** Using *HashSet<T>*

```
public void UseHashSet()
{
    HashSet<int> oddSet = new HashSet<int>();
    HashSet<int> evenSet = new HashSet<int>();

    for (int x = 1; x <= 10; x++)
    {
        if (x % 2 == 0)
            evenSet.Add(x);
        else
            oddSet.Add(x);
    }

    DisplaySet(oddSet);
    DisplaySet(evenSet);

    oddSet.UnionWith(evenSet);
    DisplaySet(oddSet);
}

private void DisplaySet(HashSet<int> set)
```

```
{
    Console.Write("{");
    foreach (int i in set)
    {
        Console.Write(" {0}", i);
    }
    Console.WriteLine(" }");
}
```

## Using queues and stacks

A *queue* is a special type of collection you can use to temporarily store some data. It is a so-called first-in, first-out (FIFO) type of collection, just like a checkout line. You access elements in the same order you added them. By getting an item, you also remove it from the queue. This is why a queue offers temporary storage. You can use a queue, for example, when you need to process incoming messages. Each new message is added to the end of the queue; when you are done processing a message, you get a new one from the start of the queue.

The *Queue* class has three important methods:

- *Enqueue* adds an element to the end of the *Queue*, equivalent to the back of the line.

- *Dequeue* removes the oldest element from the *Queue*, equivalent to the front of the line.

- *Peek* returns the oldest element, but doesn't immediately remove it from the *Queue*.

Listing 4-88 shows how to enqueue some items to a *Queue* and then loop through them.

**LISTING 4-88** Using *Queue<T>*

```
Queue<string> myQueue = new Queue<string>();
myQueue.Enqueue("Hello");
myQueue.Enqueue("World");
myQueue.Enqueue("From");
myQueue.Enqueue("A");
myQueue.Enqueue("Queue");

foreach (string s in myQueue)
    Console.Write(s + " ");
// Displays: Hello World From A Queue
```

A *Queue* is a first in, first out (FIFO) collection; a *Stack* is a last-in, first-out (LIFO) collection. Think of the undo system of an application. The last item added to the undo stack is the first one to be used when a user executes an undo action. Just as with a *Queue*, items are removed when reading them.

A *Stack* has the following three important methods:

- **Push**  Add a new item to the *Stack*.

- **Pop**  Get the newest item from the *Stack*.

- **Peek**  Get the newest item without removing it.

If you would change the example of Listing 4-88 to use a *Stack* instead of a *Queue*, you would get the reverse output as you can see in Listing 4-89.

**LISTING 4-89** Using *Stack<T>*

```
Stack<string> myStack = new Stack<string>();
myStack.Push("Hello");
myStack.Push("World");
myStack.Push("From");
myStack.Push("A");
myStack.Push("Queue");

foreach (string s in myStack)
    Console.Write(s + " ");
// Displays: Queue A From World Hello
```

## Choosing a collection

When choosing a collection type, you have to think about the scenarios you want to support. The biggest differences between the collections are the ways that you access elements.

*List* and *Dictionary* types offer random access to all elements. A *Dictionary* offers faster read features, but it can't store duplicate elements.

A *Queue* and a *Stack* are used when you want to retrieve items in a specific order. The item is removed when you have retrieved it.

*Set*-based collections have special features for comparing collections. They don't offer random access to individual elements.

Although *List* can be used in most situations, it pays to see whether there is a more specialized collection that can make your life easier.

> **MORE INFO  COLLECTION TYPES**
>
> The .NET Framework has more specialized collections. If you want to know more about these collection types, see *http://msdn.microsoft.com/en-us/library/7y3x785f.aspx*.

## Creating a custom collection

A basic collection can be implemented by implementing *IEnumerable* or *IEnumerable<T>*. That way, you implement the iterator pattern, and your collection can be used in a *foreach* statement.

If you need more features, you can look at the interfaces that are implemented by the existing collections in .NET. The ones used by the classes that you reviewed in this chapter are these:

- *IList<T>*
- *ICollection<T>*

- *IDictionary<TKey,TValue>*

- *ICollection<TKey,TValue>*

- *ISet<T>*

Of course, you can also choose to directly inherit from an existing collection. Listing 4-90 shows an example of how you can inherit from *List<T>* to add some specific functionality.

**LISTING 4-90** Inheriting from *List<T>* to form a custom collection

```
public class PeopleCollection : List<Person>
{
    public void RemoveByAge(int age)
    {
        for (int index = this.Count - 1; index >= 0; index--)
        {
            if (this[index].Age == age)
            {
                this.RemoveAt(index);
            }
        }
    }

    public override string ToString()
    {
        StringBuilder sb = new StringBuilder();
        foreach (Person p in this)
        {
            sb.AppendFormat("{0} {1} is {2}", p.FirstName, p.LastName, p.Age);
        }
        return sb.ToString();
    }
}
```

You can then use this collection like any other collection. Listing 4-91 shows how you can initialize it and then use your custom functions to manipulate it.

**LISTING 4-91** Using a custom collection

```
public class Person
{
    public string FirstName { get; set; }
    public string LastName { get; set; }
    public int Age { get; set; }
}
Person p1 = new Person
{
    FirstName = "John",
    LastName = "Doe",
    Age = 42
};
Person p2 = new Person
{
```

```
        FirstName = "Jane",
        LastName = "Doe",
        Age = 21
};

PeopleCollection people = new PeopleCollection { p1, p2 };
people.RemoveByAge(42);
Console.WriteLine(people.Count); // Displays: 1
```

### *Thought experiment*

### Choosing the correct collection

You are trying to determine the different collections that .NET uses. You try to come up with a comparison of the different collection types by performance and use case.

**1.** When should you use a generic or nongeneric collection?

**2.** What's the difference between the Dictionary- and List-based collections? When should you use one or the other?

**3.** What's the difference among the Stack, Queue, and List collections?

## Objective summary

- The .NET Framework offers both generic and nongeneric collections. When possible, you should use the generic version.
- Array is the most basic type to store a number of items. It has a fixed size.
- List is a collection that can grow when needed. It's the most-used collection.
- Dictionary stores and accesses items using key/value pairs.
- *HashSet* stores unique items and offers set operations that can be used on them.
- A *Queue* is a first-in, first-out (FIFO) collection.
- A *Stack* is a first-in, last-out (FILO) collection.
- You can create a custom collection by inheriting from a collection class or inheriting from one of the collection interfaces.

## Objective review

Answer the following questions to test your knowledge of the information in this objective. You can find the answers to these questions and explanations of why each answer choice is correct or incorrect in the "Answers" section at the end of this chapter.

1. You want to store a group of orders and make sure that a user can easily select an order by its order number. Which collection do you use?

   **A.** *List<Order>*

   **B.** *Dictionary<int,Order>*

   **C.** *HashSet<Order>*

   **D.** *Queue<Order>*

2. You are using a queue and you want to add a new item. Which method do you use?

   **A.** *Push*

   **B.** *Add*

   **C.** *Dequeue*

   **D.** *Enqueue*

3. You are working with a large group of family name objects. You need to remove all duplicates and then group them by last name. Which collections should you use? (Choose all that apply.)

   **A.** *List<T>*

   **B.** *Stack<T>*

   **C.** *Dictionary<string,T>*

   **D.** *T[]*

# Chapter summary

- You can use classes such as *Drive*, *DriveInfo*, *Directory*, *DirectoryInfo*, *File*, and *FileInfo* to work with the file system. All I/O uses *Streams*, which are an abstraction over a series of bytes.

- Asynchronous code is important for long-running operations to improve responsiveness and scalability.

- When working with a database, you can use ADO.NET to establish a connection, execute commands, and retrieve results.

- The .NET Framework has support for working with XML by using classes such as *XmlWriter*, *XmlReader*, and *XmlDocument*, or by using LINQ to XML.

- LINQ offers a uniform way of querying different data sources.

- Serializing and deserializing is the process of transforming an object to a flat file or a series of bytes, and vice versa.

- The .NET Framework offers a comprehensive set of collections that you can use in different scenarios.

# Answers

This section contains the solutions to the thought experiments and answers to the lesson review questions in this chapter.

## Objective 4.1: Thought experiment

1. You can use *DirectoryInfo* and *FileInfo* classes for searching through folders for the specified files. You can use the Path class for making sure that the locations given to you by the customer are valid.

2. You can use a search pattern when looking for files. By using a search pattern such as "*.docx," you can find all Word documents in a directory.

3. Yes. You are working with I/O in a desktop application. If you use synchronous code, the user interface appears to crash or become unresponsive each time you iterate over your folders or files. By making the application asynchronous, the user interface remains responsive.

## Objective 4.1: Objective review

1. **Correct answer:** D

    A. **Incorrect:** *File.CreateText* would create a new file each time. You only want to append some text.

    B. **Incorrect:** *FileInfo.Create* would return a *FileStream* to a newly created file. You would need to encode your data to a byte array to write it to the stream.

    C. **Incorrect:** *File.Create* is the static equivalent of *FileInfo.Create*. It returns a *FileStream* that would require encoding to write your log entries.

    D. **Correct:** *File.AppendText* adds some text to the end of a file.

2. **Correct answer:** C

    A. **Incorrect:** async/await is not usable when working with a CPU-bound algorithm.

    B. **Incorrect:** Running the code synchronously would make the user interface unresponsive.

    C. **Correct:** *Task.Run* will run the CPU-bound code on a separate thread. This will free the user interface thread to make sure that the application remains responsive.

    D. **Incorrect:** *BackgroundWorker* is retired. The new Task Parallel Library replaces it.

3. **Correct answer:** A

   A. **Correct:** UTF-8 is a general-purpose encoding format that works on many operating systems.

   B. **Incorrect:** UTF-7 is used as a protocol for newsgroup and e-mail. It's not as secure (see *http://en.wikipedia.org/wiki/UTF-7#Security) as* the other encodings, requires more space, and it's slower in encoding/decoding. UTF-8 should be used whenever possible.

   C. **Incorrect:** Because ASCII supports only a limited range of characters, it is inadequate in most cases for international applications.

   D. **Incorrect:** UTF-32 requires a lot of space for storing characters (4 bytes for each character). It is used when applications want to encode Unicode supplementary characters (for example, Chinese characters) as one single glyph. You need this only when the encoded space of such characters is important to you. If you don't need the Unicode supplementary characters, you can use UTF-8. If you do need them. UTF-16 can be used except when you have strict space requirements.

## Objective 4.2: Thought experiment

1. Using the Entity Framework can improve your development speed. You won't have to think about converting data from your database to objects. It will also manage change tracking for you and convert your LINQ queries to SQL. However, this comes at a (sometimes a significant) performance cost. If you don't really need an object model to expose your data to your clients, you could use plain SQL queries to achieve more performance.

2. For your web services, you can use *WCF.to* write regular classes and use some attributes on them to expose them as services. By separating the configuration, you can then expose multiple endpoints for different user types. You can, for example, use a JSON endpoint or an XML endpoint.

3. You can use the *XmlWriter* class for this. Because you are dealing with a lot of data, *XmlDocument* can be too slow. When you don't need to edit data but only output it, *XmlWriter* is a good choice.

## Objective 4.2: Objective review

1. **Correct answers:** A, C

   A. **Correct:** You need a *SqlCommand* to execute your update query against the database.

   B. **Incorrect:** A *SqlDataReader* is used when you select some data from your database. You don't use it when executing an update command.

C.   **Correct:** You need a *SqlConnection* to establish a connection to your database. The *SqlCommand* uses this connection to execute the update query.

D.   **Incorrect:** A Transaction is not necessary when executing only a single command. If an exception occurs, no other queries have to be canceled.

2.   **Correct answer:** B

A.   **Incorrect:** Storing your data in a plain XML file doesn't allow multiple users to read and update it at the same time.

B.   **Correct:** A relational database that stores the data with the Entity Framework mapping it to your objects helps you with quickly developing your application.

C.   **Incorrect:** A relational database is the best option to store your data. Using plain ADO.NET code would require you to manually map your objects to the database, and vice versa.

D.   **Incorrect:** The dynamic keyword can be used in scenarios in which you want weak typing. It will still throw errors at runtime if an action is not possible.

3.   **Correct answer:** A

A.   **Correct:** *XmlReader* is the fastest option when processing a lot of data. Because you only have to read it and not make any changes, this is the best choice.

B.   **Incorrect:** *XmlDocument* is not fast enough when working with a large XML file.

C.   **Incorrect:** The *XmlWriter* is used to create XML files, not to read them.

D.   **Incorrect:** Using a *FileStream* would treat the XML file as plain text. You lose the benefits of the hierarchical nature of your document. Furthermore, parsing it as plain text is not a trivial task.

## Objective 4.3: Thought experiment

1.   Although it is true that LINQ is not always as fast as a manual loop or filter, you get a lot of other benefits. LINQ to Entities translates your LINQ query to SQL, which enables you to create strongly typed queries against your database. LINQ to XML uses it to process an XML file with a more fluent syntax than if you do it by hand. The biggest advantage of using LINQ is that you can use a uniform, strongly typed way of querying against multiple different data sources. Most of the time, development time is more important than premature optimizations. If you do encounter a performance bottle-neck, you can measure your code and optimize your queries in a targeted manner.

2.   LINQ is strongly typed and easier to read than a handwritten loop or query. LINQ offers operators such as *Sum*, *Average*, and *GroupBy* that can make writing complex queries much easier.

**3.** Query syntax is translated into method syntax by the compiler. Not all operators are supported in query syntax. If you need a special operator that's available only in method syntax, you are forced to use method syntax. Query syntax is more readable and should be used whenever possible.

# Objective 4.3: Objective review

1. **Correct answers:** B, D

   **A. Incorrect:** Comparing *DateTime.Now* to the dates will give you only the dates for today, not for the whole year. Also, using *OrderBy* instead of *OrderByDescending* will give you the lowest date, not the highest.

   **B. Correct:** This will return the highest date for the current year. If your filter can't find a value for the current year, it will return '*1-1-0001 00:00:00' (DateTime.Min-Value)*.

   **C. Incorrect:** If your filter doesn't return a value, you will get an error. You should use *FirstOrDefault* instead.

   **D. Correct:** Using *Single* will throw an exception if there are multiple dates for the current year.

2. **Correct answers:** A, B

   **A. Correct:** You need to add a using statement for LINQ to make sure that all LINQ extension methods are available.

   **B. Correct:** LINQ is implemented as extension methods on IEnumerable. If your type does not implement this, you can't use the extension methods.

   **C. Incorrect:** The compiler changes your query syntax to method syntax. Using one or the other doesn't change anything.

   **D. Incorrect:** Using implicit typing lets the compiler determine the result of your query. It doesn't help the compiler find the Where method.

3. **Correct answers:** A, C

   **A. Correct:** Because of the deferred execution nature of LINQ, you execute the query twice—one for getting the number of items, and one for getting all the products. You can change your query to get both these numbers in one call.

   **B. Incorrect:** *ToList()* is necessary for running the query. If you never iterate the query, you won't get any results.

   **C. Correct:** Paging can help limit the number of items that you retrieve.

   **D. Incorrect:** Method syntax is compiled to query syntax. It doesn't make any functional difference.

# Objective 4.4: Thought experiment

1. You can use the *Binary* format, which is the smallest and most efficient. XML and JSON are human-readable, but they result in a larger file, and it's slower to serialize to it.

2. You can use the *BinaryFormatter* to serialize your data to a *Stream*.

3. Because you have some sensitive data (the logon credentials), it's important that you implement the *ISerializable* interface so you have full control over these properties. Otherwise, someone could open your binary file and extract all logon credentials from it.

# Objective 4.4: Objective review

1. **Correct answer:** B

   A. **Incorrect:** Although XML is human-readable, it's not the most optimized format. It will result in larger files then using a binary format.

   B. **Correct:** A binary format is the most efficient for storing a large amount of data.

   C. **Incorrect:** The *DataContractSerializer* is used by WCF to serialize data to XML.

   D. **Incorrect:** The *DataContractJsonSerializer* serializes your objects to JSON. JSON is used for communication between a web browser and the server.

2. **Correct answers:** B, D

   A. **Incorrect:** *XmlSerializer* outputs XML text, not binary data.

   B. **Correct:** *ISerializable* should be implemented on types that have some sensitive data.

   C. **Incorrect:** The *DataContractSerializer* is used by WCF to serialize data to XML.

   D. **Correct:** The *BinaryFormatter* can be used to serialize data to a binary format.

3. **Correct answer:** C

   A. **Incorrect:** *XmlElement* is used to configure how a member is serialized to an XML element.

   B. **Incorrect:** *XmlAttribute* outputs a member as an attribute on its parent instead of as a separate node.

   C. **Correct:** *XmlIgnore* makes sure that a member is not serialized.

   D. **Incorrect:** The *NonSerialized* attribute is used with the *BinaryFormatter* or *Soap-Formatter*.

# Objective 4.5: Thought experiment

1. A generic collection should be used when you are working with a group of items that all have the same type. It gives you better performance and it enables you to access items without casting. Nongeneric collections can be used when you want to mix objects of different types.

2. Dictionary-based collections have a key for each value they store, so they are very fast at retrieving items. They can't store duplicate items. A List stores items in no particular order. You can access items by index.

3. *Stack* and *Queue* collections can be used when you need to retrieve items in a special order (FILO or FIFO). They discard an item after it is retrieved. A List offers random access to all elements.

# Objective 4.5: Objective review

1. **Correct answers:** B, D

   A. **Incorrect:** A *List<Order>* offers random access to elements. It's not fast at selecting specific Order items by id.

   B. **Correct:** By using a *Dictionary<int,Order>*, you can easily select an *Order* by id.

   C. **Incorrect:** A *HashSet* doesn't offer random access to its items. You need to enumerate the whole set to get to an order.

   D. **Correct:** A *Queue* offers a FIFO set. You can't randomly access items, and an item is discarded after retrieving it.

2. **Correct answers:** B, D

   A. **Incorrect:** *Push* is used to add items to a *Stack*.

   B. **Correct:** Add is used on types inheriting from *ICollection<T>*. A *Queue* does not inherit from *ICollection<T>* but from *ICollection*.

   C. **Incorrect:** Dequeue is used to remove an item from a *Queue*.

   D. **Correct:** Enqueue is used to add an item to a *Queue*.

3. **Correct answers:** A, C

   A. **Correct:** You need a list to store all duplicate family name items.

   B. **Incorrect:** A *Stack* stores items in a LIFO basis. It's not suitable for storing the duplicated or nonduplicated items.

   C. **Correct:** The *Dictionary<string,T>* can be used to store the nonduplicated items on family name.

   D. **Incorrect:** You can't remove items from a regular array.

# Index

# F

# J

# K

# L

# M

# N

# U

# Y

# About the author

**WOUTER DE KORT** is an independent technical coach, trainer, and developer at Seize IT. He is MCSD certified. As a software architect, he has directed the development of complex web applications. He has also worked as a technical evangelist, helping organizations stay on the cutting edge of web development. Wouter has worked with C# and .NET since their inception; his expertise also includes Visual Studio, Team Foundation Server, Entity Framework, Unit Testing, design patterns, ASP.NET, and JavaScript.

# Now that you've read the book...

## Tell us what you think!

Was it useful?
Did it teach you what you wanted to learn?
Was there room for improvement?

**Let us know at http://aka.ms/tellpress**

Your feedback goes directly to the staff at Microsoft Press,
and we read every one of your responses. Thanks in advance!

 Microsoft